Beginning Ubuntu for Windows and Mac Users

Start Your Journey into Free and Open Source Software

Third Edition

Nathan Haines

Apress®

Beginning Ubuntu for Windows and Mac Users: Start Your Journey into Free and Open Source Software

Nathan Haines
Lake Forest, CA, USA

ISBN-13 (pbk): 978-1-4842-8971-6   ISBN-13 (electronic): 978-1-4842-8972-3
https://doi.org/10.1007/978-1-4842-8972-3

Managing Director, Apress Media LLC: Welmoed Spahr
Acquisitions Editor: James Robinson-Prior
Development Editor: James Markham
Coordinating Editor: Jessica Vakili

Distributed to the book trade worldwide by Springer Science+Business Media New York, 1 NY Plaza, New York NY 10004. Phone 1-800-SPRINGER, fax (201) 348-4505, e-mail orders-ny@springer-sbm.com, or visit www.springeronline.com. Apress Media, LLC is a California LLC and the sole member (owner) is Springer Science + Business Media Finance Inc (SSBM Finance Inc). SSBM Finance Inc is a **Delaware** corporation.

For information on translations, please e-mail booktranslations@springernature.com; for reprint, paperback, or audio rights, please e-mail bookpermissions@springernature.com.

Apress titles may be purchased in bulk for academic, corporate, or promotional use. eBook versions and licenses are also available for most titles. For more information, reference our Print and eBook Bulk Sales web page at http://www.apress.com/bulk-sales.

Any source code or other supplementary material referenced by the author in this book is available to readers on the Github repository: https://github.com/Apress/Beginning-Ubuntu-for-Windows-and-Mac-Users. For more detailed information, please visit http://www.apress.com/source-code.

Printed on acid-free paper

For Alexander, who eats everything, will try anything, and is constantly learning.

Table of Contents

About the Author

Nathan Haines is an author, instructor, speaker, and computer consultant who fell in love with Ubuntu in 2005, and helped found the Ubuntu California Local Community Team to share that excitement with others. As a current leader of the Ubuntu California Local Community team and a member of the Ubuntu Local Community Council, he works to help others share Ubuntu worldwide.

He got started in IT support during high school, when he got an after-school job helping the campus technician and later worked over the summer at his high school, then his school district, and finally at his college, learning technical writing along the way. He later taught computing classes to professionals and worked his way up to the highest levels of technical support and consumer service.

When not working with computers, he's more than likely admiring the latest Nintendo hardware, wishing he had more time for retro console and PC gaming, and indulging in linguistic curiosity by studying German or dabbling in Old English or Tolkien's constructed Elvish languages. The queue of sci-fi and fantasy books on his Kindle is probably growing instead of shrinking, although sometimes camping trips help with that.

Despite a knowledge of HTML that was forged in 1995 with Internet Explorer and Netscape Navigator 2.0, Notepad, a lot of browser refreshing, and stone knives and bearskins, he manages to keep a website online that is standards-compliant but always in need of updating at `https://www.nhaines.com/`.

As a translator and hybrid author who enjoys stiff drinks, moonlit walks on the beach, and five-star Amazon reviews on his books, he would love to hear from you at `nathan@nhaines.com` or `nhaines@ubuntu.com`.

About the Technical Reviewer

Didier Roche-Tolomelli is an Ubuntu Core Developer for many years. He started his Ubuntu journey in 2004, being active in the French Local Community Team. He then contributed more on a technical level, packaging for the desktop. Since then, he got involved in more and more core activities in Ubuntu: archive administrator and main inclusion reviewers. He is currently working at Canonical as a technical lead developer in the Ubuntu Desktop Enterprise team. During his spare time, he goes hiking, but also builds things with his hands. Recently, he started real-world hacking with 3D printing, rescuing broken items and making tailored crafted tools.

Acknowledgments

I was able to write this book thanks to the love and support of many people.

So thanks to all of the teachers and staff at school and college that got me started in computer support and technical writing—too many to mention, although I'm sorely tempted. Their encouragement of my interest in computers and programming and the opportunities they created set me down the path I'm on today.

Thanks to my family who have put up with my obsession for computers and video games even in a pre-Internet world. The cyberspace of the 1980s and 1990s that I once so clearly envisioned is very different from how we live today in how seamlessly we've woven it into our everyday lives. I think that turned out even better. Thanks, Michael and Sylvanna, Mom, John, Dad, Doris, Jon, Teasha, and Holland.

Thanks to all my friends who have meant so much to me along the way: David, Lutz, Anna, Emily, Casey, Kelly, Andy, Markus, Justin, Tom, Matt, Jerome, Patrick, Andrew, Leif Arne, Eric, Marshal, and all the others who have been a constant support and inspiration. Thanks especially to indie and hybrid author friends: Ralph, Ryan, and a couple of other Nathans, among others.

Thanks to Alexander, Blair, Claudia, and Jeffrey, because sometimes you *can* choose your family.

And of course, thanks to all of my Ubuntu family and friends: Neal, Jess, Robert, Melissa, Brendan, Lyz, Akkana, George, Steve, Richard, Jono, Stuart, George, José, Sujeevan, Daniel, David, Alan, Oliver, Ian, everyone on the Ubuntu Community Council, Gareth, Ilan, Orv, Tom, Justin, and everyone at SCaLE, and everyone else who has put up with my jokes and happily welcomed my contributions to the Ubuntu project. My work has been paid back many times over.

And thanks to everyone at Apress, who were wonderfully enthusiastic and patient throughout the entire adventure! Thanks, Louise, Christine, Jim, Mark, Karen, Jessica, James, and all the others I didn't see who worked behind the scenes to make this book the best it could be.

ACKNOWLEDGMENTS

Finally, special thanks to Christopher B. Wright, who wrote the awesome book *Pay Me, Bug!*, released it under the Creative Commons Attribution-Noncommercial-Share Alike 3.0 (CC BY-NC-SA 3.0) License, and then gave me permission to use the cover in Figure 3-21.

Images from Tears of Steel are licensed under the Creative Commons Attribution 3.0 License. (CC) Blender Foundation | mango.blender.org

Introduction

Ubuntu is a lot of things: an operating system, a software ecosystem, a development platform, a home computer solution, a server foundation, a cloud computing paradigm, an Internet of Things platform, and a community. Ubuntu and its community of developers, contributors, and enthusiasts help to make Ubuntu a first-class experience no matter where you find it.

In this book, we're looking at Ubuntu as an amazing desktop operating system. I'll nod at other possibilities here and there, but this book will help you feel at home with Ubuntu and get things done, whether you want to create business documents, relax with music or a movie, play some games, or just look at pictures of cats on the Internet.

What Makes Ubuntu So Great?

Ubuntu works a lot differently than Windows or OS X traditionally has. It has evolved separately from these proprietary operating systems, and that makes it both exotic and unfamiliar at times. And while the general concepts of windows and launcher icons are the same, there are a lot of underlying assumptions that make Ubuntu a very different experience. The main difference is the way that the Ubuntu, Free Software, and Open Source communities all come together to form the operating system you think of as Ubuntu. These combined efforts make Ubuntu a powerful way to get work done.

Ubuntu Is Built from Many Pieces

The first thing to know is that Ubuntu is built around an operating system kernel called Linux. The kernel is the program that is responsible for coordinating all of a computer's hardware and software. It manages hardware driver support, schedules how applications run and cooperate together and communicate with hardware, and takes care of a lot of behind-the-scenes details that we don't generally worry about when it comes to using a computer.

The kernel itself doesn't do anything on its own. It lets other software run in a way that can be built around the operating system and not the specific hardware. This means that a lot of other software must be written to be used with the Linux kernel and distributed alongside that kernel in order to produce a working, controllable computer system.

There are a lot of working parts, and the first thing you'll usually hear about when you look online is the GNU project. The Free Software Foundation rewrote a lot of the Unix *userspace tools*, or the command-line utilities that one would use to work with Unix using a text interface. The goal was to provide utilities that could be freely used, examined, and distributed. When the Linux kernel was first published in 1991, the GNU userspace was quickly brought to Linux, and together they made a complete, freely distributable operating system that others could build on.

Because it takes a lot of software working together to create a working system, it is common to see references to a GNU/Linux operating system. I won't use that convention in this book, but GNU tools are a major underpinning of most modern Linux-based systems, and we'll be using a lot of them in Chapter 5.

Since 1991, Linux has been bundled with other software and distributed in a way that makes it usable out of the box. Several projects began to form such distributed bundles in different ways, and these are now known as Linux distributions, or distros for short. The first distro to focus on creating a full computer system containing only Free Software was called Debian, and since 1993 it has gathered together a vast collection of freely redistributable software that runs on over 20 different computer architectures and can be further modified for use in other projects. Ubuntu builds upon Debian for each release.

Free Software is a term of art that refers to software that can be used for any purpose, commercial or private, and can be freely examined, modified, and redistributed to others. This allowed Linux to receive improvements from others and incorporate these changes so that everyone could benefit from them. It also allowed a more and more useful collection of software to be included along with the new kernel.

Ubuntu Is Linux for Human Beings

In 2004, a Debian developer named Mark Shuttleworth decided that he wanted to take Debian and focus on releasing on a consistent time-based schedule that would offer fresh software but with special attention given to polishing the user experience and providing high-quality language translations as well. Linux distros tended to include massive amounts of software that you had to choose between during installation, and it often took three to five CDs worth of data to download before you could start an install. In the early 2000s, this was a lot of information to download. One of Ubuntu's initial goals was to fit on a single CD and provide a beautiful desktop with one web browser, one office suite, one email client, and so on. By doing so, the install process was simple and streamlined, but additional and alternative software choices were still only a few clicks away.

Another major goal was to build a community that embraced the African philosophy of *ubuntu*—humanity toward others. Thus, the Ubuntu Code of Conduct (`https://ubuntu.com/community/code-of-conduct`) set clear guidelines for how community members should treat each other. The idea that everyone should be treated with respect and newcomers should be welcomed and celebrated worked to create an online community that was much friendlier and respectful than a lot of other technical communities. It was such a successful example that Ubuntu spread very quickly and many technical communities have adopted their own codes of conduct.

As Ubuntu continued to mature, it further distinguished itself from its origins. While Ubuntu still depends greatly on the Linux kernel, the GNU userspace, the Debian distribution, and thousands of other software projects, it still brings these components together in a way that offers a stunning and unique desktop experience right out of the box. This collaboration also allows Ubuntu to provide security updates and bug fixes to all of the software it installs on your computer.

Ubuntu has been working to redefine the desktop experience, and the Unity desktop shell is a brilliant and bold new interface that dedicates almost your entire screen to your applications but keeps your favorite applications, indicators, and hybrid local and online searches at your fingertips. In addition, a single 3.6-gigabyte DVD download results in a comprehensive, complete computing experience in only about four gigabytes of space once installed on your hard drive. From there you can add other software as you see fit.

By knowing some of the history of Ubuntu, we can see how it can be so different than other operating systems. But these differences are often strengths. Because Ubuntu is freely distributable, you can download and try it for free. And the install disc that you download can also be installed on a USB drive instead of a DVD, and you can even run Ubuntu directly from the disc and give it a try before you actually choose to install it. That means that the best way to learn more about Ubuntu is to dive in and just try it. But it also means that an Ubuntu disc can be used to test and recover data from computers that aren't working too well, even if they're not running Ubuntu.

A wide array of software that can be arranged to accomplish any task, dozens of supported languages, and a friendly, helpful community to turn to for support and exciting activities are just some of the things that make Ubuntu so great. The rest of this chapter will help you get Ubuntu installed and up and running so that you can experience it for yourself.

Ubuntu 22.04 LTS is the latest long-term support release of Ubuntu. It provides a platform for a lot of different experiences and will continue to receive security updates until April 2027. For simplicity's sake, this book is going to assume that you are running Ubuntu 22.04 LTS installed on a computer hard drive, and Chapter 1 is going to help you set this up. But as you explore Ubuntu and become more comfortable with it, you may want to use your computer in a different manner than Ubuntu assumes. There are various flavors of Ubuntu that come preinstalled with different software selections. They are useful in a lot of different circumstances but are all variations of Ubuntu. You could install Ubuntu and end up with the same configuration as any flavor just by adding and removing software. The next chapter will describe some of these differences as well.

If you do not already have an Ubuntu DVD, visit the Ubuntu website at ubuntu.com/ and download the Ubuntu Desktop installer. Every six months a new installer called a "point release" will be available that contains all updates to that point. At the time of publication, Ubuntu 22.04.1 LTS is the latest version.

Additional Resources

No book can cover everything, and this book cheerfully doesn't try to. Topics are covered in enough detail to get you started, but with Linux and Ubuntu, you can always dig a little deeper. Apress has an amazing assortment of books on all topics and for all skill levels and is a great place to look for comprehensive guides. In addition, there is an incredible amount of resources provided by the Ubuntu community—persons just like you who are sharing what they've learned—and I encourage you to explore them and to contribute back. We all make up Ubuntu together:

- The **official Ubuntu documentation** on your computer is also available online, along with additional community-maintained help (https://help.ubuntu.com/).

- **Ask Ubuntu** is a question-and-answer site where Ubuntu users can help each other. It's a great place to search for help and ask specific support questions (`https://askubuntu.com/`).

- The **Ubuntu community portal** is a great place to find ways to contribute back to Ubuntu and to find resources that can assist you (`https://community.ubuntu.com/`).

- Your **Ubuntu Local Community (LoCo) Team** is filled with friendly people who are crazy about Ubuntu, and they are happy to point you in the right direction if you want to meet other Ubuntu users or help share Ubuntu with others. You can find more about your local team and view upcoming Ubuntu events in your area at the Ubuntu LoCo portal (`https://loco.ubuntu.com/`).

- Your local **Linux User Group** is filled with Linux enthusiasts, many of whom are familiar with Ubuntu. Search for them online and join them at their next meeting!

- The **Ubuntu subreddit** is a fun place for readers to highlight and discuss Ubuntu news and community matters. Read the rules in the sidebar, and if I remove your support question with a gentle reminder to use Ask Ubuntu, it's not personal! (`https://reddit.com/r/Ubuntu/`)

- **Planet Ubuntu** is an aggregate of various personal and project-related blogs that share Ubuntu news regarding announcement, development, events, parties, and other interesting topics gathered from Ubuntu member blogs (`https://planet.ubuntu.com/`).

- **Ubuntu Blog** is Canonical's portal for news, partner announcements, and industry white papers and is a place to read about Ubuntu's place in the computing industry as a whole, as well as consumer products featuring Ubuntu (`https://ubuntu.com/blog`).

There's a great, big community out there, and we're all hoping that Ubuntu will help you be more productive, have more fun, and be happier. Don't hesitate to reach out if we can help! Just remember, you're a part of the Ubuntu community, too!

CHAPTER 1

Installing Ubuntu

All things considered, installing an operating system should really be difficult and arcane. It controls your computer. After starting everything up, it loads the drivers, runs every program, orchestrates how software and hardware work together, provides the computer-user interface, and determines how you will work with your machine.

But it's not.

Those days are over. Long gone are the days when you'd have to feed the computer the Initial Program Loader from punch cards, paper tape, or magnetic tape. Flicking front-panel switches to input a bootstrap program is another forgotten ghost of computing history. Searching for driver disks to have on hand to support your new graphics or sound card mostly isn't necessary anymore. Even just watching the monitor so you know when to swap to the next installation floppy or CD is a distant memory. Today, you insert a DVD or USB drive with the installer, boot up the computer, and away you go. Installing a modern operating system is done using the same pretty, graphical interface as the end result.

Ubuntu is like Windows and macOS in that the installation media contains a comprehensive set of drivers for most hardware devices found in a common home computer, and computers have enough storage space that the installer will set up a basic running system with a standard configuration. After everything's set up, you can make changes, but everyone gets the same starting point. This makes installation fast: a standard image can be installed to the hard drive. It also makes installation easy: other than language, region, time, and user information, once the installer knows where to install the OS, it doesn't need any additional information to start installing. So it starts installing while you answer those questions. And if you have an active network connection, it guesses at the region and time settings, too.

It's not time-consuming, either. Ubuntu can be installed in 20–30 minutes, depending on how fast your disks are, and if you run the installer after clicking "Try Ubuntu" from the installation media, you can even browse the Web or play Solitaire or Mines while you wait.

© Nathan Haines 2023
N. Haines, *Beginning Ubuntu for Windows and Mac Users*,
https://doi.org/10.1007/978-1-4842-8972-3_1

There are a lot of ways to install Ubuntu, so this chapter will make some assumptions. The first is that you are using the latest long-term support release of Ubuntu, which is 22.04 LTS. The second is that you are installing Ubuntu from a DVD or a USB drive that was (at least temporarily) dedicated to holding the Ubuntu installer. These same assumptions will be made throughout the entire book. If you are new to Ubuntu, this will provide a stable, reliable starting point as you become familiar with Ubuntu.

This isn't the only way to experience Ubuntu. Newer versions such as Ubuntu 22.10 will have more up-to-date software and minor enhancements, but will require updating to Ubuntu 24.04 LTS no later than July 2024. Ubuntu 22.04 LTS is supported until April 30, 2027, although Canonical offers an additional 5 years of support after that with an Ubuntu Advantage subscription. At the time of writing, this is free for personal use for up to three computers. Three months after every Ubuntu release, Ubuntu takes the latest hardware support from the latest release and all updates released for the LTS release and creates new installation images for the latest LTS. Thus, Ubuntu 22.04.1 LTS was released on August 11, 2022, and Ubuntu 22.04.2 LTS will be released on February 9, 2023. When you download an Ubuntu LTS release, it's always better to download the newest point release, because it will provide improved hardware support as well as software updates, so that you will have fewer updates to download once Ubuntu has been installed.

Tip   Find out more about Ubuntu Advantage at `https://ubuntu.com/advantage`, and sign up for a free Ubuntu One single sign-in account and get free updated support for personal use on up to three computers.

Ubuntu also has quite a few "flavors" such as Kubuntu and Xubuntu, which keep the core Ubuntu system and replace the default user interface and applications to offer a different experience that is just as reliable. All of the applications described in this book will be available and run fine on any Ubuntu flavor, but much of Chapter 2 will no longer apply because these different interfaces have varying features and distinct workflows. There are ways to add additional desktop environments to an existing Ubuntu install and gain the benefits of a flavor, and this is explained in Chapter 6. And if you later find that you prefer a different flavor of Ubuntu, you can install it directly from scratch. This will give you a cleaner, simple base that's built around your favorite interface—and you can still install any additional software you need.

This chapter guides you through the basics: preparing to install Ubuntu 22.04 LTS, performing the actual installation, and optionally switching to more advanced graphics drivers—in case you need them for gaming or additional monitor support. The remainder of the chapter will offer a brief look at additional Ubuntu flavors, giving you an idea of the differences you can expect with those interfaces during installation and daily use.

Preparing to Install Ubuntu

The first thing you'll need to do is to download and prepare installation media for Ubuntu. These are usually distributed as DVD images, but you can also prepare a USB drive as well. Installation DVDs are much easier to create than USB keys, and sometimes you will receive a copy of Ubuntu with a book, from a library, from a friend, or from a local Linux User Group or Ubuntu Local Community team. If you have any trouble with this chapter, these are very useful resources to search for. The following steps are geared toward Ubuntu, but generally apply to the other flavors of Ubuntu as well.

System Requirements

Ubuntu requires a 64-bit computer. You will also need a computer that has 3D graphics acceleration, although most computers have this feature built in.

In order to install Ubuntu, you will need to have at least 8.6 GB of hard drive space available. That said, 25 GB is a more comfortable amount to allow for additional software and storage for your own content. You'll also be happiest with a computer that has at least 8 GB of RAM, although 4 GB should also be usable on older systems. If you're installing the Ubuntu desktop on a Raspberry Pi, you'll want to use a Raspberry Pi 4 Model B or Raspberry Pi 400. The Raspberry Pi 3 works well as a server, but only has 1 GB RAM and is too slow to run the Ubuntu desktop efficiently. (Some Ubuntu flavors such as Ubuntu MATE may work well on older Raspberry Pis, although you may need to consider an older release such as Ubuntu MATE 20.04 LTS.)

You can download the Ubuntu installer from `https://ubuntu.com/download/ desktop`. It will be in the form of a DVD image with an .iso file extension. Be sure to read the Known Issues/Ubuntu Desktop section of the release notes to see if there are any issues you may want to know before you begin.

Creating an Ubuntu DVD

If you want to install Ubuntu from a DVD, insert a blank DVD into your computer. In Windows, you can right-click the downloaded file, choose "Show more options," and choose the menu option that says "Burn disc image" to write the installer to a blank DVD. In Ubuntu, right-clicking the file and choosing "Write to Disc…" will accomplish the same thing. On either OS, you will want to make sure to check the "verify" option before burning the DVD, to guard against disc burning errors.

On macOS, you can run Disk Utility and then drag the downloaded file to the left pane where your hard drives are listed. Click the Ubuntu ISO and click the Burn icon in the toolbar, and the installer will be written to the blank DVD. Make sure to enable the option to verify the burned disc.

Once the disc is burned, you'll be ready to use it to start Ubuntu on your computer. Use a felt-tip pen to label the disc "Ubuntu 22.04 LTS," with an accurate point release number (such as "22.04.1 LTS") if you downloaded a later version. With this DVD, you can run Ubuntu straight from the disc, which is a great way to demonstrate Ubuntu on a friend's computer without changing it, or to do basic computing on a computer that has malware or viruses installed or is having trouble booting up. This makes it much more useful than a simple install disc, so after you've installed Ubuntu, you may want to keep it in a safe place so you can use it or lend it to friends in the future.

Creating a Bootable Ubuntu USB Drive

Preparing a USB drive to install Ubuntu is a bit more complicated, but if you want to install Ubuntu from a USB drive, you will need a drive with at least 4 GB free. The drive will be formatted and all data will be erased, and it will function the same as an Ubuntu DVD, although some drives can be configured with "persistence," which means that settings and files will be saved to the USB drive for next time you boot from it.

Windows and macOS

On Windows or macOS (or other Linux distributions), you'll need to download a special utility to copy the installer to the USB drive. You can download the balenaEtcher from `www.balena.io/etcher/`. Once you install or run balenaEtcher, it's simple to use. Click "Flash from file," and choose the Ubuntu image you previously downloaded. Then, click

"Select target." You will see a list of removable drives. Carefully choose the USB drive you wish to write the Ubuntu installer to. Be very careful to choose the right drive, because if you choose an external hard drive, you can lose the files on that drive, and if choose your system disk, it can make your computer unbootable and lose the files on your computer. Once you have the image and target set, just click "Flash!" and balenaEtcher will prepare your USB drive.

Ubuntu

On Ubuntu, even if you are running it from a DVD or USB drive, open the GNOME Activities Overview and search for "Startup Disk Creator." Chose an inserted Ubuntu DVD or downloaded ISO file and then select a USB drive from the list, and click "Make Startup Disk" to create a bootable USB drive. Any inserted Ubuntu DVD or ISO located in the Downloads folder will be listed automatically. If the "Make Startup Disk" option is grayed out, you may need to use a different USB drive or delete some files to clear enough space.

For a Raspberry Pi

If you want to install Ubuntu on a Raspberry Pi, you will have to copy the image to a microSD card or USB drive that the Raspberry Pi will boot from. First, download the Raspberry Pi Imager from `www.raspberrypi.com/software/`. Once Imager is installed, run it and click "CHOOSE OS." If you've already downloaded the image from `https://ubuntu.com/download/raspberry-pi`, then scroll to the bottom of the list and choose "Use custom." Then, choose the img file you downloaded. If you have not yet downloaded a Raspberry Pi image, Imager can do this for you automatically. Just choose "Other general-purpose OS" and click "Ubuntu." There will be a brief delay while Imager checks for the latest versions of Ubuntu. Choose "Ubuntu Desktop 22.04 LTS (RPi 4/400)." Next, click "CHOOSE STORAGE" and pick a microSD card or USB drive to erase and install Ubuntu on. Your Raspberry Pi may or may not be set up to boot from a USB drive, so use a microSD card if you have one. Once you have selected a drive, simply click "WRITE" and Imager will set up the card or drive. Once it's finished, simply insert the card into your Raspberry Pi 4 while it's powered off, and turn it on.

Booting into Ubuntu

Every computer's startup process is different. It is determined by the computer manufacturer, but more specifically by the motherboard manufacturer. When a computer turns on, it runs special software that's built into the motherboard. Traditionally this was called the BIOS, but computers built today use UEFI.

Caution   If you are installing Ubuntu alongside Windows, it is very important to make sure you boot the Ubuntu installer using the same technology: this is probably UEFI. If you are installing Ubuntu on a new computer with no operating system or replacing Windows on an old computer, then UEFI is preferable, but legacy BIOS boot won't cause a problem.

On any Mac system, insert the disc or USB drive, turn on the power, and hold down the Option key until you see a list of drives. Choose your Ubuntu media with the mouse or arrow keys, and continue booting.

On other computers, you will need to configure the BIOS or UEFI to boot from your disc or USB drive. There is no standard way of doing this, so you may need to consult your manufacturer's documentation for instructions. First, insert the disc or USB drive into your computer, and then turn it on. You can usually watch the startup screen for messages such as "Press <ESC> for startup menu," "F9 to change boot device," "F12 Boot Menu," or something similar. These will let you choose a device to boot from for the current boot only. You only have a couple of seconds to press the key, so plan to let the computer boot at least twice for you to be able to locate and read the message. If your installed OS begins to boot, let it finish before restarting the computer, and then use the OS's shutdown feature. If your computer has no OS (or if you are going to completely replace it with Ubuntu), then you can simply reboot at any time.

The other option you have is to change the boot search order in your BIOS or UEFI configuration. This will change your settings until they you change them again, and may be the only way to choose a different boot device. For this you want to search your startup screen for messages like "DEL to enter BIOS" or "F10 to enter setup." You should be able to find a boot options or advanced menu with a boot order option. You'll want to move your boot device type to the top or front. Sometimes USB drives are only listed if they are plugged in when the computer turns on. Once you have changed the startup order, follow the onscreen instructions to save your changes and boot or exit the configuration.

When your computer reboots, you will know that you were successful if you see a black screen with a simple menu, as shown in Figure 1-1.

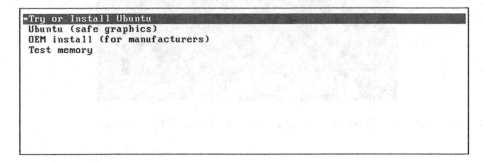

Figure 1-1. *This is the Ubuntu bootloader screen. It means your computer has booted from your installation media*

This menu allows you to do special things like run Ubuntu in a special compatibility mode (safe graphics) if your video card isn't supported. It also lets you perform an "OEM install," which can be useful if you're setting up a computer for a friend or relative. If no keys are pressed for 30 seconds, the bootloader will start Ubuntu so that you can run Ubuntu from your install media or install it on your computer. If that's what you want to do, you can simply press the Enter key with "Try or Install Ubuntu" highlighted and save yourself a few seconds.

Once you see the Ubuntu boot splash screen (Figure 1-2), Ubuntu is loading itself into your computer's memory, and, after a few seconds, the Ubuntu installer will guide you through the next step in using Ubuntu.

Figure 1-2. *This screen means your computer is loading Ubuntu*

Installing Ubuntu

Canonical Ubuntu Desktop is the flagship of the Ubuntu project. Powerful and stable with an elegant user experience, this is where you should start if you have never run Ubuntu or Linux before. It features the GNOME Shell desktop interface, LibreOffice, Firefox, and Thunderbird, and is a suitable replacement for Windows and macOS in most casual desktop computer use cases.

Beginning the Install

Once Ubuntu has finished booting, it will display a welcome message (Figure 1-3). This is the first step of the Ubuntu installer, and one of only six or seven screens you will have to interact with to install Ubuntu on your computer. On the left hand side of the installer is a list of languages. From here you can easily choose the language you are most comfortable with and interact with Ubuntu in that language for the rest of the session. If you install Ubuntu, it will be installed in the language you choose on this welcome screen, although you can install additional languages after that.

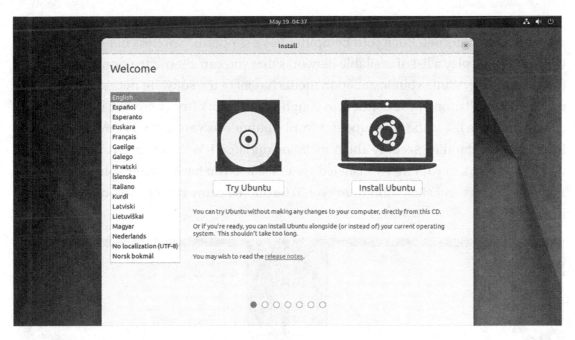

Figure 1-3. *On the Welcome screen, you can easily pick a system language and try or install Ubuntu at your leisure*

The first option, Try Ubuntu, will run a desktop interface with most of Ubuntu's features and software available to you. Software updates are disabled at first, but you can run the default selection of programs and try out the Ubuntu's custom GNOME desktop interface without installing it on your computer. This is a fantastic way to see if Ubuntu is compatible with your computer's hardware and also allows you to try out newer versions of Ubuntu or different flavors before you upgrade. (Plus, you can browse the Web or play Solitaire if you decide to install Ubuntu after trying it.) The second option, Install Ubuntu, will allow you to confirm your keyboard layout and then immediately begin the installation process.

After you click "Install Ubuntu," you can set your keyboard layout. The default selection is selected based on the language you chose on the installer's first screen (not the location on the previous screen), so it's quite likely that you won't need to make any adjustments. If your keyboard doesn't match the installer's selection, then you can either select it from the list or click "Detect Keyboard Layout" and type a series of keys that will help Ubuntu narrow down the list of likely candidates for you. This shows characters in several different languages before asking some additional yes or no questions and should help you find something that matches your physical keyboard layout. Once you have made a selection, you can test your keyboard settings in the text field before clicking "Continue."

If your computer has an active Ethernet connection, Ubuntu will try to use it to connect to the Internet. But if your computer has a supported wireless network card, Ubuntu will display a list of available networks that you can choose to connect to (see Figure 1-4). While your installation media has all of the software necessary for a complete installation, if you connect to your home network from here, the installer can download a list of the latest updates from Ubuntu's servers and will download and install any outstanding security and translation updates. It will also save your connected wireless network to your newly installed system. Once you have decided on your network settings and click "Continue," you'll be offered some choices for your Ubuntu install.

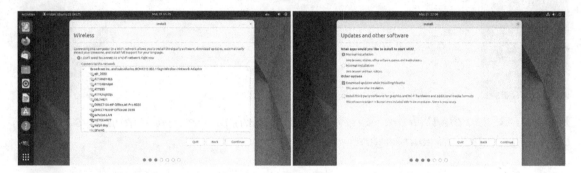

Figure 1-4. *Ubuntu will help you connect to the Internet and can download additional updates while installing*

The installer will install a basic, complete Ubuntu system, and you won't have to choose various software packages during install. However, there are two optional choices that you can make on this screen that can install additional software.

The first option is "Download updates while installing." This doesn't update the entire system, but does download a list of the latest software available in Ubuntu. The installer will automatically update core software related to the install process to help ensure that installation goes smoothly, as well as any available security and language updates for the installed system. It will also update the catalog of software updates, so that you will be ready to download and install the latest bug-fix updates after your first boot.

The other option is "Install third-party software." By default, Ubuntu is composed of software that is licensed with either a Free Software or open source license. This means that anyone can redistribute every component under relatively well-known terms. But occasionally some proprietary software is needed for a working computer system.

Software with proprietary licenses cannot always be redistributed. Many Linux users are sensitive to using proprietary software for a variety of philosophical and practical reasons. For instance, some hardware requires special drivers or firmware that is not available in source code form. This prevents them from being studied and improved upon by the community if they find any bugs or security issues. Sometimes this can be a minor inconvenience, such as when the system libraries for MP3 playback were patent encumbered. Canonical purchased a distribution license to include MP3 libraries in Ubuntu, but the license has restrictions on its source code. At other times, the lack of freely distributable software can cause frustration, such as when firmware for a wireless network card can't be included on the install media. Binary-only network card firmware can be a security vulnerability because you don't know what the card is doing. On the other hand, if you have a laptop that needs wireless communication, then you may need the binary firmware anyway.

Software such as MP3 libraries and other common video and audio codecs can be added after Ubuntu has been installed, but most new users expect this software to be included in a "complete" desktop operating system, so Ubuntu allows users to automatically install a small selection of nonfree software. The software doesn't cost any additional money for you because Canonical has taken care of all licensing concerns, so it is a good idea to select the checkbox if you aren't familiar with these issues. If you want to minimize the proprietary software installed on your computer, however, feel free to leave it unchecked. You can still add software support on a case-by-case basis later.

The next screen lets you choose how you want Ubuntu to be installed on your computer's hard drive (see Figure 1-5). If you are installing on a new computer or you want to completely replace the existing operating system, the answer is simple. Choose "Erase disk and install Ubuntu," and your hard drive will be partitioned, formatted, and dedicated to Ubuntu automatically.

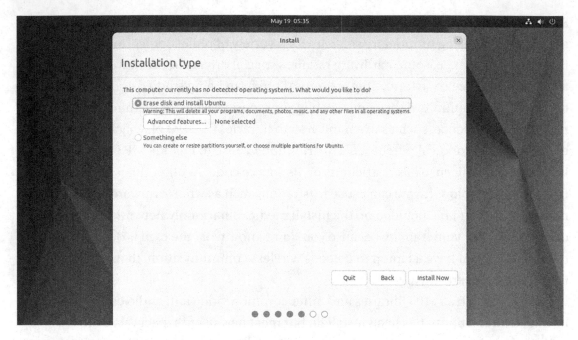

Figure 1-5. *Installing Ubuntu on a new computer is automated, but advanced formatting is also possible*

If your computer has an operating system already installed and you would like to keep it, then it should be detected here. You may have an option "Install Ubuntu alongside Windows 11," for example. This will allow you to shrink the space allocated to Windows 11 and create dedicated space for Ubuntu using a simple graphical slider. But there may be problems with computers that contain extra disk partitions for recovery or factory reset data that prevent Ubuntu from adding a new partition. And sometimes Ubuntu may not detect other installed operating systems. These scenarios will be dealt with at the end of this chapter, in the section Multiple Operating Systems. For now, be aware that unless Ubuntu offers an "install alongside" option, other operating systems and data will be lost unless you use the "Something else" option.

Under "Advanced Features," two optional settings are available when choosing to erase the drive and install Ubuntu. "Use LVM with the new Ubuntu installation" enables Logical Volume Management, which is a system to allow a computer to deal with disk storage in a more flexible way. This advanced option allows experienced system administrators to use one disk to mirror another, or to store data across multiple disks as though they were one large drive. This is traditionally used on servers more than desktops. Choosing this option will automatically configure a working system, but this book doesn't cover LVM usage.

"Erase disk and use ZFS" allows you to format your computer's hard drive using the ZFS file system. This is an enterprise-grade file system that provides advanced data integrity and file snapshot features. It is a popular file system among system admins and advanced users, but is also beyond the scope of this book.

If either of these options is chosen, then "Encrypt the new Ubuntu installation for security" sets up full-disk LUKS-based drive encryption with LVM, or enables native ZFS encryption. With this setting, a small unencrypted boot partition is created for the Linux kernel and bootloader, and the rest of the drive is encrypted and Ubuntu installed on this encrypted portion. This provides strong protection against data theft from a lost or stolen computer or hard drive by requiring a separate password to unlock the Ubuntu partition each time the computer boots.

The installer has seven screens, but the button at the bottom of this one says "Install Now." When you click this button, Ubuntu will display a window "Write the changes to disks?" with a summary of the changes being made. If you click "Continue," Ubuntu will repartition your hard drive and begin copying Ubuntu to your disk while you finish answering the install. This helps to shorten the install time, but it also means that this is the point at which you commit to the install. Clicking "Quit" now will bring up the Ubuntu desktop from the install medium, and you can start the installer again later from the dock on the left side of the screen or the icon at the bottom right of the live desktop. Clicking "Continue" on the confirmation prompt will cause a delay that can take from a few seconds on a blank hard drive to a couple of minutes if Ubuntu needs to resize existing partitions and file systems. When it has completed the partition and formatting changes to the hard drive, the next screen will appear.

Setting Regional Settings

The next screen asks for your location so that it can set your time zone and weather location. You can either click directly the map or type your location into the text field (see Figure 1-6). The map will update your location to the major city nearest to your click and highlight your time zone. Typing a city or location name into the text field will bring up a list of matches from Ubuntu's time zone database. This information not only sets your current time, but also applies any applicable Daylight Savings Time or Summer Time rules for your locale. Your time zone information is updated periodically along with other Ubuntu updates as your local Daylight Saving or Summer Time legislation changes.

Figure 1-6. *Ubuntu customizes itself based on your location and preferred language*

After you have confirmed your location, you can click "Continue" and create your user account.

Creating the Primary User Account

The only other information that Ubuntu will need from you during the installation is all about you. This is the last installer screen, and you'll enter your name, the name you want to give to your computer, your account username, and a password (see Figure 1-7).

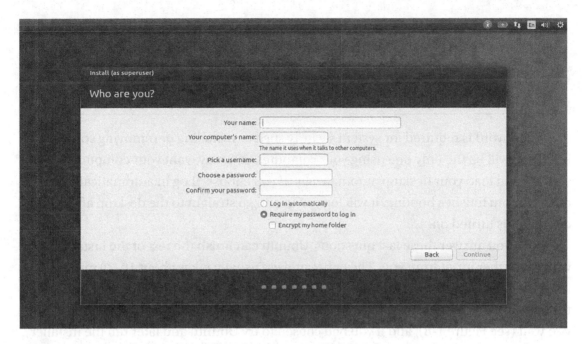

Figure 1-7. *On the last installer screen you will set up your user account and computer name*

Your name will appear on the computer's welcome screen when it boots and can contain any supported character. The computer name will also be shown on your local area network, but it can only consist of Latin letters a–z, dashes, and numbers. Your username will be the actual name of the user account your computer uses to identify you and name your personal storage folder. Your password will log you into the computer and should be something secure and unique.

Tip   Choosing a good password is a matter of balance. On the one hand, a password should be secure, but on the other hand you will be typing it in daily. A good way to strike a balance between security and convenience is to pick a passphrase. This can be something simple like "grandmother's rhubarb pie." This is very easy to remember, yet very difficult for a computer to guess because it is so long. "Rhubarb" would be guessed almost instantly because it is a dictionary word, and "rhubarb pie" would take about 12 years for a desktop computer to guess by brute force at 4 billion guesses per second. But "grandmother's rhubarb pie" would take that same desktop computer one septillion (1,000,000,000,000,000,000,00

0,000) years to crack. Feel free to throw in a number or symbol or two as well, but don't worry about making something hard for humans to read. A short password of numbers and symbols is trivial for a computer to guess. Just remember to stay away from famous quotes or proverbs.

A password is required for system security such as installing or removing software, but if you will be the only one using your computer, you may want your computer to start up and load your desktop automatically. If you choose "Log in automatically," once Ubuntu finishes booting, it will log you in and go straight to the desktop after your computer is turned on.

Once you answer these last questions, Ubuntu can finish the rest of the installation with no further input from you. The entire process usually takes about 10–20 minutes in total, depending on your computer and disk speed. A slideshow explaining some of the features of Ubuntu's included and additionally available software is presented while you wait (see Figure 1-8), and if you had chosen to try Ubuntu and later ran the installer from there, this is where you could sit back and browse the Web or play a game such as Solitaire.

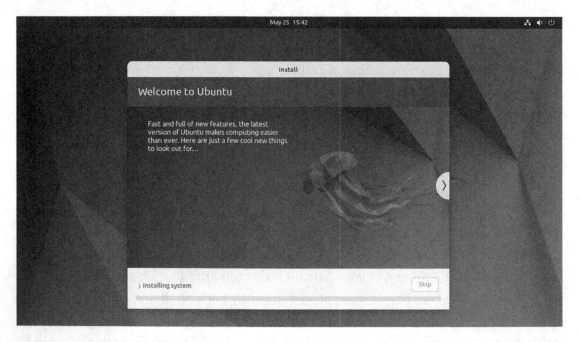

Figure 1-8. *Ubuntu displays an overview of major features while it installs*

Once the install process has finished, the installer will display a window saying that the installation is complete and you can restart your computer. When you are ready to restart, Ubuntu will shut down and then wait for you to remove the install disc or USB drive from the computer and press Enter. Then, it will reboot your computer and boot into Ubuntu. Your installation is now complete, and you are ready to proceed to Chapter 2.

Install Proprietary Graphics and Network Drivers

Ubuntu is powered by the Linux kernel and has excellent hardware support. A hardware driver is special software that communicates between the operating system and a specific hardware component of a computer. They are usually designed so that a program can tell the operating system something generic like "I want to play this sound file," and the operating system uses a software library to decode the sound format and then uses a sound driver to play it on the computer's sound card. The driver is written to work closely with the operating system so that the driver handles the hardware details and individual programs don't have to.

Because of this interface, most drivers become an extension of the operating system. In Ubuntu and other Linux-based operating systems, drivers are written as kernel modules that can be either baked into the kernel or loaded on an as-needed basis, saving memory. It is this close relationship that leads to a practical and philosophical dilemma.

Some hardware is easy to support. Most hard drives, CD-ROM drives, and USB drives, for instance, communicate using the basic ATAPI protocol. Therefore, the same generic driver supports all of these devices and is easily maintained. Other hardware such as video cards and network cards are more difficult. Two video cards from the same manufacturer may work in completely different ways, and many wireless network cards require the computer to send firmware to the network card every time they are powered on. In these cases, driver support can depend on the manufacturer.

When a driver is licensed under a Free Software or open source license, it can be examined, maintained, and improved by the developer community. This is important because it helps to ensure compatibility when new versions of the Linux kernel become available, and it ensures that any security issues or bugs can be addressed in a timely fashion once discovered. Some manufacturers only provide proprietary drivers for various reasons. These drivers are usually precompiled and can only be used as is. This makes it difficult or impossible to inspect the quality of the drivers or provide fixes

17

to problems—leaving your computer's performance and safety in the hands of the manufacturer. Therefore, Ubuntu installs freely licensed drivers whenever possible. However, some hardware has no free alternative or has both free and proprietary drivers. For this situation, Ubuntu provides a tool to make installation simple.

After Ubuntu is installed on your computer, you can run "Additional Drivers" by searching for it from the Dash. To access the Dash, press the Super key on your keyboard, or click the Ubuntu icon on the Launcher at the left edge of your screen. Additional Drivers searches your computer for hardware that has proprietary drivers available from Ubuntu and presents a list of devices and available drivers. Some drivers are optional, and others are required to use a device. For example, Figure 1-9 shows a Broadcom network card. It doesn't have a free driver available and will be nonfunctional without the proprietary driver. But the driver cannot be updated by Ubuntu, so there is no guarantee that it will see any improvements in Ubuntu 22.04 LTS. On the other hand, the driver should be fully functioning without other updates. Some hardware has free drivers with source code available, but they may or may not support all features of a hardware device. Some hardware manufacturers, such as AMD and Nvidia, work with Ubuntu to provide updated proprietary drivers, and some don't. You can always try a driver, and if there are various versions available, you can switch between them here and reboot to find the driver that best suits your needs. This is the name of a software option, as shown in the figure.

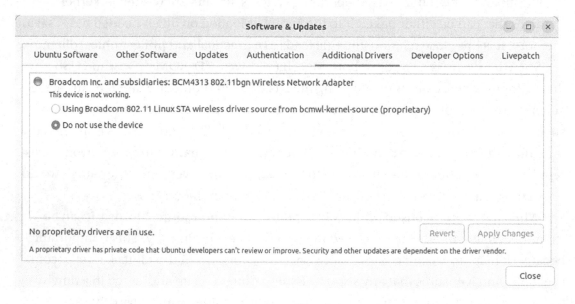

Figure 1-9. *Additional Drivers displays available and in-use drivers and simplifies installation*

Providing a choice between drivers allows Ubuntu users to choose whether they are comfortable using proprietary software that cannot be reviewed or improved Ubuntu developers. This tool also installs the proprietary drivers in a manner that ensures they will continue to be loaded when Ubuntu's Linux kernel receives updates.

Additional Ubuntu Flavors

Ubuntu 22.04 LTS comes in many additional, popular flavors—including Kubuntu, Xubuntu, Lubuntu, and Ubuntu Unity. The steps for creating and booting from each flavor's installation media are identical to that used for Ubuntu. Once you've downloaded the appropriate disc image, you can follow the steps listed at the beginning of this chapter. While the look and feel of each flavor is distinct, the installation process is extremely similar.

The following sections walk you through the installation details and provide links for more documentation about the respective flavors.

Installing Kubuntu

Kubuntu is a flavor of Ubuntu that showcases the KDE Plasma desktop environment and its rich ecosystem of software. Sporting a clean, gray, and silver look, the Kubuntu desktop features an efficient desktop that is similar to Windows in a lot of ways but also allows for serious customization options. For this reason, KDE has long been a favorite desktop environment for advanced users.

Kubuntu was the first flavor of Ubuntu to be released. While Ubuntu used to ship with the GNOME desktop environment by default, the software repositories also included KDE and related software. Users could install KDE and choose between that and other desktop environments at login. It was also possible—although a little bit of work—to replace GNOME with KDE entirely. A group of Ubuntu community members who enjoyed using KDE worked together to create a new downloadable disc and installer that would install Ubuntu without GNOME and instead provide KDE and related software right out of the box. Canonical initially sponsored Kubuntu developers directly, but in 2012 they stopped, and Blue Systems employed several key developers to continue working on Kubuntu. Canonical still provides the infrastructure used to create and release Kubuntu on the same release schedule as Ubuntu.

System Requirements

Kubuntu does not require hardware 3D graphics acceleration although most computers have this feature built in, and it makes the desktop animations much smoother.

In order to install Kubuntu, you will need to have at least 8.6 GB of hard drive space available, although 20 GB is a more comfortable amount to allow for additional software and storage for your own content. You'll also be happiest with a computer that has at least 4 GB of RAM, although 2 GB should also be usable.

You can download the Kubuntu installer from `https://kubuntu.org/getkubuntu`. It will be in the form of a DVD image with an .iso file extension. Once you have this file downloaded, you can create Kubuntu installation media using the instructions found at the beginning of this chapter. You can also find more documentation about Kubuntu and KDE at `https://kubuntu.org/support/`.

Preparing to Install Kubuntu

The Kubuntu installer automatically boots into a live desktop session from the DVD. If you click "Install Kubuntu," you are given the same options and steps to install as with Ubuntu, as shown in Figure 1-10.

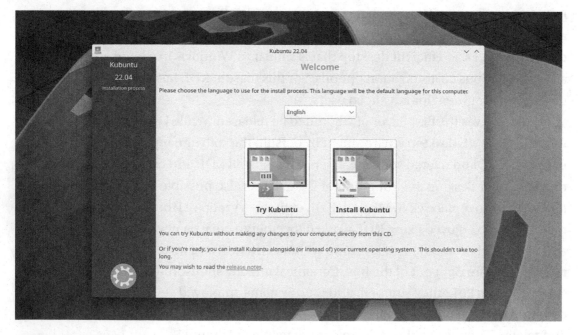

Figure 1-10. *The Kubuntu Welcome page*

Using Kubuntu

The Kubuntu desktop is fairly straightforward (see Figure 1-11). The K Menu in the bottom left of the screen will let you search and launch your applications. Like the analogous menus in Windows, Ubuntu, and GNOME, the K Menu is launched with the Super key. The older keyboard shortcut Alt+F1 will also open the K Menu, and you can click a choice or type your search immediately. Running applications will be displayed in the panel at the bottom of the screen.

Figure 1-11. *The default Kubuntu desktop is clean and ready to use or customize*

The biggest change with Kubuntu is the desktop style. The KDE Plasma desktop can be customized with widgets, which are pieces of functionality that display content and information so that you have it handy at a moment's glance. The bottom of the screen is a customizable panel that operates much in the same way as the Windows taskbar.

The default Kubuntu desktop will display any files you have in your Desktop folder. You can add other widgets as well. Widgets can provide weather information, webcomics, news, calculators, hardware information, and even web pages.

Activities are ways to customize your desktop for specific kinds of activity or work. Unlike virtual desktops (or workspaces) that simply give you more room to organize your running applications, activities provide independent desktops with completely separate widget layouts. Typically, you might have one activity set up for casual computing, one for work, one for software development, and so on. Each can have its own set of widgets and panel configuration, and automatically launch specific programs as well. They aren't active unless you're using them, so unused activities won't slow down your computer.

KDE and GNOME both strive to be comprehensive desktop solutions with different design goals. Therefore, Kubuntu comes preloaded with KDE apps that integrate more easily into the established look and feel of KDE (see Figure 1-12). For instance, Kubuntu ships Elisa instead of Rhythmbox and Kate instead of Gedit. These applications are more or less equivalent, but they do have different features and different workflows.

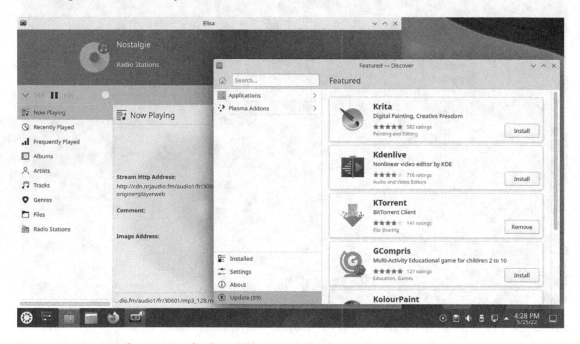

Figure 1-12. *Kubuntu includes different default applications than Ubuntu. They are just as powerful*

Because Kubuntu is simply Ubuntu with a different selection of software, you can install the same applications on any Ubuntu flavor. This means that you can install Elisa on Ubuntu or Gedit on Kubuntu. A default install is just a shortcut to a specific type of desktop and workflow. You are never limited to the default choices. In fact, if you prefer Ubuntu Software to KDE's Discover, you can even install that yourself. They use the same update system internally and will not conflict with each other.

KDE itself has always been famous (or infamous, depending on your perspective) for the sheer number of complex settings you can change. And while the default settings are a great starting point, you can still change most of the behavior (see Figure 1-13). If you find that standard Ubuntu with its GNOME desktop doesn't fit the way you work, with a little bit of configuration, KDE might be the perfect environment for you.

Figure 1-13. *KDE is loved for its customizability. You can change the window style, animations, and much more*

Installing Xubuntu

Xubuntu is a flavor of Ubuntu that showcases the Xfce desktop environment and a variety of lightweight software. Sporting a striking gray and silver theme, the Xubuntu desktop is efficient and appeals to a more classic and minimalistic aesthetic than either Ubuntu or KDE. Xfce is also not as resource intensive as the other desktop environments and is ideal for slightly slower computers or systems without supported 3D acceleration.

In the beginning, Xubuntu emerged as an alternative to Ubuntu that was ideal for slow computers with limited amounts of RAM. While it is no longer the most lightweight flavor of Ubuntu, it still remains a popular choice as a modern but basic computing experience that can easily be added on to.

System Requirements

Xubuntu does not require hardware 3D graphics acceleration although most computers have this feature built in, and where present it makes the desktop animations much smoother.

In order to install Xubuntu, you will need to have at least 8.6 GB of hard drive space available, although 20 GB is a more comfortable amount to allow for additional software and storage for your own content. You'll also be happiest with a computer that has at least 1 GB of RAM, although 2 GB will be much more usable.

You can download the Xubuntu installer from `https://xubuntu.org/download/`. It will be in the form of a DVD image with an .iso file extension. Once you have this file downloaded, you can create Xubuntu installation media using the instructions found at the beginning of this chapter.

You can also find more documentation about Xubuntu and Xfce at `https://xubuntu.github.io/xubuntu-docs/`.

Preparing to Install Xubuntu

The Xubuntu installer is nearly identical to Ubuntu's, but is in the style of the XFCE interface. The slideshow after the final step introduces some of Xubuntu's features (see Figure 1-14).

Figure 1-14. *The Xubuntu installer's slideshow gives information and a tour about how to use the interface*

Using Xubuntu

Xubuntu's desktop looks like a simplified version of Ubuntu and GNOME2's desktop before Ubuntu 11.04 (Figure 1-15). In the top left corner of the screen is the Whisker Menu, which you can open by clicking the icon, pressing the Super key, or by pressing Ctrl+Esc. This is the main application launcher and displays your favorite applications when first opened. You can browse the different categories by clicking the right side of the Whisker Menu (see Figure 1-16).

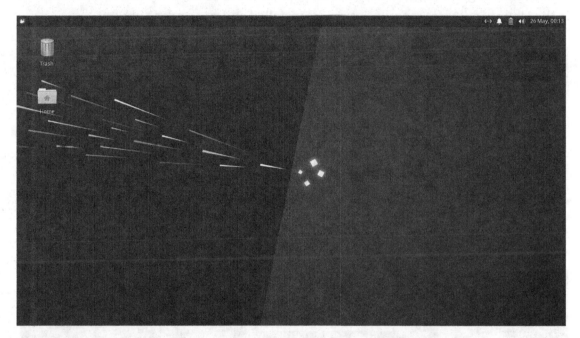

Figure 1-15. *The default Xubuntu desktop is functional and light*

As with most other modern operating systems, you can also type the name of the program you would like to run, and the list of applications will be filtered as you type. Right-clicking an application in the menu lets you add or remove an application from your favorites. Your currently running applications are listed in the top panel, to the right of the Whisker Menu icon.

Xfce has less options than the more complex desktop environments because it seeks to stay small and simple. The desktop does have some customization options, which you can quickly access by right-clicking the desktop and choosing "Desktop Settings" from the pop-up menu. From there you can change the way the desktop behaves as well as remove the default icons that are present.

Many applications will be familiar. The default web browser and mail client are Firefox and Thunderbird, respectively, and they work as well as ever. But other applications are chosen for their efficiency. LibreOffice is installed by default, and reads and writes Microsoft Office formats as well as the standard OpenDocument formats. Music and video playback is provided by Parole, and Internet Relay Chat support is provided by HexChat.

Additional software is provided by GNOME Software, although you can also use Synaptic Package Manager as an alternate interface, and indeed any software available in the Ubuntu software repositories can be installed and run under Xubuntu.

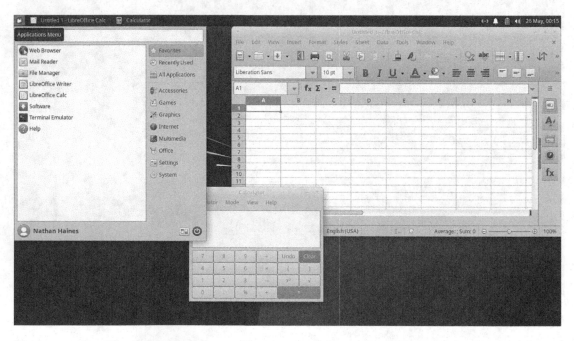

Figure 1-16. *The Whisker Menu allows you to launch applications, change settings, and shut down the computer*

Xubuntu was once the best way to run Ubuntu on computers that just weren't up to the task of Ubuntu's interface and default applications. Today, users who want a comfortable desktop that is simple and minimalistic use Xubuntu as a classic interface that still offers the hardware and software compatibility of Ubuntu.

Installing Lubuntu

Lubuntu is a flavor of Ubuntu that showcases the LXDE desktop environment and a variety of lightweight software. Sporting a refined dark theme, the Lubuntu desktop is a classic desktop that is designed to use as few resources as possible while still providing a contemporary computing experience. While complex web browsing is necessarily memory and processor intensive, all of the other default applications are quite efficient.

Lubuntu arose as an even more lightweight option after Xubuntu began adopting more and more GNOME and other heavy applications that made it difficult to run on older machines. Lubuntu now provides one of the fastest and most comfortable experiences for older systems out of all of the various Ubuntu flavors; however, as with all other Ubuntu flavors, it requires a 64-bit PC.

System Requirements

Lubuntu does not require hardware 3D graphics acceleration although most computers have this feature built in, and where present it makes the desktop animations much smoother.

In order to install Lubuntu, you will need to have at least 8 GB of hard drive space available, although 15 GB is a more comfortable amount to allow for additional software and storage for your own content. You'll also be happiest with a computer that has at least 512 MB of RAM, although 1 GB will be noticeably more comfortable. As usual, the more the merrier, so I would recommend 3 GB of RAM for systems intended for web usage with complex sites such as YouTube, Facebook, and Google Docs.

You can download the Lubuntu 22.04 LTS installer from `https://lubuntu.me/downloads/`. It will be in the form of a CD image with an .iso file extension. Once you have this file downloaded, you can create Lubuntu installation media using the instructions found at the beginning of this chapter.

You can also find more documentation about Lubuntu at `https://manual.lubuntu.me/stable`.

Preparing to Install Lubuntu

When you boot the Lubuntu install media, you will be brought to the default Lubuntu desktop. From here you can try out Lubuntu, or you can double-click the "Install Lubuntu 22.04 LTS" desktop icon to launch the installer. The Lubuntu installer's slideshow is much like Ubuntu's, with the minimalistic style of the LXDE interface, and the slideshow after the final step introduces some of its features (see Figure 1-17).

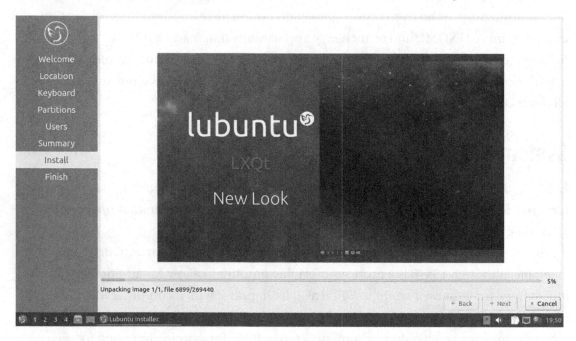

Figure 1-17. *The Lubuntu installer's slideshow provides an overview of the desktop*

Using Lubuntu

Lubuntu is a simple desktop that looks very similar to a classic Windows desktop (see Figure 1-18). The panel at the bottom of the screen contains the menu that contains your installed applications which can be clicked on or opened by pressing the Super key, a virtual desktop switcher, two quick launch icons for the file manager, and to show the desktop, and your running programs are listed to the right. Lubuntu ships with Openbox as its window manager and uses the older term "iconify" to refer to minimizing a window. You'll see this term if you right-click a window's title bar. Choosing "Roll up/down" in that window menu will reduce the window to only its title bar. Clicking once a rolled up title bar will restore that window. Aside from these charming quirks, the interface should be quite familiar to most computer users.

Figure 1-18. *The default Lubuntu desktop is functional and light*

Lubuntu does include Firefox as its standard web browser, but lighter applications replace the standard Ubuntu offerings. There is no default email client, but Thunderbird is available, as well as the lightweight Sylpheed or Claws Mail clients. LibreOffice is the default office suite, but the lightweight FeatherPad text editor is perfect for small text documents and PCManFM is a fast, responsive file manager (see Figure 1-19). VLC provides a simple but powerful means to play back both music and video files. With a fairly minimal selection of default software, you have what you need to get started, but it's also a perfect base to build your optimal desktop experience upon.

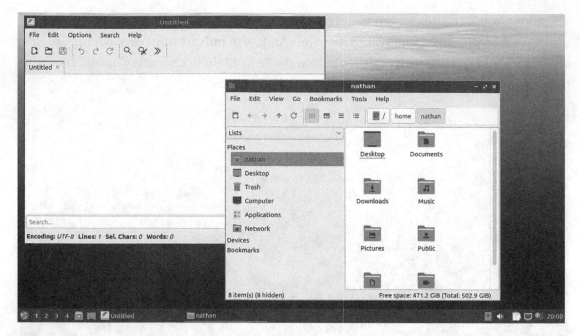

Figure 1-19. *FeatherPad text editor and PCManFM file manager are fast and powerful*

Additional software is provided by Discover in the System Tools menu, and any software available in the Ubuntu software repositories can be installed and run under Lubuntu.

Lubuntu is now the least hardware-intensive flavor of Ubuntu and is a pleasant way to bring new life to computers running older versions of Windows that are no longer supported. With the advantage of modern software and security updates, Lubuntu can keep older computers useful as well as safe.

Installing Ubuntu MATE

Ubuntu MATE is a flavor of Ubuntu that showcases the MATE desktop environment for those who were happier with the classic GNOME 2 environment. Using the Ubuntu themes with cool green highlights—but offering you a choice of alternate accent colors including Ubuntu's classic orange—the MATE desktop is a solid work or gaming environment and has additional built-in layout options that can mimic Windows, macOS, or Ubuntu's Unity. MATE also is ideal for slightly slower computers or systems without supported 3D acceleration. In addition, it is an excellent option for running on a Raspberry Pi 2, 3, or 4 computer.

System Requirements

Ubuntu MATE is available for 64-bit PCs and both 32- and 64-bit Raspberry Pi devices, and you should install the 64-bit version if your Raspberry Pi will run it. Ubuntu MATE does not require hardware 3D graphics acceleration although most computers have this feature built in, and where present it makes the desktop animations much smoother.

In order to install Ubuntu MATE, you will need to have at least 8.6 GB of hard drive space available, although 16GB is a more comfortable amount to allow for additional software and storage for your own content. You'll also be happiest with a computer that has at least 4 GB of RAM, although 1 GB will also be usable. If you're installing Ubuntu MATE on a Raspberry Pi, you'll need an SD card with greater than 8 GB capacity, although with the price of SD card storage constantly decreasing, you may want to think of 16 GB or 32 GB as a minimum and go from there. As with any SD card that will be used extensively, it's better to spend money on a high-quality name brand card rather than maximize storage.

You can download the Ubuntu MATE installer from `https://ubuntu-mate.org/download/`. It will be in the form of a DVD image with an .iso file extension. Once you have this file downloaded, you can create Xubuntu installation media using the instructions found at the beginning of this chapter. If you are installing on a Raspberry Pi, then a preinstalled system image will be in the form of a compressed disk image with an .img.xz file extension. This is the same image that the Raspberry Pi Imager will download, so there's no need to download it beforehand unless you want to image the SD card yourself or perform multiple installs. Detailed information about Raspberry Pi compatibility, including hardware recommendations and an installation guide, are available at `https://ubuntu-mate.org/raspberry-pi/`.

You can also find more documentation about Ubuntu MATE at `https://ubuntu-mate.org/about/` and `https://ubuntu-mate.org/support/`.

Preparing to Install Ubuntu MATE

The Ubuntu MATE installer is nearly identical to Ubuntu's. The slideshow after the final step introduces some of Ubuntu MATE's features (see Figure 1-20).

Figure 1-20. *The Ubuntu MATE installer's slideshow gives information and a tour about how to use the interface*

Using Ubuntu MATE

Ubuntu MATE's desktop looks a lot like Ubuntu's GNOME 2 desktop before Ubuntu 11.04 (Figure 1-21). In the top left corner of the screen is the Brisk simple menu, which you can open by pressing the Super key or by clicking with the mouse. Pressing Alt+F1 opens the simpler Applications menu at your mouse cursor location at any time. This is the main application launcher, and it displays a menu of application categories with applications in submenus. You can begin typing the name of the application you wish to run, or browse the different categories by hovering over them with the mouse or navigating with the arrow keys.

Figure 1-21. *Ubuntu MATE has an extremely comprehensive welcome screen on first run*

This layout should still be familiar to anyone who has worked with Windows 95 or later. Your currently running applications are listed on the bottom panel, and you can click on an application to switch to it.

The Welcome screen offers quick access to many configuration opens that let you get started fast. For example, not a fan of green? Click "Change Theme" and choose between various Ubuntu themes (called "Yaru") which have a variety of accent colors in both light and dark variants. Click "Desktop Layout," and you'll be able to quickly switch between Ubuntu MATE's default "Familiar" layout, the nostalgic "Mutiny" layout that mimics Ubuntu's Unity interface, the "Redmond" layout that will make any Windows user feel at home, or the "Cupertino" layout which makes Ubuntu MATE feel similar to macOS. There are more themes, and a lot more options that can be refined in MATE Tweak, but the above four layouts will make most users at home as they become more familiar with Ubuntu.

Many applications will be familiar. The default web browser is Firefox, and the default mail client, Evolution, is a comprehensive email, address book, calendar, and to-do manager that will be familiar to anyone who's used Microsoft Outlook at the office. LibreOffice is installed by default, and reads and writes Microsoft Office formats as well as the standard OpenDocument formats. Music and video playback is provided by Rhythmbox and Celluoid.

A curated selection of software is provided by Software Boutique in the Menu ➤ Administration menu. You may need to enter your password if the Welcome and Software Boutique applications have been updated. Click on the various category icons on the top of the window. Additional software is provided by GNOME Software, which you can download as "Software" under the "More Software" category. Any software available in the Ubuntu software repositories can be installed and run under Ubuntu MATE.

The MATE interface is extremely flexible and can be highly customized, but there are several default layouts which are included for your convenience (Figure 1-22). They are styled to look like Windows, macOS, Ubuntu, Fedora, openSUSE, and more. Use the Menu ➤ Preferences ➤ MATE Tweak menu option, and click "Panel" to see the various panel layouts available. Aside from the default layouts, there are many other options available to you, and you can save your own custom panel layout for later.

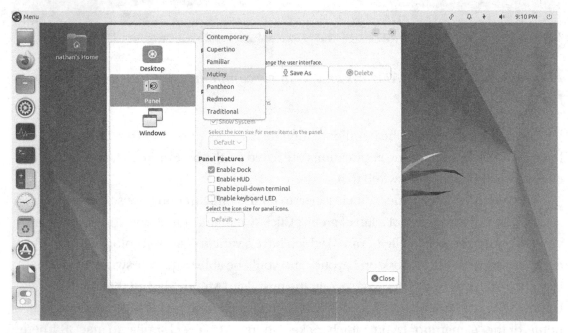

Figure 1-22. *MATE Tweak can help make Ubuntu MATE more familiar to your customary operating system*

Ubuntu MATE is the perfect blend of a powerful desktop with feature-filled defaults software and an efficient system that will run on older computers and Raspberry Pis as well. It is also ideal for users who have used GNOME in the past and are happier with the older customizable but less resource-intensive interface. The classic user interface is a great way to enjoy the power and functionality of Ubuntu on any computer.

CHAPTER 1   INSTALLING UBUNTU

Installing Ubuntu Unity Remix

Ubuntu Unity Remix is a remix of Ubuntu that reunites the Ubuntu desktop with its former Unity desktop interface. For users who want to maximize their monitor space or who are feeling nostalgic, this is the perfect flavor for productivity and ease of use.

When the GNOME Project stopped working on GNOME2 and looked toward GNOME3 and a GNOME Shell interface, there was a lot of disagreement about the future of the desktop. Some projects, like MATE, continued to refine the GNOME2 experience and make it their own. Canonical and the Ubuntu community developed Unity as an easy-to-use, minimal interface that once polished began to be refined for phone and tablet devices. After 6 years, Ubuntu decided to adopt GNOME Shell once again. The Unity interface provided in the Ubuntu Unity Remix offers Unity 7, without the mobile enhancements that were contained in Unity 8 for phones, tablets, and desktops.

With a launcher on the left side of the screen that can be set to automatically hide and appear when the mouse pushes past the left edge of the screen, and a single top panel that contains easy-to-use indicator icons on the right, the current application's menu bar, a heads-up display (HUD) for searching those menus, and that combines with the window controls, title bar, and menu for maximized windows on the left, Unity gets out of your way and lets you use your screen space for what you really want: your applications.

System Requirements

Ubuntu Unity Remix does not require hardware 3D graphics acceleration although most computers have this feature built in, and acceleration greatly enhances the Unity experience.

In order to install Ubuntu Unity Remix, you will need to have at least 8.6 GB of hard drive space available, although 20 GB is a more comfortable amount to allow for additional software and storage for your own content. You'll also be happiest with a computer that has at least 2 GB of RAM, although 4 GB will be noticeably more comfortable.

You can download the Ubuntu Unity Remix installer from `https://ubuntuunity.org/download/`. It will be in the form of a DVD image with an .iso file extension. Once you have this file downloaded, you can create Ubuntu Unity Remix installation media using the instructions found at the beginning of this chapter.

You can also find more information about Ubuntu GNOME at `https://ubuntuunity.org/`.

Preparing to Install Ubuntu Unity Remix

The steps for creating and booting from Ubuntu Unity Remix installation media are identical to that used for Ubuntu at the beginning of this chapter.

Using Ubuntu Unity Remix

Ubuntu Unity Remix is very similar to Ubuntu in terms of default software selection, but the user interface is provided by Unity instead of GNOME Shell (see Figure 1-23). The interface is designed both to emphasize simplicity of the interface and enhance your focus on the currently focused application. This makes Unity a very unique experience from that of Windows or Ubuntu, but a little more focused than macOS.

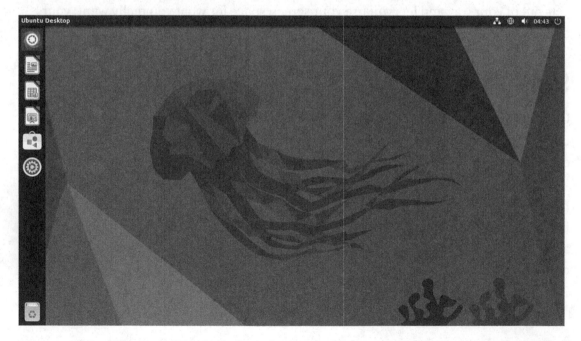

Figure 1-23. *Ubuntu's Unity desktop looks similar to GNOME Shell or macOS, but behaves quite differently*

Pressing the Super key or clicking the Dash icon at the top left of the screen opens the Unity Dash. This displays your most often launched applications as well as recently opened files and folders, and you can type to search your installed applications and local files. You can use the search lenses at the bottom of the Dash to specifically look for applications, files, movies, music, or photos. You can press Enter to open or run the first search result, or you can use the arrow keys to navigate through the results. Dragging an application icon to the Unity Launcher on the left side of the screen will pin it to the Launcher for easy access in the future. Pressing Escape will clear your current search or, if the search field is blank, will close the Dash. Pressing the Super key while the Dash is open will also close the Dash.

The top panel will display the name of the currently focused application on the left. When you have an application open, its menu will be hidden. To view the menu, you can move the mouse over the top panel and click to interact (see Figure 1-24), or you can use standard accelerator keys such as Alt+F for the File menu, Alt+E for the Edit menu, and so on. Holding the Alt key will display the menu and underline the relevant accelerator key for each menu.

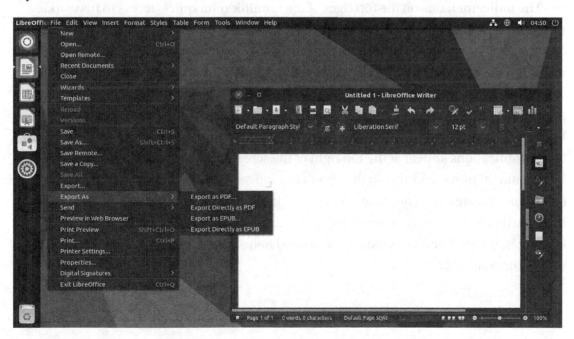

Figure 1-24. *Unity keeps your current applications menus at the top of the screen*

Tapping Alt will bring up a heads-up display (HUD) (see Figure 1-25) that will allow you to type and search through the active application's menu system. You can run the top result by pressing Enter at any time, or by using the arrow keys to select another result and run it with Enter. As a bonus, the results will show the menu hierarchy for each command so that you can find the menu with mouse later, if you prefer.

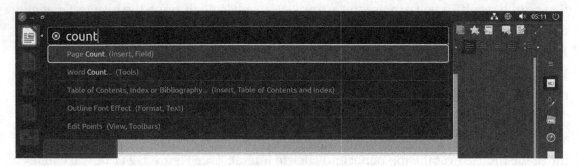

Figure 1-25. *Unity's HUD lets you type your command instead of hunting for it with the mouse*

The indicator icons on the top right of the monitor offer quick access to networking, sound input and output levels, your calendar and other time zone clocks, and system functions such as system settings, logging out, and shutting down the computer. As a bonus, you can scroll your mouse wheel over the sound indicator, or middle-click your mouse to change or mute and unmute the system volume, and most media players will show playback controls under the sound menu while they are running (see Figure 1-26). This offers quick access to pause or resume media when you need to focus. Unity notifications appear at the top right of the screen, but are ephemeral: they're for informational purposes only, so they don't last longer than a few seconds, and if you bring your mouse over a notification, it will fade and your pointer will click "through" it. While this is different than Windows, macOS, and Ubuntu's default GNOME Shell interfaces, it soon becomes second nature, and helps you to ignore notifications when you're concentrating.

Figure 1-26. *Unity's indicator icons give you quick access to your computer's status and other commands*

Additional software is provided by Software in the Launcher or the Unity Dash, and any software available in the Ubuntu software repositories can be installed and run under Lubuntu.

Ubuntu Unity Remix provides an elegant desktop environment that takes advantage of years of usability research by Canonical and the Ubuntu community while still being familiar and accessible. If you prefer this way of interacting with your computer, this is the most convenient way to enjoy the Unity experience.

Installing Ubuntu Server

Ubuntu Server is a special installation of Ubuntu that doesn't include a graphical interface and contains a smaller selection of preinstalled software. This allows the software you do choose to install to make the most of your hardware. Ubuntu Server is one of the most popular operating systems available for servers and in the cloud, and is very easy to install.

System Requirements

Ubuntu Server is available for 64-bit PC-compatible computers as well as several other architectures, including ARM64 and Raspberry Pi computers.

In order to install Ubuntu Server, you will need to have at least 5 GB of hard drive space available, although 20 GB is a more comfortable amount to allow for additional software and storage for your own content, depending on your intended use of the server. Ubuntu requires 512 MB of RAM, but the recommended amount of RAM likewise depends heavily on the work you will be doing on the server.

You can download the Ubuntu Server 64-bit PC installer from `https://ubuntu.com/download/server`. It will be in the form of a DVD image with an .iso file extension. The steps for creating and booting from Ubuntu Server installation media are identical to that used for desktop Ubuntu. You can download Ubuntu Server ISOs for other platforms, such as 64-bit ARMv8, PowerPC64, IBM System z series mainframes, and preinstalled Raspberry Pi images from `http://cdimage.ubuntu.com/ubuntu/releases/22.04/release/`.

You can also find more documentation about Ubuntu Server at `https://ubuntu.com/server/docs`.

Installing Ubuntu Server

When you boot the Ubuntu Server installer, Ubuntu will offer a simple menu and provide options for installing Ubuntu, or utility functions such as booting from the next drive, entering your computer's UEFI configuration utility or testing your memory (see Figure 1-27). The options you see will depend on whether or not your computer is an older BIOS system or a newer UEFI system.

The original Ubuntu 22.04 LTS installer will install Ubuntu with the original hardware kernel, but with Ubuntu 22.04.2 and later, you'll also have the option to install Ubuntu server with the HWE kernel. HWE stands for "hardware enablement," and while standard Ubuntu software will continue to be minor updates from 22.04, the HWE kernel is the Linux kernel from the latest Ubuntu release, on a 3-month delay. This allows you to install Ubuntu 22.04 LTS on newer hardware that was not supported or available in April 2022. The HWE kernel will continue to be updated to the latest Ubuntu release's kernel every 6 months starting with 22.04.2 LTS in February 2023.

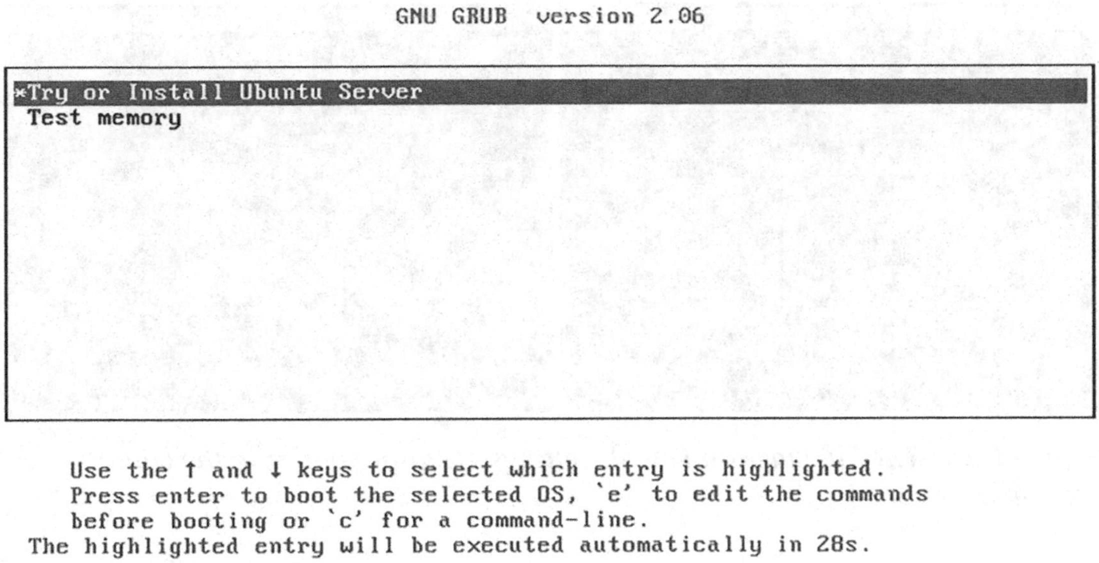

```
GNU GRUB  version 2.06
```

```
*Try or Install Ubuntu Server
 Test memory
```

```
Use the ↑ and ↓ keys to select which entry is highlighted.
Press enter to boot the selected OS, 'e' to edit the commands
before booting or 'c' for a command-line.
The highlighted entry will be executed automatically in 28s.
```

Figure 1-27. *Ubuntu Server's installer will let you test your server's memory on older, BIOS-based computers*

The installer is an easy-to-use, menu-based program that will walk you through the various settings needed to install an Ubuntu server. You can use the arrow keys to move between options and the Tab key to move between sections (such as lists, options, or confirmation buttons), and note that there is a help menu at the top of every screen that will offer more information about the installer, the screen you're on, or access to a Linux command prompt. It will even offer instructions for connecting to the installer via SSH, which allows you to perform the install and monitor the installation progress from another computer.

On the first page of the Ubuntu installer, you will choose your language by highlighting it with the arrow keys and pressing Enter (see Figure 1-28). Ubuntu will be installed in the language you choose on this screen. Next, Ubuntu will check to see if the installer has been updated. It is almost always a good idea to use the latest installer, but you can look at the installer's changelog online if you want to be more discerning. If you do update to the new installer, the installer will restart and pick up where it left off. After that, you will be asked to verify your keyboard layout. If you have a keyboard that doesn't match your selected language, you can select it from a list of languages and layout variants, or you can choose "Identify keyboard" to have the installer attempt to detect it.

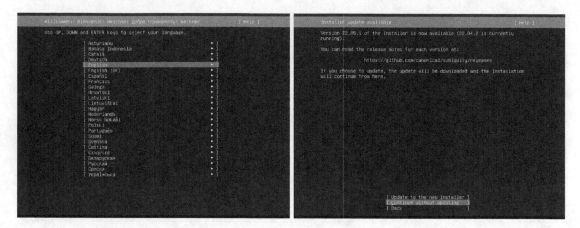

Figure 1-28. *The language and locale settings are quite similar to the Ubuntu desktop installer*

Next, you can choose between two base installations. "Ubuntu Server" is a standard set of applications that provide a comfortable server command-line environment. It will take up approximately 6.6 GB of space. The "minimized" will skip installing comfort features that aren't needed on systems that humans won't log into regularly—such as documentation, core utilities, and standard scripting languages—and will only take up 2.2 GB of space once installed. If you do have a minimized Ubuntu Server install that you wish to start logging into interactively, you can run "sudo unminimize" at the command line and follow the prompts to restore the removed content.

Next, the installer will display any detected network interfaces with autoconfigured settings, and allow you a chance to customize or disable the network settings for each interface. In corporate environments, most servers are assigned IP addresses that do not change, either by setting it up here or by assigning it to the server's network card on the corporate DHCP server. But if you are setting up a server on your home network or a virtual machine, you'll probably just want to accept the default setting, which is to use DHCP ("dynamic host configuration protocol"). This means that you won't accidentally use an IP address that might confuse your router, but it also means that your server's IP address *may* change from time to time. You may also be able to assign a "static" or "fixed" IP address for your server in your home router's settings, if you're concerned about the address changing. On the next two screens, you'll finish up your network configuration. If you're installing on a home network, leave the proxy address blank and choose "Done." Likewise, there's no reason to change your Ubuntu archive mirror unless you have problems with the default mirror.

The installer will then begin to load disk partitioning rules and present you with some partitioning options. Unless you know how you would like to partition the disk, it's safe to choose the guided option. The first option, "Use an entire disk," will allow you to pick a drive on your system and will create a partition table and several partitions automatically, with 1.75 GB being reserved for boot files, and the rest of the drive's space allocated for use by the server. By default, Ubuntu will set up Logical Volume Management (LVM), and optionally you can add encryption, so that you will be asked to enter a password on the server's keyboard on every boot. While the server is powered off, all data on the drive will be protected. The final option, "Custom storage layout," allows you to manually define a partitioning scheme and partitions as well as mount points for each partition. Follow the onscreen prompts to set up your hard drive. If you are not familiar with partitioning in Linux, you should simply choose "Use an entire disk." Once you choose "Done" and press Enter, the installer will summarize the changes that will be made to your drives and allow to review them and make changes before continuing (see Figure 1-29). Once you choose "Done" on this screen, you will be asked to confirm that you are ready to modify your drives. Once you choose "Continue" from that prompt, installation of the core Ubuntu system will begin. This will take at least several minutes.

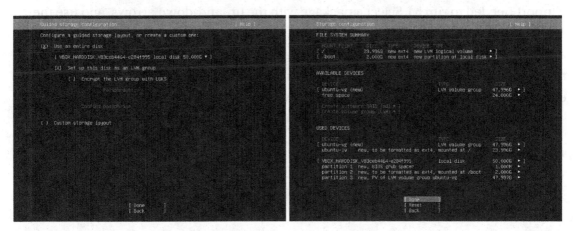

Figure 1-29. *Setting up a hard drive is essential but can cause data loss. Double-check the confirmation screen*

Next, the server install will ask for the full name of the user that will have administrative access to the server. Enter your full name, then press Tab or Enter, and then choose a name for your server. Next, name your user account. Because there is no graphical interface on the server, you will need to remember the username you enter here for future use. Next, you should enter a password. Once you enter in your

information and choose "Done," you will be taken to a screen where you can set up
SSH remote access to your server, which lets you work on the server from any computer
on your home network (or with configuration of your home router, from the Internet
as well). If you decide to install OpenSSH server, you can import your public SSH keys
automatically from your GitHub or Launchpad accounts. If you do this, Ubuntu will turn
off password authentication to make your server more resistant against unauthorized
access. If you want, you can reenable the feature.

After the core system has been set up, the installer will configure the package
manager, which will keep Ubuntu updated. If your network requires proxy settings, enter
the information when prompted; otherwise, simply press Enter. Ubuntu will download
updated package information and download and install any available language updates.

The Ubuntu installer will then offer a list of popular snap packages that can be
automatically installed (see Figure 1-30). They're a collection of fun or useful server
software that is automatically kept up to date directly from the software vendor. For
instance, you can install the Nextcloud snap, and your server will automatically
download and configure a LAMP stack and Nextcloud server (a file synchronization and
collaboration server, along with the web server, database, and programming language
support needed to run it). Select a package with the up-and-down arrows, and use the
spacebar to toggle it on or off. Pressing Enter will show a short description of the package
as well as any alternate versions available. Many snap packages have multiple "channels"
that let you stay on one major version of the software and receive updates. Once you
choose "Done" and press Enter, the installer will then install the rest of the Ubuntu
server software, including downloading and installing any outstanding security updates.

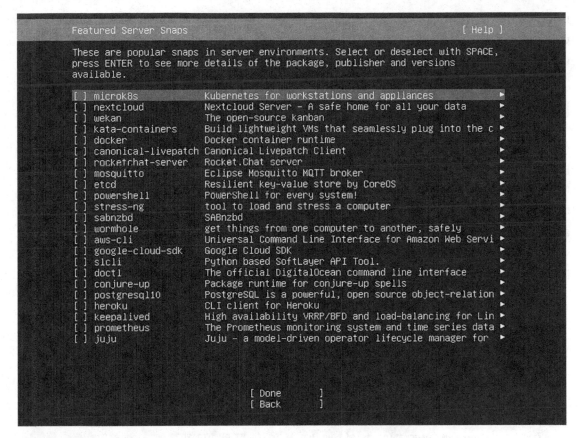

Figure 1-30. *Ubuntu Server makes preparing a new server for common tasks nearly effortless*

This is the bulk of the installation process and will take the longest amount of time in the process. Once it is finished, the installer will perform cleanup tasks and then allow you to view the full installation logs or reboot into your new server.

Snap packages are perfect for a server that is going to be used as an appliance—that is, it's configured for one main task only. But if you're looking for a more traditional or flexible server experience, you'll probably want to install various Ubuntu packages instead (or in addition to a preconfigured snap). For this, the "tasksel" program provides many different roles that can be added to an existing Ubuntu system. A role is a predefined set of software to support a use case, for example, "LAMP" will set up Apache, MariaDB, Perl, PHP, and Python so that you're ready to set up a web server. Or you can install rolls for virtual machine hosts, mail servers, and all kinds of other common types of servers. Once the roll is selected and the software packages are installed, they're updated along with your other Ubuntu packages. You can type "man tasksel" on the command line of a running Ubuntu server for more information about this useful way to get a server up and running quickly.

Using Ubuntu Server

After it boots, Ubuntu Server will display a series of startup messages and then a login prompt. The first time you boot your server up, it may finish some configuration. If the screen stops scrolling for 30 seconds, but you don't see a login prompt, just press the Enter key and it should appear. If not, just wait patiently for another minute or two and then try Enter again. Entering your username and password and the login prompt will display some system statistics and then the command prompt. From here you can interact with your new server via the command line (see Figure 1-31).

```
Ubuntu 22.04 LTS ubuntu-book tty1

Hint: Num Lock on

ubuntu-book login: nathan
Password:
Welcome to Ubuntu 22.04 LTS (GNU/Linux 5.15.0-40-generic x86_64)

 * Documentation:  https://help.ubuntu.com
 * Management:     https://landscape.canonical.com
 * Support:        https://ubuntu.com/advantage

  System information as of Sun Jun 26 05:44:37 AM UTC 2022

  System load:  0.0               Processes:              153
  Usage of /:   28.1% of 23.45GB  Users logged in:        0
  Memory usage: 2%                IPv4 address for enp0s3: 10.0.2.15
  Swap usage:   0%


13 updates can be applied immediately.
To see these additional updates run: apt list --upgradable


The programs included with the Ubuntu system are free software;
the exact distribution terms for each program are described in the
individual files in /usr/share/doc/*/copyright.

Ubuntu comes with ABSOLUTELY NO WARRANTY, to the extent permitted by
applicable law.

To run a command as administrator (user "root"), use "sudo <command>".
See "man sudo_root" for details.

nhaines@ubuntu-book:~$ _
```

Figure 1-31. *The first three lines welcome you to your server, and logging in displays the server status at a glance*

Server administration is an entire book in and of itself, but the Ubuntu Server documentation linked at the beginning of this section and the "tasksel" command can get you started with a few simple projects. With Ubuntu running on an older PC or a dedicated virtual machine, you can learn at your own pace. Ubuntu Server is a small and compact operating system you can build a server on, and with the popularity of both the server and cloud installs, the skills you learn using Ubuntu can easily be put to use in production environments.

Installing a Minimal Ubuntu System

A minimal Ubuntu system is a special install of Ubuntu that contains the very bare minimum of software required to boot and compose a standard Linux environment. This system doesn't include a graphical interface and can be used as a base for systems where resources are at a premium. Minimal Ubuntu installs can be performed using the Ubuntu Server installer.

System Requirements

In order to install a minimal Ubuntu system, you will need to have at least 5 GB of hard drive space available, although 10 GB is a more comfortable amount to allow for additional software and storage for your own content. Ubuntu minimally requires 512 MB of RAM, but the recommended amount of RAM depends heavily on the work you will be doing on the server.

You can download the Ubuntu Server installer from `https://ubuntu.com/download/server`. It will be in the form of a DVD image with an .iso file extension. Once you have this file downloaded, you can create Ubuntu Server installation media using the instructions found at the beginning of this chapter.

Installing a Minimal System

The steps for creating and booting from Ubuntu Server installation media are identical to those listed in the previous section. Once you've booted with your installer, you can follow the steps listed in the Ubuntu Server section of this chapter until you get to the "Choose type of install" screen that allows you to choose a minimal install (see Figure 1-32).

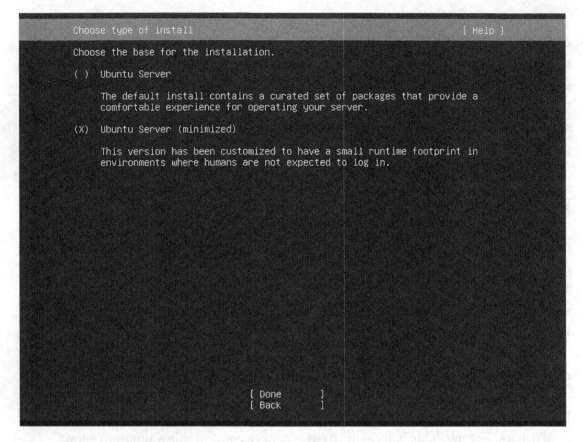

Figure 1-32. *Selecting a special install mode is the only difference from an Ubuntu Server install*

You can also find more documentation about Ubuntu Server at `https://ubuntu.com/server/docs/`. It will equally apply to a minimal system because of the command-line interface.

Using a Minimal Ubuntu System

A minimal system is useful for any number of interesting and esoteric uses where resources are limited, whether it be for a small server running on older hardware or a platform to build more complicated software. A minimal install can be an excellent way to put together a lean system using your preferred lightweight window manager. It can even be a good way to install packages one by one to see how a standard Linux environment is built from many components. With only a core selection of software installed, you can choose exactly the software you want to work with while still enjoying all the benefits of Ubuntu—a robust package manager, 5 years of security updates, and a comprehensive selection of precompiled software packages. You can even run "sudo unminimize" later if you decide you want to add in the core utilities and documentation that are typically found on a modern Linux command line.

While Ubuntu is often thought of as a great choice for beginning Linux users, it is also a compelling choice for expert computer users. A minimal Ubuntu Server install is a perfect starting point for self-teaching or serious do-it-yourself projects.

Multiple Operating Systems

Dedicating a computer to a single operating system is always the simplest way to use a computer. But there are many reasons this might not be practical. First and foremost is a situation where you only have one computer and you still need your old operating system. In this case, installing two operating systems on one computer can be a way to work with a new operating system while still being able to use the first one.

The first thing to know is that a computer can only run one operating system at a time. When the computer starts, the bootloader is responsible for loading the rest of the operating system. On older computers, the motherboard's BIOS will check each drive, in the order it was configured to, for a bootloader. On newer systems using UEFI, it will check all drives for legacy bootloaders or EFI bootloaders, and will boot the one it was configured to. (This means that you can easily pick Ubuntu or Windows by name from a list on a UEFI system.) If the computer finds a valid bootloader, it will load the bootloader and run it. From there, the bootloader is responsible for loading the rest of the operating system and handing over control to it. Ubuntu uses the GRUB bootloader by default, and if you install Ubuntu on a computer with an existing operating system, it will detect them and add them to a startup menu so you can choose which to run when you boot your computer.

The second thing to know is that each operating system will be installed and set up independently on its own drives or drive partitions. Each operating system will have its own settings, and normally they will not interfere with or affect one another. Sometimes disk storage can be shared as long as each operating system can read the same file systems, but the home or primary user folders cannot be directly shared between two different operating systems.

Caution   You should always keep up-to-date backups of your files and computer data. But if there were ever a time to have a recent backup, it's when resizing file systems, creating partitions, and installing bootloaders. Make sure your files are backed up before making any changes to your computer!

Dual Boot with Ubuntu and Windows

Most PC-compatible computers come with Microsoft Windows preinstalled. This is useful for many reasons—notably that you can take the computer out of the box and turn it on and it will start up and boot into a working interface. This was not always the case with home computers. However, Windows is expensive, and there are many programs that run best when running directly on Windows while it is running directly on the computer hardware (as opposed to a virtual machine). It is often useful to be able to keep Windows installed on a computer even when primarily using Ubuntu.

Ubuntu can often be installed alongside Windows without special concerns, but sometimes legacy formatting restrictions can cause installation problems. On a new computer, it is always best to install Windows first, and then install Ubuntu next, because Windows is designed to be the only operating system on a computer and the Ubuntu installer is designed to work alongside other operating systems if they are present. A dual-boot Ubuntu installation proceeds as outlined earlier in this chapter until the fourth screen, which asks for the installation type (see Figure 1-33).

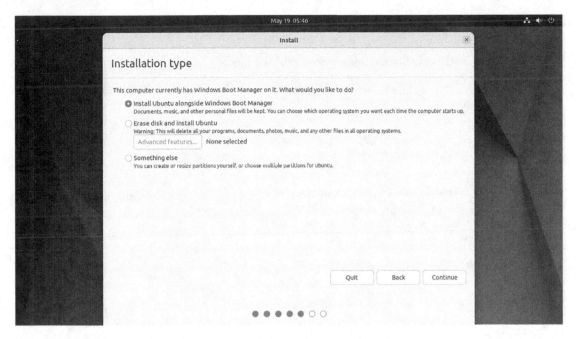

Figure 1-33. *Ubuntu does its best to detect any existing operating systems on a computer*

Ubuntu offers to either install itself alongside your existing operating system or replace it entirely. It is noteworthy to mention here that if Ubuntu does not correctly detect your existing operating system on this screen, continuing will probably erase it as well.

Caution   If the Ubuntu installer says "This computer currently has Windows on it," but does not offer "Install Ubuntu alongside Windows," then continuing will erase Windows and all your files. Very often, rebooting your computer into Windows and then restarting Windows (instead of performing a shutdown) will allow Ubuntu to resize your Windows file system. On older systems, you may need to delete the system recovery partition manually. See "Custom Partitioning" below for more information.

Ubuntu must be installed into its own dedicated file system. If you choose to install alongside Windows, the installer will create these file systems automatically. If you have installed Windows manually and left empty space unallocated for Ubuntu, the installer will simply use the entire remaining disk space. Otherwise, Ubuntu will show you a screen that displays your hard drive and allows you to adjust the amount of space allocated between Windows and Ubuntu (see Figure 1-34).

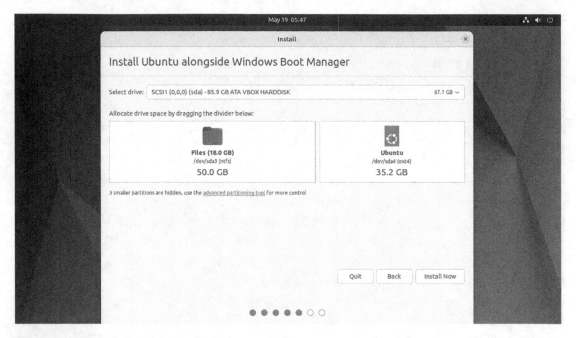

Figure 1-34. *Sliding the divider will determine how much disk space Ubuntu and Windows will have available*

Ubuntu will reserve 1 GB of disk space for virtual memory. This allows your computer to temporarily load more information than it has available RAM. Accounting for this extra dedicated space and room for more programs, you should give Ubuntu at least an additional 10 GB for itself, on top of the amount of disk space you want to use to store your own files. You can use the mouse to drag the divider and resize the Windows and Ubuntu file systems. If you want to install Ubuntu onto a different hard drive, you can select it from the drop-down list at the top of the installer window. A second hard drive is a good way to install Ubuntu on a desktop computer. Once you click "Install Now," the Ubuntu installer will shrink the Windows file system, shrink its containing partition, create several new partitions for Ubuntu, and then create new file systems. This action is irreversible and begins the rest of the Ubuntu install. The installation procedure from this point on continues as detailed earlier in this chapter.

When you start your computer after Ubuntu is installed, Ubuntu's bootloader, GRUB, will give you 10 seconds to choose a different operating system before Ubuntu is started (see Figure 1-35). You will also have the ability to run Ubuntu with advanced options, such as with an older kernel if an update gives you hardware compatibility problems, a safe graphics mode, or a rescue mode that provides a text interface you can use to repair a broken Ubuntu system.

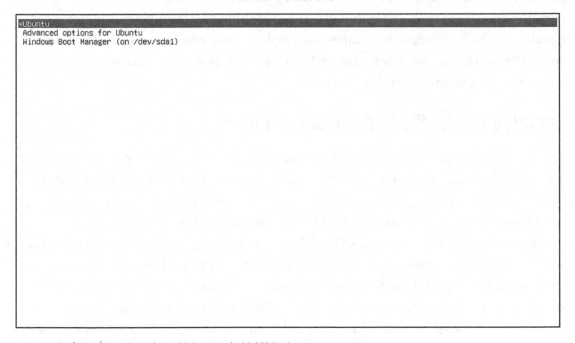

Figure 1-35. *Ubuntu will allow you to choose an operating system to boot when your computer starts*

Custom Partitioning

For over a decade, a more powerful partition scheme called GUID Partition Table (GPT) has been available, and in the past couple of years has become a common format for new computers. This allows you to create an unlimited number (for all practical purposes) of partitions on a disk. You will not run into any limitations with Ubuntu and other operating systems with drives that have been initialized to use GPT.

In the recent past, however, many computer hard drives used a partition scheme called Master Boot Record (MBR). This uses a simple partition table at the beginning of the drive that defines the way the drive is dedicated to different file systems. Unfortunately, MBR was created in 1982 to support the massive new 10-MB hard drives that would soon be available on the IBM PC XT computers. Because of this, the original specification only allows for four primary partitions to be created. Creating more partitions requires using one of these "primary" partition slots to define an "extended" partition, which can hold an unlimited number of additional "logical" partitions. Because this part of the partition table has remained unchanged ever since, Windows computers are limited to only four drive letters per disk unless some partitions are created in the extended partition space.

Ensuring the Ability to Reinstall Windows

Traditionally, computers come preinstalled with Windows on a single primary partition, and a computer manufacturer may have created additional primary partitions to store backup, recovery, or diagnostic tools. This can cause a conflict because these are always created as primary partitions to allow the computer to boot directly into them.

Beginning with Windows Vista, Windows began creating a dedicated boot partition to increase reliability. Most new computers with Windows preinstalled now contain two Windows primary partitions: a "recovery" partition that allows the owner to reinstall Windows to its factory-shipped condition and a "backup" partition created by the manufacturer to assist the user in creating full computer backups. This means that there are no more partitions available for Ubuntu, and most computers do not come with separate Windows install discs.

If this is the case, Ubuntu will not display an option to install alongside Windows. You will have to make a decision to modify the partition layout yourself. Personally, I order the installation media from my manufacturer for about $20 plus shipping and remove the backup and recovery partitions. Some manufacturers install a tool that allows you to create a recovery disc using blank DVDs. Another alternative would be to download the Windows 10 or Windows 11 setup disc directly from Microsoft. This will allow you to reinstall Windows again in the future. But if you do not want to do this and want to be able to reinstall the version of Windows that came with your PC, you will need to install Ubuntu to a different drive.

By default, Ubuntu also replaces the bootloader on your first hard drive to allow your computer to automatically start up. If you uninstall Ubuntu in the future, your computer will not be able to fully boot from the hard disk without installing a new bootloader. You can use a Windows recovery disc or setup disc to do this and choose "Automatic Repair." Windows should reinstall its own bootloader, and you will be able to boot directly into Windows again.

Using the Graphical Partitioning Tool

If Ubuntu cannot install itself automatically because there are no available partitions or if you want to specifically choose a different disk or bootloader target, you can choose "Something else" from the Installation Type screen and click "Continue." Ubuntu will start a graphical partition editor (see Figure 1-36).

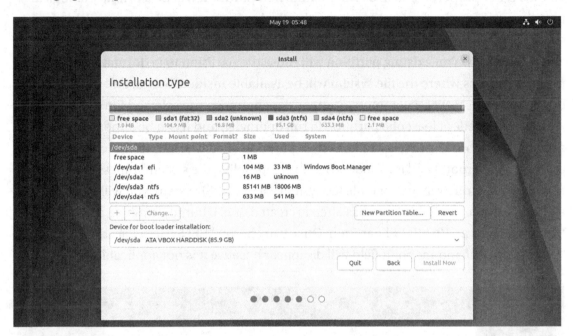

Figure 1-36. *A typical dual-boot partitioning scheme. Ubuntu will share the EFI boot partition with Windows*

The partition editor will list all hard drives and partitions. Ubuntu doesn't use Windows drive letters, but instead refers to physical hard drives in the order in which they are connected to the computer. The first IDE or SATA hard drive will be named /dev/sda, the second /dev/sdb, and so on. (An NVMe connection will look like /dev/nvme0n1.) Each partition on a hard drive is numbered and added to the physical drive name. Primary partitions are numbered from 1 through 4, but on an MBR disk, logical partitions always begin at number 5 even if there are lower numbers available. Unless notified, no changes will be made to your hard drive until you click "Install Now."

On an MBR disk, if you already have four primary partitions, you will have to remove at least one to install Ubuntu. You can do this by selecting it and clicking the minus (-) button under the partition list. You may also need to resize an existing partition to create more room to install Ubuntu. In Figure 1-36, /dev/sda1 is the Windows boot partition, and /dev/sda3 is the system partition that is named C: in Windows and contains the operating system and all user files. By selecting /dev/sda3 and clicking "Change...," the partition can be given a smaller size, which creates free space for Ubuntu.

By clicking "free space" and clicking the plus (+) button, you will be able to create a new partition (see Figure 1-37). The Ubuntu installer will also allow you to choose various other properties, such as whether the new partition will be a primary or logical partition and whether it should be located at the beginning or end of the available free space. "Use as" will indicate what file system should be created inside the partition, and if changed on an existing partition will cause the partition to be formatted. "Mount point" describes where the file system will be available inside Ubuntu, and the drop-down list will list several common locations depending on the selected file system.

Ubuntu needs at least one partition to run optimally, and it can be either a primary or a logical partition. The first is a main system partition of at least 8.6 GB, which is mounted at "/" (read as "root") and is formatted as "Ext4 journaling file system" unless you have a reason to use a different compatible file system. On an UEFI system, you will also need an EFI partition, but if Windows has already created one, Ubuntu will share it. By default, Ubuntu creates a 512-MB EFI partition. Once you choose "EFI System Partition" from the "Use as:" list, the mount point field will disappear because it is not applicable.

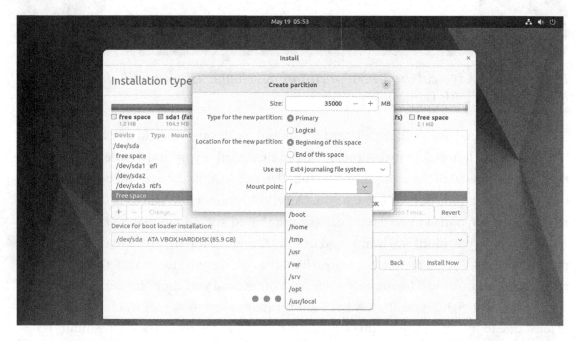

Figure 1-37. *The partition editor lets you choose settings such as file system type and mount point*

Additional Partitioning Scenarios

There are other reasons to set up custom partitions. For example, creating dedicated /boot or /home file systems or especially dedicated /var file systems on servers can be very useful. A dedicated /home file system is helpful because it contains all of your user data and program settings, so it allows you to completely reinstall Ubuntu without losing any of your personal data. A separate /var file system on a server prevents the main disk from filling up with logs or other data and causing the operating system to fail.

The bootloader can also be installed on a different disk. By default, it will install to the first hard drive, but if you want to install Ubuntu on its own hard drive and choose to boot from it during startup, you may want to install the bootloader to the same hard drive as Ubuntu instead, or even to a specific partition. This is most useful for computers that have an easy-to-access BIOS or UEFI boot manager.

Once your partitions are set up properly, you can click "Install Now." This will write the changes to disk and begin the Ubuntu installation. The installation procedure from this point on continues as detailed earlier in this chapter, and every boot will display the operating system selection menu shown in Figure 1-35.

Dual Boot with Ubuntu and macOS

If you have an Intel-based Mac, you can run Ubuntu on it. Ubuntu 22.04 LTS doesn't have an installer for Apple Silicon-based Macs (which have an Apple M1 or M2 chip), and while plenty of work is being done to support them in the future, for the time being there is no easy way to run Ubuntu on an Apple Silicon Mac with full hardware support. Instead, you may want to consider installing Ubuntu in a virtual machine like Parallels or VirtualBox. This section will give instructions for Intel-based Macs only, although if you do manage to get Ubuntu running on an Apple Silicon-based Mac, the rest of the book will apply.

All Macs come with macOS preinstalled, and thanks to the Unix-like nature of the operating system and the purpose-built hardware, most Apple users are very happy staying with the default software. Upgrades are extremely reliable, thanks to the limited hardware and software combinations. So for many users who want to install Ubuntu on their Mac, it will be their first time installing an operating system. Luckily, it's still a pretty easy process, and dual booting ensures that you can still boot into macOS for top speed.

Although all Intel-based Macs are basically PC-compatible systems, there are still some differences to a traditional PC. They all boot using EFI, not BIOS. And bootable Mac hard drives are partitioned using the GPT partitioning scheme. But Ubuntu has limited support in resizing Apple file systems. For this reason, I like to make room for an Ubuntu install in macOS before running the installer.

From the macOS desktop, with Finder as the current application, choose the Go menu and then Utilities. Then, double-click Disk Utility to launch that application. When it appears, it will show all of your hard drives and partitions in the left pane. You'll want to select the actual disk that you wish to modify, not a partition. The partitions have friendly names that you are used to working with such as "Macintosh HD" and are indented underneath the disks, but the disks begin with their storage capacity (see Figure 1-38).

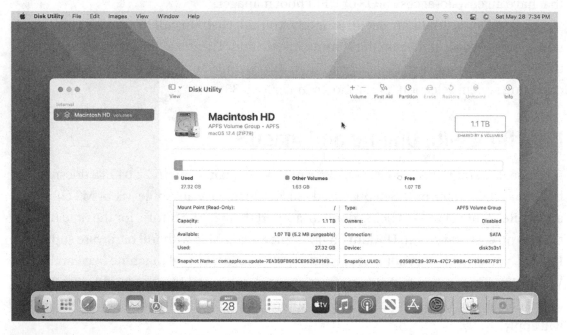

Figure 1-38. *Disk Utility shows you disks and partitions and allows to you format and resize them*

Once you've selected the drive, you'll see six options at the top of the right pane. The third option, "Partition," will let you resize your macOS partition and create room for Ubuntu. You can click a displayed partition to select it, and then drag the resize handle at the bottom corner of the partition to graphically resize the disk, or you can simply change the number in the size field. You can estimate the amount of space needed for Ubuntu by taking 10 GB of space for Ubuntu plus the amount of RAM installed on your machine, and increasing that by the amount of storage you want. I recommend at least 30 GB for a simple desktop install. Once you have freed enough space, click the "Apply" button. Disk Utility will ask if you want to partition the disk, and should state "Partitioning this disk will change one of the partitions. No partitions will be erased." and list any partitions that will be resized. Then, it is safe to click the "Partition" button.

Once the resize operation finishes, you can reboot your Mac. By holding the Option key, you will be able to choose to boot with your Ubuntu installation media. An Ubuntu installation proceeds as outlined earlier in this chapter until the fourth screen, which asks for the installation type (see Figure 1-39).

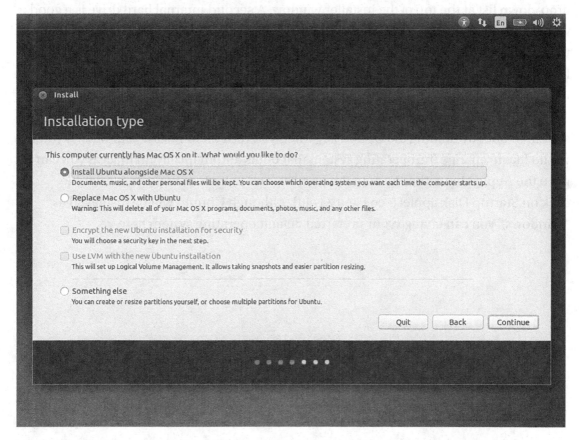

Figure 1-39. *This screen shows that Ubuntu detected your macOS install*

Ubuntu offers to either install itself alongside your existing operating system or replace it entirely. It is noteworthy to mention here that if Ubuntu does not correctly detect your existing operating system on this screen and say "Install Ubuntu along side macOS," continuing will probably erase it as well.

Ubuntu must be installed into its own dedicated file system. If you choose to install alongside macOS, the installer will create these file systems automatically. If you resized your partitions with Disk Utility and left free space unallocated, the installer will simply use the entire remaining disk space. Otherwise, Ubuntu will show you a screen that displays your hard drive and allows you to adjust the amount of space allocated between macOS and Ubuntu.

If you want to install Ubuntu onto a different hard drive, you can select it from the drop-down list at the top of the installer window. A second internal hard drive is a good way to install Ubuntu on a desktop Macintosh computer. Once you click "Install Now," the Ubuntu installer will create several new partitions for Ubuntu, and then create new file systems. This action is irreversible and begins the rest of the Ubuntu install. The installation procedure from this point on continues as detailed earlier in this chapter.

Once Ubuntu has finished installing, you will be able to choose which operating system to boot by holding the Option key when you turn on or restart your Mac. If you would like to change the operating system that boots automatically, in macOS you can go to the Apple Menu, then System Preferences, and in System Preferences double-click on Startup Disk applet (see Figure 1-40). Although Ubuntu will be displayed as "Windows," you can change your preferred default operating system here.

Figure 1-40. *macOS's System Preferences* ➤ *Startup Disk tool lets you customize your default OS*

Summary

Ubuntu can fulfill many tasks, and that leads to various ways to install it. Because each computer and each user is different, there is no one right way to install Ubuntu. However, most users will be able to start with Ubuntu itself, go through a simple install process, and have a working computer with no difficulty at all.

The best thing about being able to install an operating system is that it gives you the ultimate freedom over your computer. Not only can you confidently install Ubuntu using these instructions, but after you are comfortable with the operating system, you can refer back to this chapter to read about the various flavors of Ubuntu that are available as well.

CHAPTER 2

Getting Started with Ubuntu

One of the best things about Ubuntu is that it's ready for use as soon as it's installed. As soon as you reboot, you can get almost anything done immediately, and new applications are just a couple of clicks away. Some of the power of Ubuntu is in its differences from other operating systems.

Ubuntu is best approached as its own experience, without comparison to other operating systems—in fact, all operating systems are best approached this way. Therefore, the rest of the chapters in this book talk about Ubuntu directly. But it's hard to leave behind the habits and experience we've formed from working with computers. You're probably fairly handy with a computer running Windows or OS X. This chapter will help you take what you already know and apply that knowledge to Ubuntu, so that you feel comfortable more quickly. And it will help you work more closely with your other computers as well. It's a lot like a travel guide, complete with a phrasebook!

Tip　All modern operating systems using the desktop model of interaction have the same fundamentals. You can think of switching between them a bit like visiting a different country. There are different languages and customs, but with a bit of preparation, you can fit right in.

Try to think of learning a new operating system like the same kind of adventure, and you'll find the experience a lot more fun—and enjoyable.

63

© Nathan Haines 2023
N. Haines, *Beginning Ubuntu for Windows and Mac Users*,
https://doi.org/10.1007/978-1-4842-8972-3_2

Setting Up Your Computer

The first time you boot up Ubuntu and log in, Ubuntu will display a welcome screen that will help you set up your computer to work for you (see Figure 2-1). First, you'll have an option to link some online accounts to your Ubuntu desktop. For instance, if you link your Google account, clicking the clock at the top of your screen will display upcoming appointments in your Google Calendar. Linking a Nextcloud account will give you quick access to your files without needing to install the Nextcloud client. You can link some accounts and click Next, or you can click Skip. There are more account types available in the Settings application, and you can always connect to (or unconnect) accounts there later.

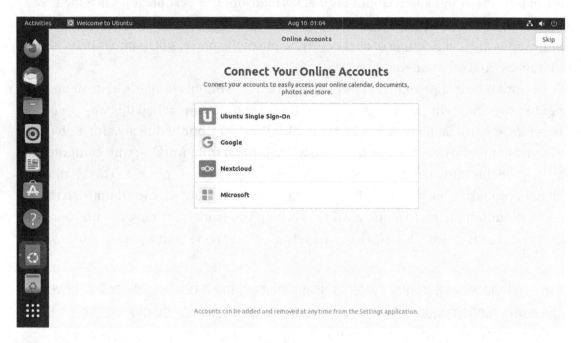

Figure 2-1. *Connecting Ubuntu to your online accounts gives you access to your data in the cloud*

The second screen prompts you to set up the Ubuntu Livepatch service from Canonical. This allows your computer to automatically protect itself from security vulnerabilities in the Linux kernel that powers everything else. This keeps you protected until you can install an updated kernel via the standard software update process and restart your computer. This isn't urgent for home desktop use, but for business desktop and server use, it's a really nice feature. Livepatch is free for every individual for up to three computers. If you didn't connect an Ubuntu One account on the previous screen, Ubuntu will help you log in if you click "Set Up Livepatch..." Or, you can click Next to continue without setting up Livepatch. You can always set it up later in the Software & Updates application.

The third screen allows you to help Ubuntu understand how it's being used by periodically sending information about your system to Canonical. This helps Ubuntu developers better understand how it's being installed and used. Ubuntu occasionally publishes a report about how many users are running Ubuntu, where, which versions, and so on. The information isn't personally identifiable, and you can see what information is transmitted by clicking "Show the First Report." You can also choose the option "No, don't send system info," and no information will be sent. Click Next when you've chosen to send or not to send information about your system.

The fourth screen (see Figure 2-2) allows you to turn on Location Services in Ubuntu. This uses a service by Mozilla (which provides the Firefox browser in Ubuntu) to determine your location. If you turn on location services, GNOME applications can request this information. It isn't used very often, but for instance GNOME Weather will use this information to automatically show your local weather in addition to the locations you have manually set. Ubuntu can also use this information to automatically adjust your computer's time zone while you are traveling. Click the switch next to "Location Services" to enable this feature, or leave it disabled, and click Next.

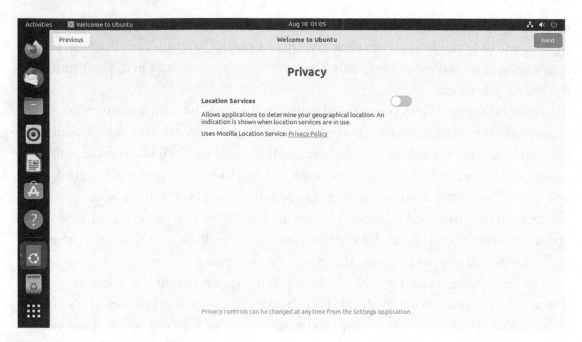

Figure 2-2. *You can allow Ubuntu to detect your location so that programs can provide tailored information*

The last screen (see Figure 2-3) shows a variety of popular third-party software that is available directly from their developers to be installed on your Ubuntu system. You can click an icon to launch Ubuntu Software and view the entry for each program, and you can click the arrows on the side of the window to advance to the next page. There are typically two pages of software titles that are recommended, and Ubuntu Software may start slowly the first time as it updates its software catalog. Any application you install will automatically receive updates once installed. Once you are done viewing this list of software, you can click "Done," and you will find yourself at the Ubuntu Desktop.

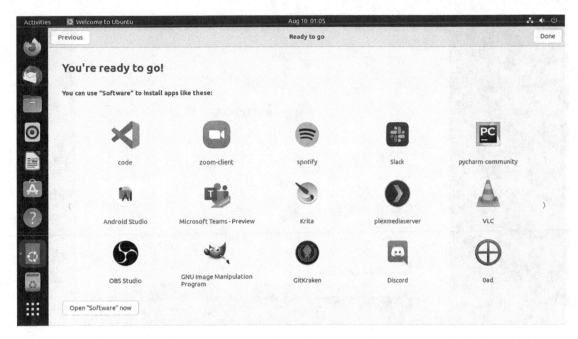

Figure 2-3. *Hundreds of applications have been packaged especially for you to use with Ubuntu*

Ubuntu Desktop

The Ubuntu desktop is simple and elegant right out of the box. Your new Ubuntu system has several programs preinstalled, and the desktop interface is called GNOME Shell along with several enhancements. Along the left-hand side of your screen is the Ubuntu Dock. Along the top of the screen is the top bar. On the left it has an Activities overview button and an application menu with the name of the currently focused program that can be clicked on for more details about the application. In the center is the clock, which you can click on for a list of notifications, a calendar, and upcoming appointments. On the right are individual application indicator menus and the system menu. Every application window has several window controls on the top right of its title bar, just like Windows (see Figure 2-4).

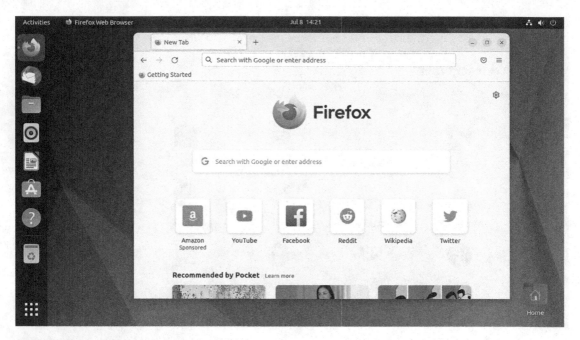

Figure 2-4. *This is the default Ubuntu desktop with a web browser running*

Ubuntu Dock

On the left edge of the screen is the Ubuntu Dock. This is where you can pin and launch your favorite applications, and see which applications are running. Clicking the Activities button at the top left of the screen or pressing the Super key (the Windows Logo or Command key) opens the Activities overview, and the bottom icon in the bottom left of the screen shows a list of the desktop applications installed on your computer (except the ones that are pinned to your favorites in the Dock). You can click an app icon to launch the corresponding application. Running applications will have a pip on the left, and will display two or three pips if two or three windows are open, or four pips for four or more windows. Clicking a running application's launcher icon will focus that application and its window to the foreground. If an application has more than one window open, clicking the icon again will display the windows as thumbnails. You can then click a thumbnail to bring that window to the foreground, or click the X button in the thumbnail's top right corner to close that window. Middle-clicking, or holding Shift or Ctrl and clicking a running application, will launch a new window of that application.

Right-clicking on an application icon will display a quick menu that lists application-specific commands. Different commands may be available depending on whether the application is currently running. The quick menu will also list all open windows, which can be selected with the mouse. The "Quit windows" option will close all open windows of that application.

Adding an application to your favorites keeps the icon displayed on the top half of the Dock when it is not running. This gives you instant access to your favorite and most-commonly used applications at the top of the Dock with a single click. Simply drag the icon to the top of the Dock to add it to your favorites. You can also right-click on an icon while the app is running or in the applications list and choose "Add to Favorites." To remove an app from your favorites, you'll have to right-click its icon and choose "Remove from Favorites."

You can rearrange your list of favorite apps by dragging them around the top half of the Dock. You can hold down the Super key and press a number key to automatically run or (switch to, if it's already running) the corresponding launcher icon, so arranging them can help you launch applications even more quickly. However, GNOME Shell doesn't display these numbers when you hold down Shift, so you will have to count the icons yourself.

You can make the Dock disappear until you need it by turning on the auto-hide feature. To do this, run Settings from the Activities overview or the system menu at the top right of the screen. Click the Appearance option on the left of the Settings application, and turn on "Auto-hide the Dock." This setting takes effect immediately, so you can test it out before closing Settings. By default, the Dock will be visible unless you have a window that would overlap it. When hidden, the Dock will appear when you push the mouse pointer "past" the left side of the screen. This gives you fast access to the Dock without it getting in the way of running applications.

The bottom of the Dock shows mounted storage devices (such as hard drives or USB storage) that are attached and ready to use (called "mounted" in Ubuntu), and you can right-click on a storage icon and choose "Unmount" to get it ready to remove. The last icon in the Dock before the application list is your Trash folder. You can click on it to view (and restore) deleted files that have not yet been removed from your computer, but you cannot drag files onto it.

Activities Overview

The Activities overview (see Figure 2-5) is designed to streamline the way you work with your computer. You can bring up the Activities overview by pressing the Super key on your keyboard, clicking on the Activities button on the top left of the screen, or by pressing three fingers on your computer's touchpad or touchscreen and gesturing upward. You can use it to view all open windows, manage workspaces, and search for installed applications, recently opened files and folders, and other information like city time zones, weather, or emojis and other special characters. The most useful things to know are that you can simply begin typing to search for information, pressing "Enter" activates the first result listed at any time, and you can use the arrow keys to select results as well as the mouse. Pressing Esc will clear the search field and bring you back to the initial Activities overview mode.

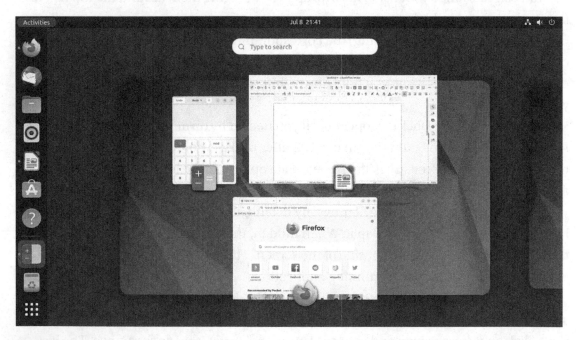

Figure 2-5. *The Activities overview shows your open windows and any active workspaces*

In the Activities overview, you can simply click on a window to focus it and bring it to the top of your other applications. You can also drag them from one monitor to another, or to different workspaces. A workspace is a way to group windows together in a collection of related activities, and you can use them to work on certain tasks without the clutter of having unrelated windows in the Activities overview or task switcher. In addition to dragging a running application to a new workspace, from the Applications list, you can drag an icon to any existing workspace at the top of the screen, and it will open on that workspace. Workspaces are covered in detail in Chapter 6 under Using Multiple Workspaces, but for now you should know that you can move between workspaces by clicking on them or scrolling through them in the Activities overview screen with your mouse wheel, additional workspaces do not take up additional memory or computing resources, and there will always be one empty workspace on the right that you can begin using by dragging a window to it.

When performing a search from the Activities overview (see Figure 2-6), the results are custom-tailored to the information they provide. For instance, clicking on an application result will launch the application. Clicking on a file result will open it, and other types of results will open in their corresponding application. Clicking on a Characters result will automatically copy the character to your clipboard so you can simply paste it into another application.

Figure 2-6. *The Activities search will return many kinds of information*

This search and the application grid, which you can access at the bottom of the Dock or by pressing Super+A, are the primary ways that you'll start applications that you have not pinned to the Dock. In the application grid, you can scroll through multiple pages of apps by using the mouse wheel or clicking and dragging the mouse to the left and right (or, if you have a touch-sensitive display, by swiping to the left and right).

You can customize the application grid by dragging the icons around to rearrange them. Not only can you reorder the icons or drag them to different pages, you can also drag one icon on top of another to create an app folder, which you can name. For example, you can click on the Utilities folder to see how important but seldom-used applications are all grouped together to be easy to find without cluttering the application grid.

Clock, Calendar, and Notifications

The top center of your primary monitor shows a clock with your current local time. Clicking on the time opens the Notification Window (see Figure 2-7). This window serves several purposes. First, it shows any application notifications that have recently occurred. Second, it shows today's date along with a monthly calendar. You can use the arrows to the left and right of the month to flip between months. If you have integrated any online accounts, appointment data from the cloud will be synchronized, and dates with scheduled appointments will be indicated with a small dot beneath the date. Clicking on a date shows you that day's appointments.

Figure 2-7. *Ubuntu shows a calendar, upcoming meetings, and notifications such as media playback controls*

Clicking on a notification will open the corresponding application. Some notifications are dynamic. For instance, Rhythmbox and Firefox will display playback controls for any media they are currently playing. Other applications can add relevant information as well. For instance, any additional time zones you add to Clocks will add the current local time for those time zones beneath the calendar. Likewise, if you install GNOME Weather, your local weather forecast for the next 5 hours will be displayed as well.

When you need to concentrate, you can click the "Do Not Disturb" switch at the bottom of the notification window. This will cause GNOME to hide any future notifications until you turn Do Not Disturb mode off.

System Menu and Indicators

The top right corner of your screen will show the System menu. This is dedicated to your computer's hardware functions and your desktop preferences.

At the top of the System menu are volume control sliders. If you have speakers attached to your computer, you will be able to quickly adjust your computer's volume. If an application is accessing your computer's microphone, you will also see a slider for that as well. If the maximum volume is still low, you can open Settings, click "Sound" in the left side of the application, and turn on "Over-Amplification" to allow values over 100%. This can cause audio quality loss or damage to speakers, headphones, or your hearing, so use this option only when necessary.

Tip   The System menu offers an additional shortcut: move your mouse over the volume or microphone icon, and use the scroll wheel to quickly raise or lower your computer's volume levels.

The next section of the System menu gives you access to hardware settings. Clicking on your wired network, your wireless network, or your Bluetooth icon will allow you to disable the hardware feature or open up Settings to that settings category.

Your current location or power savings status is also displayed, and if you are using GNOME's Night Light feature to reduce blue light, you can disable it until tomorrow (or reenable it sooner), turn off the feature all together, or view your Night Light settings.

The last section allows you to quickly launch Settings for a comprehensive list of various preferences you can change, or lock your screen, which will also put your monitors in power-saving mode. Selecting "Power Off/Log Out" will let you close all applications and return to the login screen. You can also reboot your computer or completely power it down.

Certain applications will add indicator icons to your panel. These are displayed to the left of your System menu. The way you interact with these icons will vary from application to application. Most allow you to simply click on the icon to display a contextual menu with various commands. Sometimes middle-clicking an icon will open (or close) an application window. Most modern applications treat a left or a right mouse click as the same thing, but older software—especially software originally designed for Windows—will expect a right click before showing a menu. If you've spent a lot of time interacting with the little icons in Windows' notification area (commonly but inaccurately called the "system tray"), then you'll be at home in Ubuntu as well.

Customizing Ubuntu

Ubuntu has a very professional, clean look, but the little details always add up. There are several settings that you can set on your Ubuntu desktop without making major changes to the operating system. Some of the most versatile change the appearance of your Ubuntu desktop (see Figure 2-8). Simply click the System menu and click Settings (or press the Super key, search for Settings, and click the app icon) to load the Settings app, and then click "Appearance" on the right side of the window.

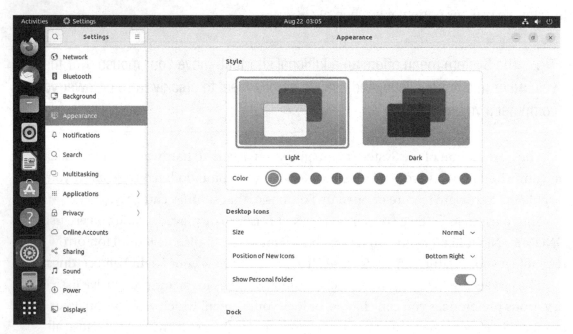

Figure 2-8. *You can quickly customize Ubuntu to suit your preferences*

The Style section contains what will be the most popular settings for every reader. Ubuntu defaults to a light theme that gives a bright, clean look to the Ubuntu desktop and makes it really easy to see which application is currently focused. But dark themes are increasingly popular on phones, and Ubuntu's dark theme keeps the Ubuntu interface from blinding you at night. Newer GNOME and GTK applications can detect your preferences and will automatically change their colors to provide a dark interface. Because this is a new feature, not all applications will automatically support dark mode.

In addition, Ubuntu offers ten pleasing accent colors for your desktop. If orange isn't your style, you can pick a different color for your icons and menus. While the choices are limited, the new accent color feature in Ubuntu 22.04 LTS ensures that the theme will be compatible with older and newer applications.

Note that while I personally prefer dark mode on my own computer (since I'm a night owl), this book sticks with the default light mode because it makes the figures easier to read. Feel free to change these settings until you find a combination that you enjoy the most.

Other notable settings options are the Background settings. You can change your desktop's background image, and note that that change you make will only apply to the current style you have activated: light or dark, so you can choose a different wallpaper for each style. Ubuntu comes with a color and grayscale background with the release's mascot (Ubuntu 22.04 LTS is codenamed "Jammy Jellyfish"), and also includes an additional ten images voted on from a selection provided by the Ubuntu community for each release. You can also click "Add Picture..." on the header bar to choose your own picture.

"Displays" lets you manage your computer's monitor settings, but the Night Light feature lets you turn on blue light reduction. You can schedule this to automatically activate between sunset and sunrise, or you can set a custom schedule. You're also able to adjust how strong the effect is. As a writer, I use it as is, friends who create photos or other art avoid it altogether, but the choice is yours.

The last feature I want to highlight is the screen long feature. You can see this in Settings by clicking "Privacy," and then "Screen". By default, Ubuntu automatically locks your screen after 5 minutes of no keyboard or mouse activity. This is great for a laptop or business computer, but it's a little aggressive for a home computer. You can set Ubuntu to set blank your screen (and put your monitor in power-saving mode) after a delay between 1 minute and 15 minutes. You can also tell Ubuntu to never blank your screen. By default, Ubuntu also locks your desktop session at the same time it blanks your display. You can add an additional delay of 30 seconds, a couple of minutes, half an hour, or 1 hour before your desktop session is automatically locked. While your screen is locked, running applications will continue to run just as before, but you will have to enter your password to regain access to your desktop session.

Ubuntu won't blank your display while you are watching a video, and you can immediately lock your screen by pressing Super+l (lowercase l). Your desktop session will be locked until you enter your password on the lock screen.

Managing Windows

Every application is displayed inside a window. At the top of the window is either a traditional title bar (as in Windows or macOS) or a larger and more versatile "header bar," which combines the functions of a title bar with a traditional menu bar and toolbar. You can move a window by dragging it by its title bar or header bar. Most application windows have three window controls on the right side of the title or header bar. In order, these hide (or minimize) the window, maximize the window to take up the entire screen, or close the window. Moving your mouse pointer to the window's edge or corner allows you to resize the window to any size you like.

You can also resize windows by dragging a window to the top, left, or right of your screen. Dragging to the top of the screen maximizes a window. You can drag it down from the panel to restore the previous window size. Dragging a window to the left or the right snaps it to that half of the screen, and is perfect for displaying two windows side by side. If you snap one window to the left half of the screen and another to the right half of the screen, you can resize both windows at the same time by dragging their shared border. Dragging a snapped window away from the edge of the screen by its title bar or header bar restores the previous window size as well.

You can switch between windows by pressing Alt+Tab. If you continue holding Alt, the window switcher will appear, and you can choose any running application as long as you are holding Alt. Each time you press Tab, you will cycle forward through the list to the next running application. Releasing Alt when the desired application is highlighted will switch to that application. Alt+Shift+Tab moves in reverse. You can also click a displayed window icon with the mouse to switch to it while you are holding Alt.

If you have multiple windows open in the same application, you can easily switch between them by pressing Alt+` (backtick) on a US keyboard. If your keyboard layout is set to match your physical keyboard, you can press the leftmost key above the Tab key even if it is not the backtick key. The application switcher will display all open applications, with the current application's windows below. This works the same as the window switcher, and Alt+Shift+` will move backward through the list. You can also use the arrow keys while holding Alt: Up to move to the application switcher, Down to display the application's open windows, and left and right to move around. You can let go of Alt to select a window, or click a displayed window with your mouse.

Installing and Updating Software

Ubuntu is a comprehensive operating system. As discussed in the last chapter, the Ubuntu operating system consists of a Linux kernel, the standard GNU userspace, X or Wayland for the graphics display system, and tens of thousands of other Free Software and open source projects. All of the software that comes with Ubuntu has been built from its source code directly on Ubuntu and packaged for delivery and installation. (Technically, some proprietary software and drivers were not compiled by Ubuntu, but they are installed and updated in the same manner.) This includes not only the software included on your installation media and in a newly installed Ubuntu system but thousands upon thousands of other applications that are available from the Ubuntu software repositories.

Ubuntu also provides a variety of applications that are published especially for Ubuntu and other Linux distros as "snap" packages. These software applications are compatible with any supported version of Ubuntu, and updates come directly from the software developer, independent of Ubuntu's release schedule. For the most part, you won't need to worry about how the software has been prepared for you. Ubuntu software brings all these sources together in one place.

Ubuntu Software

The easiest way to install new software is through the Ubuntu Software store (see Figure 2-9). This is a catalog where you can browse, search for, and install new software that is provided by Ubuntu. You are also provided with reviews and ratings from other Ubuntu users and can write your own as well. This is the best way to install software if you don't know exactly what you're looking for.

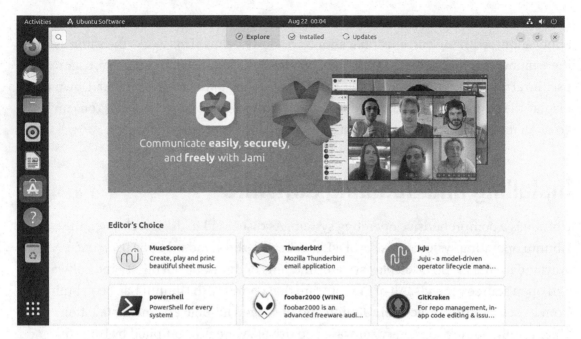

Figure 2-9. *Ubuntu Software provides a catalog with thousands of free applications*

Ubuntu Software provides a look at thousands of software packages. Because the packages are located in the Ubuntu software repositories, it always downloads and installs the most up-to-date version of an application for the current Ubuntu release. In addition, anything installed will receive updates through the Software Updater along with all other software. This makes Ubuntu Software an easy way to install software, and will be the primary method of installation used for the rest of this book. Some software is not displayed in Ubuntu Software, and when this software is featured in this book, instructions for installing in a Terminal window will be given. You can see Chapter 6 for a full explanation of what it means to install software via the command line, and how it can be a faster way to install software if you know precisely what you are looking for.

Snaps

Ubuntu now uses the "snap" packages to allow third-party developers to offer their applications to Ubuntu users. Snaps are mostly restricted to their own files and data, which provides protection against undiscovered security flaws or undetected malicious software. Over time, more and more software will be available via snaps—including newer versions of software included in Ubuntu, like LibreOffice and VLC. These applications do not replace or conflict with Ubuntu-provided software and are automatically upgraded when newer versions are published. This means, for example, that Firefox on Ubuntu is provided directly by Mozilla!

Other Sources

If you download software for Ubuntu directly from a website, you'll be provided with a .deb file. This is a Debian package file and is used by Debian and Ubuntu to allow your operating system to install and uninstall software cleanly by using the Debian package manager. You can simply double-click on the .deb file, and Ubuntu Software will open and display the information inside the Debian package. You can choose whether or not to install the software from that screen. With the exception of certain packages like Google Chrome and Steam, which add their own repositories to Ubuntu's list of software repositories, software you install manually will not receive automatic updates with bug or security fixes and in any case have not been reviewed by Ubuntu developers, so make sure to only install software you trust.

Updating Ubuntu

The Ubuntu repositories are where all Ubuntu-provided software is contained and is shared between desktop, server, and cloud versions of the operating system. In principle, the only differences between these versions are the default set of installed software packages and some system settings. This means that all software on your system in your default install as well as all software you install from Ubuntu Software (when the source is not the Snap Store) is maintained and supported by Ubuntu (see Figure 2-10).

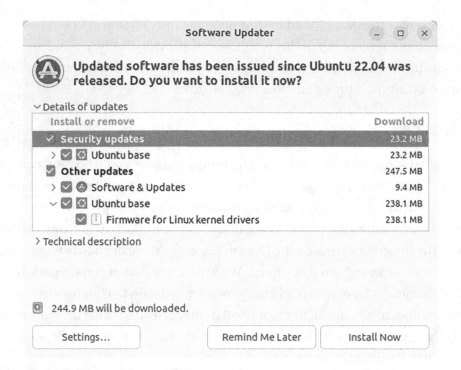

Figure 2-10. *Software Updater tells you about software updates. This is the detailed view*

Your computer will check for Ubuntu updates on a daily basis. Once a week, Ubuntu will inform you about recommended updates. These updates will only provide maintenance updates to fix bugs, not major newer or "feature" releases of software. If security updates are available, Ubuntu will notify you immediately. Installing the updates is automatic once you click "Install Now" and only requires your password authorization to begin.

The Software Updater provides updates for all software contained in the Ubuntu repositories, and acts as a single way to make sure all of your applications are secure and up to date. All updates are signed and verified by the Ubuntu developers so you can be assured that updates are trustworthy.

Snaps are updated independently, and the snap subsystem will check for updates four times a day. Installing updates via Software Updater will also start a check for updated snaps just before it exits. Snaps are updated automatically, as long as the application isn't running (see Figure 2-11).

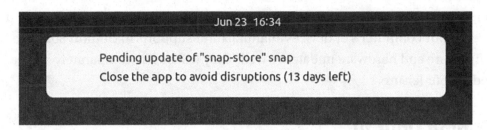

Figure 2-11. *Snaps cannot be updated while they are running. Ubuntu will notify you and check again later*

If you receive a notification of a pending update, you can simply continue using the application. Just remember to close it when you're done with it. Ubuntu will update it the next time it checks for updates to your computer's snap packages. If it still hasn't been able to update a running snap after 14 days, Ubuntu will forcibly close the application and begin the update process.

The easiest way to update a snap package is to close it, and then open Ubuntu Software and click on "Updates" at the top. You can see the individual snap packages and other updates available and update them individually or altogether (see Figure 2-12).

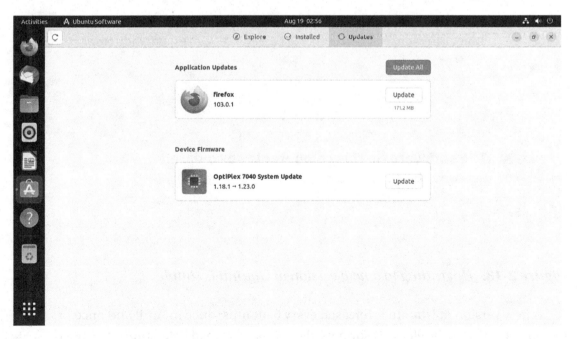

Figure 2-12. *Ubuntu Software can update snap packages, and often your computer's firmware as well!*

Simply click "Update" to download and install the latest update of your installed software. If your computer's or devices' manufacturer supports it, Ubuntu Software can install firmware and hardware updates as well. They will be listed separately and can be updated at your leisure.

Upgrading Ubuntu

Because all software provided by Ubuntu is also maintained by the Ubuntu community (or is isolated, thanks to snap packages), this makes OS upgrades simple as well. Ubuntu will notify you when a new version of Ubuntu is available. If you do not upgrade at that time, the Software Updater tool will also offer you the chance to upgrade (see Figure 2-13).

Figure 2-13. *Upgrading to a new version of Ubuntu is simple*

A new version of Ubuntu is released every 6 months: once in April and once in October. Every fourth release is supported for 5 years instead of 9 months (with an additional 5 years of support available with a free Ubuntu Pro subscription) and is considered a long-term support (LTS) release. Ubuntu 22.04 LTS is the release covered in this book, and the next LTS release will be Ubuntu 24.04 in April 2024.

When a new version of Ubuntu is released, the Software Updater will notify you of the available update. LTS releases, by default, will only notify you once the next LTS release is available, and only after a delay of 3 months when all updates are rolled into a "point" release (such as Ubuntu 22.04.1 LTS). This allows for any major bugs to be addressed, and postrelease updates to settle down with the help of early adopters. This allows you to enjoy a stable system at all times.

When you are notified of a newer version of Ubuntu, it's important to install all updates still pending for your current release and back up your files. Once your software is up to date, you can click the "Upgrade..." button in the Software Updater. This will display the release notes for the new version of Ubuntu. After reading the release notes, you can choose to continue with the update. This is a lengthy process that downloads a very large amount of data and cannot be interrupted once it begins.

This upgrades all software on your computer with newer versions. For the most part, it actually uses the same methods as minor software updates—a testament to the power of Ubuntu's software packaging systems. While it should be safe to browse the Web or play a simple game, you should make sure your system is plugged into AC power if you are upgrading a laptop, and refrain from doing any important work on your computer during the upgrade. Once finished, reboot immediately. Your system will restart and you will be running the new version of Ubuntu.

Managing User Accounts

Ubuntu was designed to handle multiple users on a single computer, and it is easy for each user to have his or her own account where each user's settings and program data can be stored separately from the others'. While any installed applications are available to every user, application settings are stored in each user's home folder. Things like mail, personal files, language settings, and desktop and wallpaper preferences are user-specific. Giving each computer user a dedicated account allows each user to use the computer without affecting other users' experience. A user can even log in and use Ubuntu while another user's programs continue running in the background!

Creating a new user account can be done from the System Menu ➤ Settings, scrolling down the list on the left and on "Users" applet. This applet displays all user accounts installed on the system, and the panel is initially locked (see Figure 2-14). While locked, you can only make changes to your own user account, such as changing your display name or password.

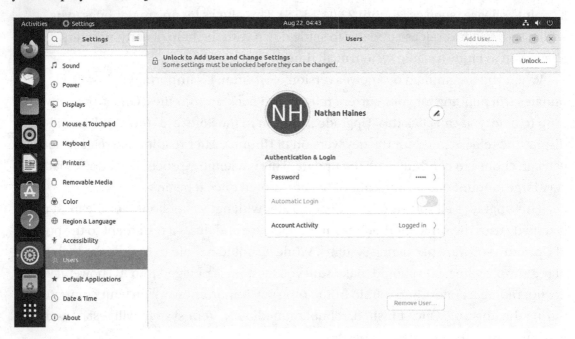

Figure 2-14. *User Accounts is where accounts can be added, removed, and modified*

Adding, removing, or changing other user accounts modifies the operating system's settings, and requires administrative access. You can click the "Unlock" button near the top right of the window. You will be prompted for your password, and then you will be able to modify other user accounts. (If you are not using an account with administrative privileges, you can select an account that does have administrative privileges and provide that account's password instead.) The applet will automatically lock again after 15 minutes of disuse. The "Add User..." and "Remove User..." buttons also become available.

To add a new user, click the green "Add User" button in the Settings header bar. The "Add account" window will appear, and you can choose between a "Standard" account and an "Administrator" account (see Figure 2-15). A user with an administrator account is able to install or remove software with his or her password just like the user account created during installation. Standard accounts cannot authorize system-level changes, and an administrator user will need to authorize any such action taken by the standard user when prompted. The "Full name" field shows the display name of the user that will be shown on the Ubuntu welcome screen, and the "Username" field must start with a letter and only contain letters, numbers, and periods ("."), dashes ("-") and underscores ("_") and no spaces or other symbols. The down arrow to the right of the username field will display some suggested usernames based on the Full name field. The username is used for the user's home folder, so something simple is often better.

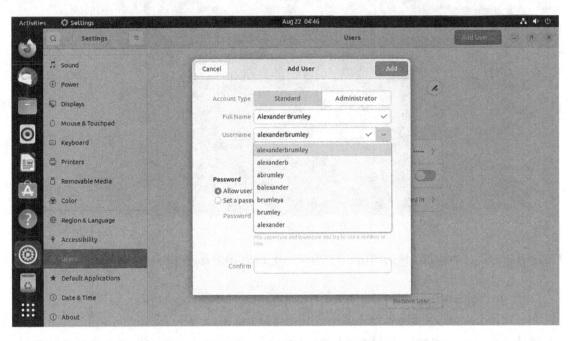

Figure 2-15. *A new account can be added to the computer in seconds*

The new account needs a password. By default, Ubuntu will simply prompt the user to create a secure password the first time they log in. You can also set a secure password before creating the account. Once you have decided how to handle the password, click the green "Add" button in the window's header bar.

Finding Things in Ubuntu Instead of Windows

If you're coming from Microsoft Windows (Figure 2-16), you should find Ubuntu fairly easy to adapt to.

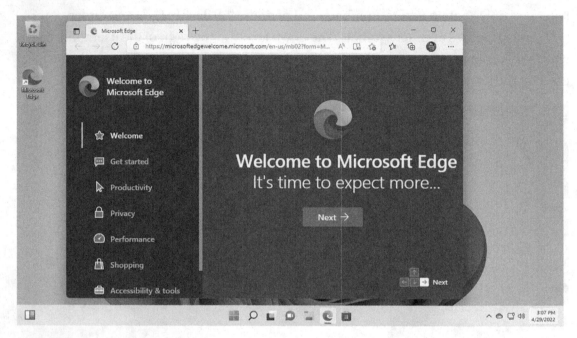

Figure 2-16. *A typical Windows 11 desktop with one web browser window open*

Here are some guidelines that should help you make the transition:

The Windows Logo key is called the Super key in Linux. The Alt key is still called Alt but is also sometimes referred to as Meta. These names refer to modifier keys used on Unix terminals long before Windows or PCs existed:

- The Windows Taskbar is replaced by the Ubuntu Dock on the left side of the screen. The Dock can be moved to the bottom or right of the screen, and the icons can be resized in Settings, under Appearance. The system notification area (sometimes called the system tray) on the right side of the Windows Taskbar is similar to the indicator icons at the top right corner of the screen in Ubuntu. The Action Center in Windows 11 is duplicated by the Notification window at the top center of Ubuntu's desktop.

- The Start Menu and Start Screen are replaced by the Activities overview search and the application grid. File search is provided by both the Activities overview and by running the Files application and pressing Ctrl+F. The Control Panel and Settings apps are replaced by the Settings application. Task Manager is replaced by System Monitor available in the application grid.

- Changing the desktop wallpaper image can be performed by right-clicking the desktop and choosing "Change Background...." The theme and accent colors can be changed via Settings ➤ Appearance. Custom themes are not supported by Ubuntu or GNOME and require third-party software. An accessible, high-contrast theme is available in Settings ➤ Accessibility by enabling the "High Contrast" option.

- Windows are controlled similarly in both Windows and Ubuntu. The system menu in Windows is accessed by clicking the window icon or the top left corner of the title bar, and in Ubuntu it can be accessed by pressing Alt+Space or right-clicking a title bar in Ubuntu.

- The Windows File Explorer file manager is replaced by the Nautilus file manager, labeled "Files" in the Ubuntu Dock and application grid. The C: drive in reference to the system drive is known as the root directory. Disks and external storage drives are not assigned drive letters but are mounted inside the existing file system, usually under /media/username. Folders are often referred to by the older term "directory"—especially on the command line. The user folder is known as the home folder. Hidden files begin with a . (period) and are often called "dot-files." The Windows registry is replaced by a combination of text configuration files, often in /etc for system-wide settings and dot-files in each user's home folder for user-specific settings, usually in a hidden directory such as .mozilla or .config.

- The functionality of the Microsoft Store is provided by Ubuntu Software. Windows Update and updates from the Microsoft Store are replaced by Software Updater, which tracks maintenance and security updates for all applications installed via Ubuntu Software or otherwise installed from the Ubuntu software repositories (such is as on the command line with `apt`). Third-party applications installed as snap packages are updated automatically.

Finding Things in Ubuntu Instead of macOS

If you're coming from macOS (Figure 2-17), Ubuntu will feel extremely familiar.

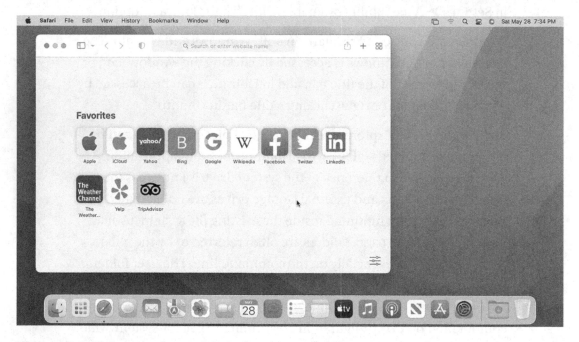

Figure 2-17. *A typical macOS desktop one Web browser window open*

Here are some guidelines that should help you make the transition:

- The Option key is used for Alt but is also sometimes referred to as Meta. These names refer to modifier keys used on Unix terminals long before Mac OS or OS X existed. The Command key is used for the Super key.

- The Dock is replaced by the Ubuntu Dock on the left side of the screen. The Ubuntu Dock can be moved to the bottom or right of the screen, and the icons can be resized in Settings, under Appearance. The menu bar extras are similar to the indicator icons at the top right corner of the screen in Ubuntu.

- Launchpad is replaced by the Activities overview and application grid. Spotlight-like file search functionality is provided by the Activities overview, and File search is provided by running the Files application and pressing Ctrl+F. System Preferences is replaced by the Settings menu under the application grid or System menu. Activity Manager is replaced by System Monitor in the application grid.

- The Apple Menu is replaced by the System menu at the top right of the screen.

- Changing the desktop wallpaper image can be performed by right-clicking the desktop and choosing "Change Background...." The theme and accent colors can be changed via Settings ➤ Appearance. Custom themes are not supported by Ubuntu or GNOME and require third-party software. An accessible, high-contrast theme is available in Settings ➤ Accessibility by enabling the "High Contrast" option.

- Windows are controlled similarly in both macOS and Ubuntu. The Maximize control in Ubuntu functions like the full-screen control in macOS. Additional window controls in Ubuntu can be accessed by pressing Alt+Space or right-clicking a title bar. In Ubuntu, the App Menu features can sometimes be found by right-clicking the application's Launcher icon as well as clicking the Application menu.

- Finder is replaced by the Nautilus file manager, labeled "Files" in the Ubuntu Dock and application grid. The Mac drive in reference to the system drive is known as the root directory. Disk and storage drives are mounted in the existing file system, usually under `/media/username`. Folders are often referred to as directories—especially on the command line. The user folder is known as the home folder.

- The functionality of the App Store is provided by Ubuntu Software. Software Update and automatic updates from the App Store are replaced by Software Updater, which tracks maintenance and security updates for all applications installed via Ubuntu Software or otherwise installed from the Ubuntu software repositories (such as on the command line with apt). Third-party applications installed as snap packages are updated automatically.

Connecting to a Windows Desktop Remotely

You may find it useful to run Windows programs during your transition to Ubuntu, or you may want to use Windows-only programs from time to time. Luckily, Ubuntu comes with a remote desktop client preinstalled. Remmina Remote Desktop Client can connect to other computers in a variety of different ways, including Remote Desktop Connection, VNC, and SSH. Remote Desktop Connection (also known as Terminal Services) is available in Windows 10 Pro and higher editions, and SSH is available in all Unix- or Linux-based operating systems. In order to connect to a computer remotely, it must be powered on and not sleeping or hibernating.

Your first step is to set up your Windows system to accept remote desktop connections. This is fairly simple, and you can do so by right-clicking Computer or This PC in the Start Menu or File Explorer and choosing "Properties" from the context menu. When the System Properties window appears, you can click the "Remote" tab or the "Remote desktop" option and make sure that the "Allow remote connections to this computer" or "Remote Desktop" option is enabled. If you have trouble logging in, make sure that "Allow connections only from computers running Remote Desktop with Network Level Authentication" (recommended) is unchecked. In Windows 11, you can access this setting by clicking the down arrow next to the "Remote Desktop" feature switch.

You can run Remmina by searching for its name or "remote desktop" in the application grid. The first time you run Remmina, it will display a window with an empty list of remote computers. You can save various profiles for connecting to remote computers and double-click them in the future. To begin, click the "New connection profile" icon at the top left of the header bar. To set up a connection to a Windows computer, you'll need to know the IP address of the computer or the host name if your router supports Windows host name resolution. You'll put this in the Server field, and you can also enter your Windows username and password to the profile to save time when connecting. If you are connecting over the Internet, consider keeping the color depth at 256, but if you are connecting to another computer on the same network, you may want to increase the color depth to 16-, 24-, or even 32-bit color.

Changing the connection name and clicking "Save" will save the connection for later. You can connect to the same computer in the future just by double-clicking the entry when Remmina starts up. Clicking Connect will connect to the Windows machine (see Figure 2-18). In most respects you will be able to interact with Windows just as though you were running it on your local machine. Other users may or may not be able to use the remote machine while you are connected, depending on your version of Windows.

Figure 2-18. *You can connect to remote Windows machines and use them with ease*

The toolbar on the left allows you to scale the display to match the size of your Remmina window ("Toggle dynamic resolution update") or enter full-screen mode (Right Ctrl+s) and focus on Windows only. You can customize these options in the toolbar or in the connection preferences to tune the experience to your preferences.

Sharing Office Documents with Others

On Ubuntu, you'll start off with LibreOffice. This full-featured office software is more than capable of opening, editing, and saving Microsoft Office documents. But by default it uses the Open Document Format to save its files in. This standard format is now supported by all modern office software, but legacy office software may have limited support.

LibreOffice supports saving files in many various formats. By default, an edited document will be saved in its original format. However, you may find it convenient to offer files in different formats to ensure an optimal viewing experience for others.

In LibreOffice, you can choose "Save As..." from the File menu. You can either type a file name with a standard extension (".odt" for Open Document Text format, ".doc" for Word 97 format, ".docx" for Microsoft Word 2007 XML format, ".html" for HTML, and so on) or choose a specific format from the drop-down list under the folder view. Clicking Save will save a copy of the document and continue saving under the new filename and format. Word formats are useful for sharing files that must be edited by users with Microsoft Office, which may have limited support for the Open Document format.

If you would like to ensure that the other user can view and print a document precisely as you formatted it, but you do not need or want them to edit it, you can save a copy of the file as a PDF. This is available via the "Export as PDF..." option under the File menu in LibreOffice, and will create a file that represents a printed document that can be viewed and printed by others on any operating system with a PDF viewer.

Note   In producing this book, my editors needed Word 2010-format documents and provided Word template files. However, I don't own a modern copy of Microsoft Word and use Ubuntu exclusively. I opened the template in LibreOffice and saved it in Open Document Text format and started typing. When I finished a chapter, I would save it as Microsoft Word 2007–2013 XML (DOCX) format and send it to my editors. Each of us was able to use our preferred tools to deliver this book into your hands.

Sharing Photos and Graphics with Others

Graphics images are among the easiest files to share between operating systems, as the Internet has seen to it that the most common and useful file formats are supported and shared between all modern operating systems. Therefore, most formats should work without issue. I will simply add a note about each of the most common file formats.

JPG files are the most common format around. This is a "lossy" format, which means that it saves space by not encoding all of the data perfectly when it's compressed. This format is designed for real-world photographs and takes advantage of how the human eye works. This does mean that editing and saving JPG files results in a slight loss of quality that can build up over time. For a finished photograph that does not need to be edited more than once or twice, JPG is the clear winner. For art with large single-color fields or line art, the compression can interfere with the image quality.

GIF is a fairly ancient file format that was developed to be easy for the slow computers available in 1987 to process. GIFs have only 256 colors, and therefore tend to be low quality, but they are often used online to show short animations. For any other purpose, they are a bad choice, even if they work everywhere.

PNG was developed as a response to a patent lawsuit regarding the GIF format, and is probably the most versatile image format around today. With good lossless compression, the resulting files are not subject to quality loss over multiple edits, and while photographs result in much larger file sizes in JPG, line art is much smaller and more crisp than GIF. This is a perfect format for works in progress and can be opened in almost every image browser.

TIFF was an early black and white-only format that was developed as a common format for desktop document scanners. It is still often seen as a format for scanners and faxes. While the format became quite versatile for grayscale and color documents and can flexibly hold lots of notes and other information about a scanned document and can even use JPEG compression for documents, it's probably better to choose JPG for a final file or PNG for a file that will be edited by others.

Formatting Disks to Work with Other Operating Systems

Computers store data on hard disks, floppy disks, CD, DVD, and Blu-ray discs, magnetic audio tape, paper tape, solid-state disks, and flash memory, and the physical formats have changed tremendously since the 1940s. The logical formats have changed even more rapidly. I'll use an analogy to help illustrate how computers and disks work.

A disk is like a ruled piece of paper. You might have a single sheet or various sizes of notepads. They can be opened and viewed by anyone. Internal and external hard disks, optical discs, and media cards are all like a notepad.

When you write in a physical notepad, the notepad doesn't really care what you write. You can write in English or German. Japanese kana represents sounds. Hebrew characters represent sounds but are written from right to left. Chinese ideograms represent ideas. All of these can be written between the lines on the same notepad. But only some of these ways of writing will make sense to readers. These writing systems are like the disk format and file system, and the readers are like the operating system.

The first Windows and Mac computers were typically used in offline, homogeneous environments. This meant that in the days before networking was widespread, Microsoft and Apple were free to develop their own way of reading and writing data to a disk in a manner that was efficient and supported the way their software worked. For this reason, Windows computers first supported only FAT file systems written to a nonpartitioned or MBR-formatted disk. Mac computers supported HFS file systems on a full or Apple Partition Map-formatted disk. As their needs became more complex, Windows computers began supporting NTFS and GPT, and Apple computers began supporting FAT and NTFS so they could read and write Windows-formatted disks, and started using HFS+, APFS, and GPT. But priority was given to the native file formats on each system.

Linux grew up in a networked world where it needed to read a lot of different file formats. So while the Linux "extended file system" was developed to serve its needs better than the Minux file system it started with and Ubuntu today uses the fourth version of this system, ext4fs, Linux also often needed to read Windows- and Mac-formatted disks. This resulted in rich file system support that Ubuntu users benefit from today. The upside is that Ubuntu can read almost any disk format that it sees. But Windows and macOS are still very limited in the formats that they support. Here are some tips for formatting disks so that they can be used on Windows and Mac computers.

Both Windows and macOS can read MBR- and GPT-formatted disks. MBR is good for small media devices, but GPT should be used for any system hard drive you install Ubuntu to, and is required for drives larger than 2.1 TB. Apple Partition Map can only be read by macOS and Ubuntu, and has been replaced by GPT on macOS.

File system support is trickier. The only format that Windows and OS X both support for reading as well as writing is FAT32. This format can be read in almost any consumer device on the market, but can be prone to corruption if a computer or device loses power while writing, and also has a file size limit of approximately 4 GB. Especially for video and backup files, this can be restricting.

The native Windows format is NTFS, and Ubuntu can read and write this format reliably. However, OS X can only read NTFS and not write to it. For sharing between Windows and Ubuntu computers, however, this is a very robust and reliable format.

The native macOS format is APFS. Ubuntu doesn't have trouble reading the previous default format HPFS+, but Ubuntu can't read APFS-formatted disks without installing additional software, and cannot write to them at all. Windows cannot read either disk format without third-party software.

With this maze of compatibility issues, FAT32 and NTFS remain the best choices for USB drives and portable hard drives.

The write-once-only nature of early optical discs posed special problems, and therefore early CD-ROMs used a file system called ISO 9660. This was extended in a few different ways to support long file names and was eventually replaced by UDF, or Universal Disc Format. The upside is that CD, DVD, and Blu-ray data discs use these formats exclusively. This means that optical discs can be read by any computer with a compatible disc drive. So you'll never need to worry about formats—your burning software will take care of that decision.

Summary

Using a new operating system can be very much like living in a different part of the world with different customs: much is still familiar, and just a little bit of context can make your environment much more comprehensible.

Ubuntu has its own strengths and works very well with others. Whether you move to Ubuntu only or use it along with other operating systems, Ubuntu is flexible enough to work with other computers over the network or via floppy disk. Armed with this knowledge, you're ready to begin using Ubuntu as a part of your everyday routine.

CHAPTER 3

Productivity at Home and Work

A fresh Ubuntu installation is reasonably complete. The included applications and tools form a comprehensive computer system that can be used for all basic daily computer use and more. But Ubuntu's software repositories are home to thousands more software packages that can transform your computer into a powerful tool to boost your productivity. The possibilities are nearly endless.

One of the strengths of the default software—from the Firefox Web browser to the Thunderbird email client to the LibreOffice office suite—is familiarity. This world-class software is common on Windows and Mac computers and is familiar enough even if you haven't used it before. Instead of focusing on the default applications, this chapter covers additional software that can enhance the most common tasks that users will want to accomplish: from advanced email management to note-taking, time management, organization, file backup, and working with web apps and mobile apps. Each is available through Ubuntu Software.

Writing Documents Without Distractions Using FocusWriter

Writing is one of those activities that is really personal. There are a lot of different ways of writing, and every writer has his own preferences and rituals. Personally, I like to write outlines and notes with a fountain pen in a notebook, which is how this very book started out. Then, I like to switch to a word processor for most of the actual writing. LibreOffice is a great way to format documents, and I used it exclusively to write this book. But the features and toolbars can also be distracting.

© Nathan Haines 2023
N. Haines, *Beginning Ubuntu for Windows and Mac Users*,
https://doi.org/10.1007/978-1-4842-8972-3_3

A lot of creative writers prefer to use simplified writing environments. Early word processors were very simple with little to no interfaces for menus, toolbars, and status bars (sometimes referred to as "chrome"). While pressing F11 in Text Editor and Ctrl+Shift+J in LibreOffice or opening a terminal and running nano (see Chapter 5) will reduce distractions, there's a purpose-built word processor that's designed with writers in mind.

FocusWriter is a minimalistic word processor that fills your entire screen (see Figure 3-1). Unlike other similarly focused text editors and word processors, FocusWriter opens OpenDocument Text and Rich Text Files as well as plain text. It also supports simple text formatting. The default theme is a white editing area with a nice wooden writing desk as a border, and there are several other themes: a stormy sky, a misty forest, professional, muted-blue background, a green-on-black theme that evokes old monochrome phosphor monitors, a space nebula, a somber cityscape, and a tranquil sky above peaceful clouds. But you can create your own themes as well: the background can be set to any photo or solid color, and the editing area's font and foreground and background colors can be customized as well.

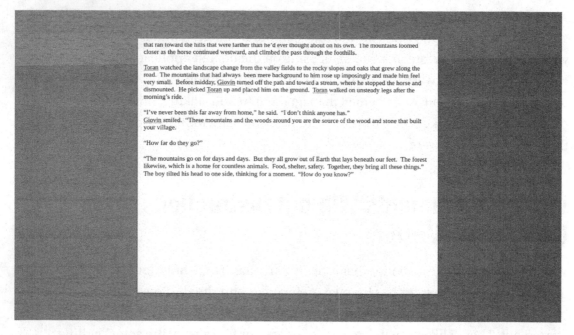

Figure 3-1. *FocusWriter provides a distraction-free environment for writing*

The lack of other windows and indicators allows you to focus on your writing without distractions. Basic shortcut keys for copying and pasting work, as well as formatting with the usual shortcut keys such as Ctrl+B for bold text, Ctrl+I for italic text, and so on. The word processor keeps track of your word count and time spent writing, and also allows you to set an alarm or timer to help you keep track of your progress. This is perfect for using the Pomodoro technique or setting up a word count goal for events such as National Novel Writing Month.

Despite the empty look of the writing area, FocusWriter does have an interface that appears as needed. By bringing the mouse up to each edge of the screen, you will access a different interface feature. In the application, only one feature is visible at a time. The composite screenshot below (see Figure 3-2) displays all edges at once, for illustrative purposes.

The top of the screen contains the menus and a fully customizable toolbar. You can rearrange and add or remove toolbar buttons and labels in the menu system under Settings ➤ Preferences... ➤ Toolbar.

The left side of the screen shows a scene selector with all "scenes" present in the current document. Scenes are separated by "##" on a single line per standard writing convention, but the scene separator is easily customized in the preferences as well. For example, I prefer "-*-" in my own writing, and you can change the divider to anything that works for you. The scene selector allows you to quickly jump between portions of your document. The right side of the screen displays a standard scroll bar and can be used to manually scroll through your document.

The bottom edge of your screen shows you all open documents as well as statistics for the current document. If you've set a time or word count as a daily goal in the preferences, it also displays your goal progress as well. The right side of the status bar shows the current progress of any active timer or alarm as well as the current time.

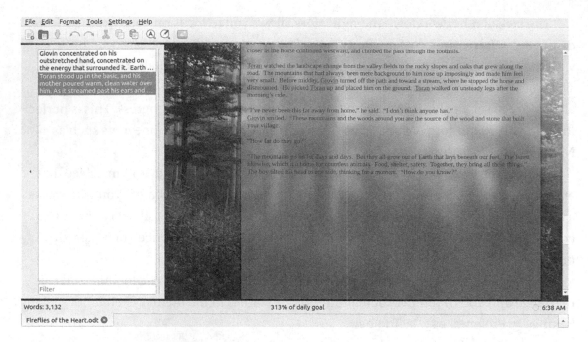

Figure 3-2. *Each edge of the screen provides a different tool for working with your documents*

Because the interface is so simple, it is worth reviewing FocusWriter's settings. You can have FocusWriter highlight the current line your cursor is on or the surrounding lines, and there are very flexible statistic and daily goal settings that you can customize to your needs. There's even a "Typewriter sounds" feature that plays the sound of a typebar hitting paper when you type letter keys and a carriage return and bell when you press Enter. Combined with a suitable theme, you can really make your own distraction-free writing environment!

FocusWriter is a fun and easy way to cut out distractions and write creatively. With a little background music or white noise and a serene landscape background, the only thing missing to fuel your writing time is a mug of tea or coffee.

Managing Your Personal Finances Using HomeBank

Managing money is a major life skill, and it's a lot easier if a computer can do all the math for you. There are several financial management programs available in Ubuntu, but one of the simplest to use is HomeBank.

HomeBank is a single-entry home accounting program, and it keeps track of your account balances and transactions (see Figure 3-3). You can import QIF, OFX, or QFX files exported from Quicken, Microsoft Money, or You Need A Budget, and you can also import OFX files downloaded from your bank. This can help you get a head start in populating your data.

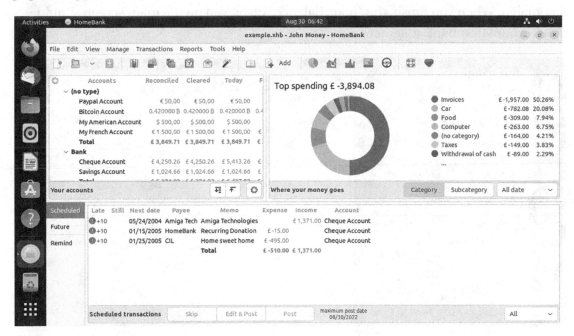

Figure 3-3. *A high-level overview of your current account balance and recent spending*

When you first run HomeBank, you'll see a welcome dialog. Creating a new file will walk you through entering your personal information and your first account. "Accounts" can track any type of money, whether it is cash at hand, money stored in a bank account, or the monetary value of an asset or liability. You can also set up accounts to be excluded from the budget or reports if you want to track something separately.

Once you have HomeBank set up, running the application will show the main window. It shows all of your accounts sorted by category, with the bank-reconciled and current balances as well as a balance that includes transactions you've entered but which take place in the future. It also shows a pie chart of your spending by category, which you can adjust to show for the last month, the current month to date, by quarter, rolling 30, 60, or other day period, and otherwise customize to your preferences. At the bottom of the screen, you'll see upcoming transactions that are scheduled as bills.

Double-clicking on an account will show the account window. It works just like a check register (see Figure 3-4). Adding transactions adjusts your balance. Aside from the date and amount, you can also enter payee and category details as well as a memo.

This allows you to keep track of your account balances. Reconciliation is handled manually, so you'll need to compare your transactions with a printed bank statement. You can select a transaction and click the reconcile button from the toolbar to mark it as reconciled. When you finish, the "bank balance" displayed on the main screen should match your latest bank statement.

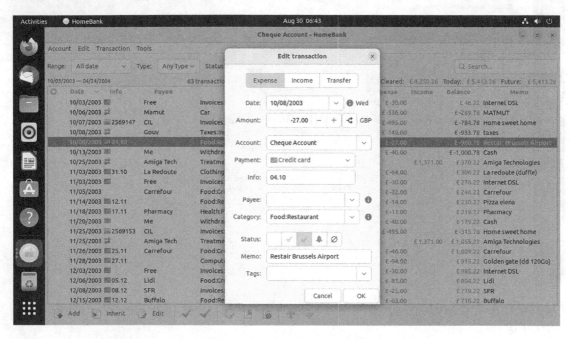

Figure 3-4. *Entering transactions works just like a standard check register*

HomeBank also allows you to set up your budget expectations with the budget dialog, and you can adjust budget amounts for each category on a month-to-month basis. The main window offers several reports, and clicking the respective toolbar button will display a report window. By default it shows an informative but bland list view, but you can choose between various chart views for each report.

An extremely useful feature of HomeBank is the ability to view a vehicle cost report. This allows you to track not only repair and maintenance costs but also your fuel economy. Be sure to use Edit ➤ Preferences from the menu, select "Locale," and choose "Use miles for meter" and "Use gallon for fuel" under "Measurement units" if you want to view your fuel economy in terms of miles per gallon.

Altogether, HomeBank is a simple yet powerful way to track your finances. While smart spending practices are still your responsibility, having your spending data and friendly reports available will help you keep on track of your money and stick to your financial goals.

Managing Your Professional Email, Contacts, and Calendar Using Evolution

Evolution is a deluxe email and personal information management software in Ubuntu. In addition to email, it also manages your contact list, calendar appointments, and to-do lists as well. It is equivalent to Microsoft Outlook and is very similar in organization. For many years it was the default email manager in Ubuntu, but it was replaced by Thunderbird in an effort to make the default desktop more simple and lightweight. However, if you can make use of the extra functionality in Evolution, you will find that this application will make your life a lot more simple.

The first time you launch Evolution, the Evolution Account Assistant will appear. This setup wizard will guide you through the process of setting up your first email account. For this, you will likely need the details of your email provider's server settings; however, popular public providers may be set up automatically. The very nice thing about setting up your email with an IMAP account is that you can continue using Evolution along with Thunderbird, Outlook, Windows Mail, or your phone and view the same email on each device. Once you have set up your mail account, Evolution will launch and prompt you for your account password. Then, you'll see the main Mail window (see Figure 3-5).

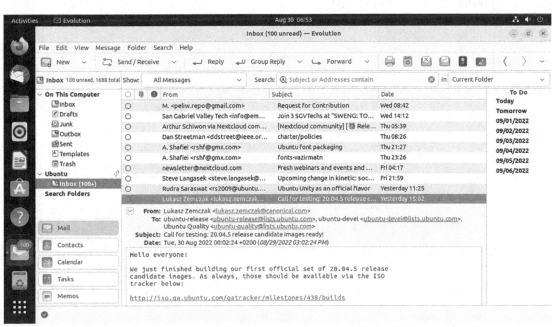

Figure 3-5. *Evolution is a very capable email and personal information manager*

Evolution can handle multiple email accounts from different servers, and each account has its various folders listed on the left side of the window. The right side of the window has the message list for the currently selected folder and a preview pane for the current message below the message list. The message view is particularly useful because it groups email by reply in a threaded view, which you can toggle on or off by choosing the menu option View ➤ Group By Threads or pressing Ctrl+T. This is very handy for mailing lists or long email discussions on a single topic.

On the bottom left of the window, you'll see buttons that allow you to switch to other modes as well. Evolution supports multiple contact lists, calendars, a task list, and various memos and to-do lists.

Contact view lists your contacts, and you can track user details both locally and by syncing them with online address books provided by Google, LDAP servers, or over WebDAV. This allows you to utilize your phone and work contacts while keeping them separate from each other. Clicking the down arrow to the right of the "New" button on the contacts view allows you to create a new address book, and the "Type" drop-down menu allows you to choose an online data source for your address book.

The Calendar view allows you to view and edit appointments and other schedule data as well as a task list. In addition to your local calendar, you can also add CalDAV, Google, ICS, and weather sources that you can display one at a time or in aggregate on the calendar display (see Figure 3-6).

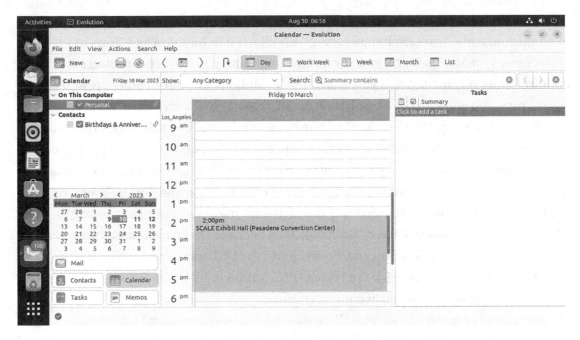

Figure 3-6. *Calendar view shows schedules from multiple calendars side by side*

The nice thing about Evolution's multiple calendar support is that you can easily import shared calendars as well. This lets you view your friends' or coworkers' public calendars and coordinate your schedules. You can easily display or hide any calendar's appointments by clicking the check box beside the calendar on the left-hand side of the window.

The monthly thumbnail calendar lets you navigate to dates quickly, and dates with appointments are displayed in bold. You can change the Calendar view from day, work week, week, month, or agenda-style list by clicking the toolbar buttons. The task list on the right can be resized with the drag handle to make more room for the Calendar view, or removed by using the menu option View ➤ Layout ➤ Show Tasks and Memos pane.

Task view lets you set up working tasks that you can schedule start and due dates for, record priorities and notes, and eventually mark canceled or completed. Tasks can easily be marked completed by clicking the check box next to a task on either the calendar or task view.

Memo view is similar to task view except there is no priority or completion status. Memos are virtual sticky notes you can use to keep miscellaneous information around. They can be searched or printed from this view.

One very nice feature of Evolution that isn't available by default is the ability to connect to a Microsoft Exchange server. This allows it to function as a drop-in replacement for Microsoft Outlook for business use, and you can send and accept appointments via email. When you search for "Evolution" in Ubuntu Software and click on its entry, you will see that the software detail page has a header called "Add-ons" which lists "Exchange Web Services" as one of the additional Evolution features. You can select the check box next to the add-on and enter your password when prompted to install it automatically, or you can install the package `evolution-ews` via the command line. The next time you launch Evolution and click the down arrow next to "New" on the toolbar and choose "Mail Account," the Evolution mail configuration assistant's "Receiving Email" page will have "Exchange Web Services" as an option in the server type list. After you enter your username and paste the URL for the web email portal under "Host URL," you can click the "Fetch URL" button to fill in the OAB URL field and continue setting up your email account as normal.

Evolution is a heavy-duty email client that can be used to manage your email; schedule appointments with yourself and other; take advantage of your existing Google and work email, calendars, and address books; and keep track of work tasks and other information. If you are used to Microsoft Outlook, then Evolution can smooth your transition over to Ubuntu. You can even manage your work email in Outlook and your personal email in Thunderbird if you prefer—both programs coexist peacefully on the same computer.

Managing Your Calendar with Thunderbird

Thunderbird is a nice, simple messaging client. Famous for email, it also handles Usenet, RSS, and instant messaging as well. Most computer users use online calendaring tools via their web browser, but it can be extremely convenient to have this tool on your desktop as well. If Evolution is too heavy for your comfortable use, you can use the default calendar functionality in Thunderbird instead.

The calendar plug-in for Thunderbird is called Lightning, which was so popular that Thunderbird adopted it and includes it by default. It adds the "Events and Tasks" menu to the tab bar and a "Today Pane" and dedicated Calendar and Tasks tabs to Thunderbird. You can toggle the Today Pane on and off from the bottom right corner of the Thunderbird window, and you can open the Calendar and Task tabs by clicking the respective icon on the left side of the Thunderbird window just under the menu bar.

On the bottom left of the Calendar tab (see Figure 3-7), you'll see a list of calendars, with "Home" being the default calendar. You can right-click here and choose "New Calendar…" or click the "+" icon beneath the calendar on the left to create a new calendar, and you can create either a local or remote calendar. Choosing "On the Network" allows you to add an ICS, CalDAV, Sun Java System Calendar Server, or a Google Calendar for synchronization. These are set up and maintained separately from any accounts you may have set up in the Online Accounts section of Settings.

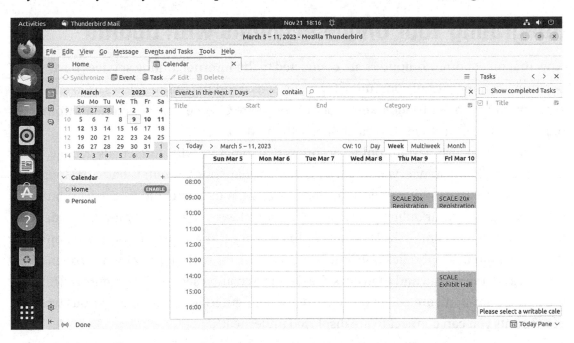

Figure 3-7. *Calendar view shows schedules from multiple calendars side by side*

To add your personal Google Calendar, right-click in the calendar list, and choose "New Calendar…." Select "On the network" and click "Next," and then type your Google account into the "Username" field. The "Location" field will automatically fill in with "gmail.com," and you can simply click the "Find Calendars" button. A new window will appear and ask you for your Google account and password. Enter this information and follow the prompts to sign in, and then click "Allow" when Google asks you to grant Thunderbird permission to access your Google account. Thunderbird will show a list of your calendars from Google, and you can choose which ones to integrate into Thunderbird. You can click the "Properties" button to change the calendar name, its color, and how frequently Thunderbird will check for updates. Once you have selected the calendars you want and click "Subscribe," the calendars will be added to

Thunderbird, and your appointments will be synchronized to your computer. From then on, when you create a new event and select your Google calendar during creation, the event will appear on the Web and any other device where you use your Google account.

Lightning is a great Thunderbird feature that adds basic calendar support to the email client. You can use it to manage your appointments and keep your schedule synchronized across all of your devices.

Integrating Your Online Accounts with Ubuntu

Now that most home computers are connected to the Internet, online services have become a routine part of computing for many of us. Working online allows us to talk and share photos with our friends, keep track of and share Google Drive documents from any online computer, and sync our calendars with the Web.

Ubuntu supports various online accounts that integrate with some of its default applications. For instance, you might use Flickr to share photos with friends, or Google Docs to collaborate on documents, or Google Calendar or Nextcloud to manage your schedule. Adding your online accounts to Ubuntu allows you to bring your online data to your computer seamlessly. Ubuntu's Online Accounts manager allows for easy online data integration. Simply click the System menu in the top-right corner of the screen, click "Settings" in the menu, and then click the Online Accounts section (see Figure 3-8). The top of the right-hand area displays all currently configured accounts, and various types of accounts you can connect to are displayed underneath.

Different accounts integrate with various kinds of features. For instance, Ubuntu Single Sign On is used for Canonical's Livepatch service; Nextcloud is used for documents, contacts, and calendars. You can always add or remove accounts at any time.

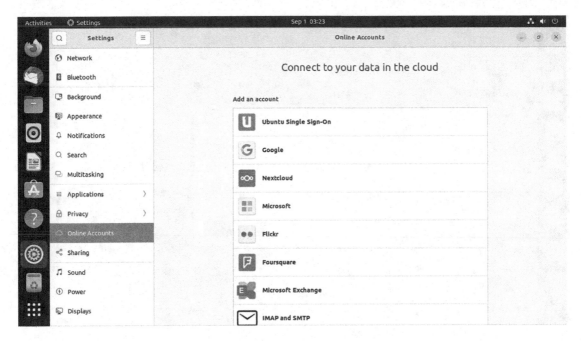

Figure 3-8. *Ubuntu brings your online accounts directly to your desktop*

Each online account can actually integrate with your desktop in various ways. A Flickr account integrates with Shotwell. This means that when you add your Flickr account to Ubuntu, when you're organizing your photos with Shotwell, you can send them to your Flickr account directly from Shotwell.

Google is another example of a service that has many different services. Adding your Google account will give you access to your Google Drive files in Files. You'll be able to publish photos in Shotwell to your Google Photos account by selecting a photo or photos and clicking the "Publish" button on the toolbar. Ubuntu also synchronizes your Google Calendar events. When you click the clock at the top center of your screen, the calendar will show dates with events from your Google Calendar along with events you've added in Evolution or Thunderbird. If you have Evolution installed, your Gmail email and contacts along with your calendar will be automatically integrated into Evolution with no further setup.

Ubuntu's online accounts support allows you to sign into your online services in one place and integrate them into your Ubuntu desktop. But the Online Services applet keeps you in control of what information you share with your local applications. Each account can be added or removed, and services can be enabled or disabled on a per-service basis (see Figure 3-9).

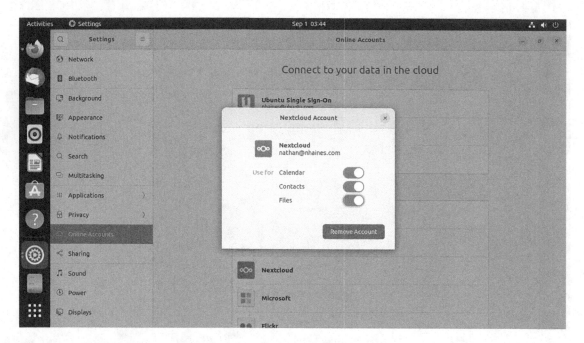

Figure 3-9. *You're in control of the data you share with your computer and online*

Clicking on an account shows the various types of date that Ubuntu applications can use. Your Google Calendar data will appear in the clock menu, but without Evolution installed, Ubuntu won't use your Gmail data. So if you don't already have it, you might choose to install Evolution or disable Gmail integration. (Mozilla Thunderbird does not use Ubuntu Online Accounts integration and works independently.)

This integration technology provides seamless integration of local and online data in Ubuntu, and makes working with your data fast and easy to find.

Organizing Your Thoughts with Mind-Mapping Software Using Freeplane

Mind-mapping software is a great way to organize thoughts and notes in a structured manner that is still flexible enough to experiment and brainstorm. This category of software is increasingly popular in creative circles, and is a great way to explore an idea because you can begin thinking in broad terms and then come back to each category and focus on more specific concepts.

Freeplane is a popular mind-mapping tool in Ubuntu, and can be used to create mind maps. The software works rather simply, with a broad concept or topic in the middle, and then you add "elements" to represent subconcepts. A map can range from simple to very complex. The included documentation comes in the form of a mind map and demonstrates some of the variety of formatting options, categories, icons, and hyperlinks that can be included in each element. The default document that opens the first time you run Freeplane demonstrates most of these capabilities (see Figure 3-10).

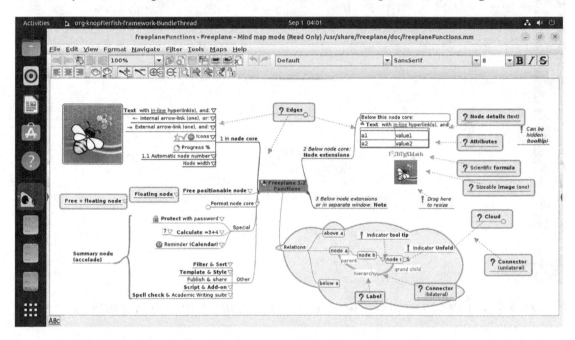

Figure 3-10. *Freeplane has many advanced formatting options available*

Using the software is fairly simple. In a map, you can hover your mouse pointer over a node or click a node to select it (the selected node will have a blue border around it) and start typing to replace the label, or double-click the node to edit the existing label. Once you have your main concept (e.g., "drinks"), you can add nodes that branch off of the main node. Pressing the Insert key will create a child node branching from the selected node and place the cursor so you can begin typing a label for it. If the parent node is "drinks," you might add "tea." Typing a name and pressing Enter will leave the new node selected. Moving your mouse back over the main node again and pressing Ins, you might add "coffee." Pressing Enter twice after typing a node name will create a "sibling" node automatically. Under "coffee" you might add "americano," but by pressing Enter twice, you can add "espresso," "latte," and so on without having to move the mouse back to "coffee" and press Ins again. Hovering over tea, you could add "black," "white," "green," and "oolong." As you think of variations on each category, you can always go back and add more child nodes. "Earl Grey" might go under black tea, or you might add a new node called "flavored" and leave each category for types of leaves. (See Figure 3-11.)

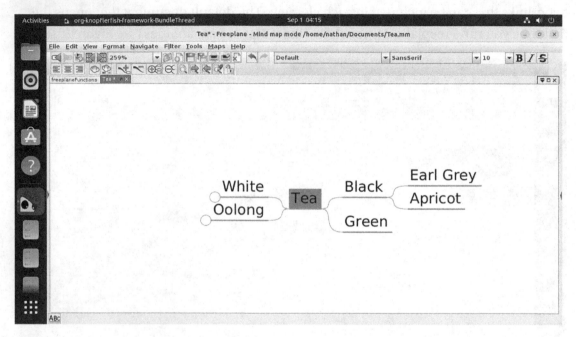

Figure 3-11. *You can organize any kind of information using Freeplane*

Removing a node is as simple as clicking or hovering your mouse over it so a blue border appears and pressing the Del key. A confirmation window will pop up and ask if you really want to delete the node. Deleting a node will also delete all child nodes it contains.

You can edit nodes as well. Selecting a node by clicking or hovering allows you to rename it. Dragging a node to a different node will attach it as a child to the new node. Right-clicking on a node allows you to set a lot of different options. Exploring the documentation will help illustrate the possibilities (pressing F1 brings up a very comprehensive tutorial), but you can add or remove various predefined icons, change the formatting or style, and even export a branch as a new mind map if you decide you want to expand on a concept more fully on its own.

A nice thing about Freeplane is that it has a large number of export options. You can export a mind map as an HTML, XHTML, or Java applet for adding to a website, an OpenOffice.org Writer file that can be opened in LibreOffice, an image, and many other formats. This makes sharing mind maps with others extremely easy.

Freeplane is a nonconventional organizational and planning tool that is useful for keeping track of projects, Internet research, and organizing all manner of research for authors of both fiction and nonfiction. It may just be the tool that helps channel your creativity.

Personal Wiki Note Taking Software Using Tomboy

Everyone likes to keep notes handy. These simple reminders can be practically anything—lists, memos, or tiny documents that are not quite worthy of text or LibreOffice files because they are small or somehow related. Just as sticky notes are a way of life for some, keeping notes on the computer brings a new level of convenience to the desktop.

Tomboy is an easy-to-use note manager that combines the simplicity of sticky notes with the power of wiki software. You can install Tomboy from Ubuntu Software, where it is listed as "tomboy-ng." When you open Tomboy, you'll see a welcome screen with a summary of your Tomboy status. While this is one way to interact with Tomboy, the main way is to use the Tomboy icon on the top panel, to the left of the System menu. You can click "Don't Show for normal startup" if you don't need this status window every time you start. Clicking the Menu button on any Tomboy window or on the Tomboy tray icon gives you several options, and one of them is "New Note," where you can start your first sticky note. The bottom of the menu lists your existing notes. Every note that you open will appear in its own window (see Figure 3-12).

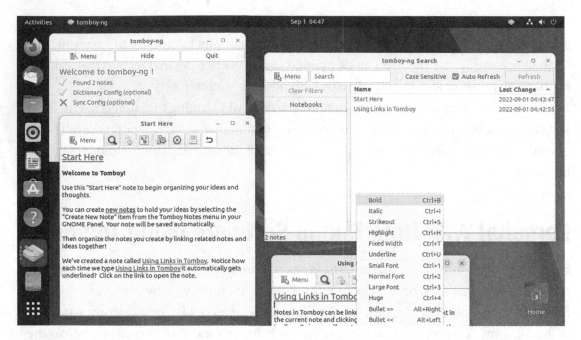

Figure 3-12. *Tomboy lets you create simple notes that can link to each other*

This note taking software is easy to use. The "Search" window displays all notes sorted by notebook, and you can use the search bar to search the full text of any note. At any time, pressing Ctrl+N will create a new note. Then, you can click on the blue, underlined title at the top of the note to change its name. The first line of any note will become its title, and it may take a couple of seconds for this to reflect in the formatting. Typing underneath the title will let you create the body of the note, which can be formatted by choosing a format and typing, or selecting regions of text and clicking the "Text" button in the toolbar (see Figure 3-13) to choose your formatting, which is indicated by the "abc" icon. The shortcut keys for formatting are mostly standard, but you can view them in the "Text" formatting menu for reference.

One of the unique features of Tomboy is the ability to link notes together. You can select text and click the "Link" button in the toolbar (represented by a dotted downward arrow) to immediately create a new note with the title of the text you selected. This note is linked to the previously selected text and can be opened again by simply clicking the link. This allows you to expand on ideas in unlimited detail and keeps individual notes simple while making it easy to organize collections of notes.

Notes can further be sorted into notebooks, which provide for further organization. Simply clicking the "Notebook" button in the toolbar of any note allows you to select an existing notebook or create a new notebook. Lastly, notes can be exported to HTML format by clicking the gear icon on the note toolbar and then shared via email or on the Web.

Tomboy also includes a dedicated indicator applet so that it stays running even after you close the last note. You can use this menu in the top right side of the screen to quickly create a new note or open a recently opened note.

Keeping track of the little pieces of information we gather throughout the day can be tricky. Tomboy helps you organize and manage this information and keep notes cross-referenced with a simple, easy-to-use note editor with powerful formatting and simple linking between notes.

Installing Additional Language Support

One of the easiest features to take for granted is language support. Anyone who speaks English is pretty lucky in that most computer software is written entirely in English by default. But anyone who is bilingual is aware at how different menus, terms, concepts, and even simple text can be from one language to another.

Ubuntu is surrounded by a global community of developers and users, and this global community also speaks dozens of languages. One of the ways that Ubuntu embraces these members is through robust and comprehensive language support. Dozens of languages can be chosen right at installation so that Ubuntu users can feel right at home. It can be easy to forget how foreign a computer can be when it isn't in one's primary language (see Figure 3-13).

Figure 3-13. *Even the familiar becomes strange when it's in an unfamiliar language*

One last thing to remember is that using Ubuntu in a different language is a fantastic way to practice your language skills, and the language tools and text entry will assist you whenever you are working in multiple languages.

Language support in Ubuntu covers a variety of areas, and they are all important. The foremost, naturally, is translated and localized software. Figure 3-13 shows Ubuntu as it appears in German. The web browser shows *Suche oder Adresse eingeben* instead of "Search or enter an address." The menus are all in German: *Datei* instead of "File," *Bearbeiten* instead of "Edit," and so on. LibreOffice names new documents *Unbenannt 1* instead of "Untitled 1." Fonts capable of displaying a language's native script are so important that while the Ubuntu font supports the extended Latin, Greek and ancient Greek, and Cyrillic alphabets, other fonts fill in where needed for other languages.

Localization is the next detail. Germany uses specific formats and spellings that are distinct from other languages, but even from other German-speaking regions (see Figure 3-14). The clock in the top right of the screen shows 24-hour time instead of the 12-hour time popular in the United States. Numbers use commas as decimal points and periods as thousands separators so that Jupiter takes 4.332,59 days to orbit the sun instead of 4,332.59 days. And even the standard folders in the home folder are named differently. Pictures are found in the *Bilder* folder, the Desktop is now the *Schreibtisch*, and the Trash is now stored in the *Papierkorb*. The first time you log in after setting a new language, your computer will ask whether you want to add the standard folders in the new language. Your system will begin using these new names as defaults, but the existing content will not be moved. Some languages have more dramatic changes. Right-to-left languages such as Arabic and Hebrew display properly, and the direction of progress bars also orients themselves from right to left. The calendar changes. The week might start on Monday instead of Sunday. A locale might not use the Julian calendar at all and use an alternate calendar instead. These details all add up to give a computer a native feel in any given language and location.

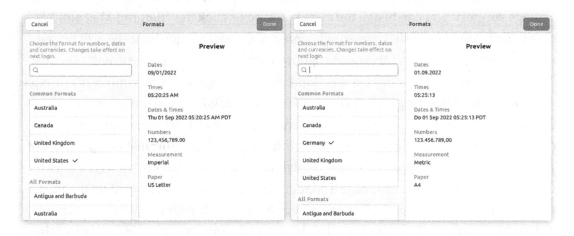

Figure 3-14. *Locales affect numbers, dates, calendars, measurement units, and currencies*

The last component of language support is text input. At a basic level, this means various keyboard layouts to support the hundreds of physical keyboard designs available throughout the world and at various times in computing history. The Spanish keyboard has an Ñ key, and the top letter row of a German keyboard starts with QWERTZ instead of QWERTY and has keys for Ä and ß. The top letter row of Greek keyboards starts with ;ΣΕΡΤΥ instead of QWERTY. A matching keyboard layout means that the characters that appear on your screen match the characters printed on your keyboard keys. The input indicator on the top right of the screen shows the current layout, if more than one has been configured. "en" for English, "de" for German, and so on. Clicking on the indicator allows you to select between installed layouts or show the currently selected keyboard layout. This is valuable because it may not match your physical keyboard at all. (Or, sometimes worse, it may almost match your physical keyboard layout, but have some surprises around the edges!)

Configuring Language Support

You can check your current language support and add or remove additional languages by launching "Language Support" from the application grid. The Language Support window appears and displays "Checking available language support" as Ubuntu verifies the language tools available for your language and locale. For instance, an Ubuntu system installed with English (United States) support is missing spelling dictionaries and locale format settings for Australian, British, Canadian, and South African English. Running Language Support will declare that "This language support is not installed completely," and clicking "Details" will show the software packages required to complete language support. You can install the extra software or click the "Remind Me Later" button. If you do not install these extra languages, the extra English locales will not be fully available, but of course this can be ignored unless you wish to use them.

After language support has been verified, the Language Support window is available. It displays all installed languages in order of preference, with the current setting displayed in black. You can drag and drop languages to order them in preference. The first language will be used for the computer interface, and any untranslated portions of a program will be displayed in the next available language in order of preference. There may be a brief delay when you make a change. These changes will take effect the next time you log into your desktop, but do not require a reboot. Your language settings only affect your session while you're logged in, but you can apply your settings to the entire system if you are an administrative user. This will localize the computer startup and login screen, but other user accounts will retain their current language settings. You will need to enter your password to authorize the change.

Clicking "Install/Remove Languages..." will allow you to add or remove support by language, which will install the associated locale settings as well. The new window lists all supported languages, and you can use each language's check box to select or unselect it. Click "Apply" to automatically download the translations, locales, and any necessary fonts and remove any unselected languages. You will need to enter your password to download and install the new software.

The Regional Formats tab on the Language Support window allows you to select the locale settings for your computer. This affects all sorts of formatting (see Figure 3-14, although the Language Support window shows a slightly condensed view), and the drop-down list will display all regions currently available for the installed languages. This can be set up independently of the display language and will only affect your account. You can likewise make this change system-wide with the "Apply System-Wide" button and your password.

Configuring Your Input Sources Settings

Input sources affect how you use your keyboard to enter text into the computer. In the most straightforward setup, you can simply select the layout that matches your keyboard so that the character printed on any given key matches the character that appears on your screen when you press it. Certain languages with complex scripts have more elaborate text entry systems called Input Method Editors. Other keyboards have special keys or features. However you prefer to enter text, Ubuntu has a setting for you. You can launch "Settings" from the application grid or from the System menu at the top right of your screen. Then, scroll down and click the "Keyboard" option from the left.

The Input Sources section shows a list of various input sources you can use (see Figure 3-15). These correspond to various keyboard layouts. You can click the + button to add a new layout or click the three vertical dots to the right of an installed layout and click "Remove" from the context menu. The context menu can also be used to view the selected keyboard layout. These can then be cycled through at any time by holding Super and pressing Space to cycle through the enabled options, or by clicking the input icon in the top right of the screen and selecting one directly (see Figure 3-15).

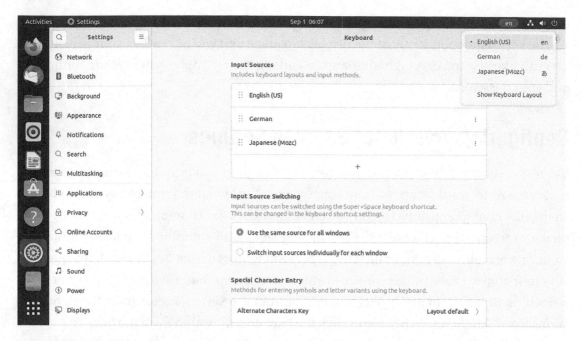

Figure 3-15. *The Text Entry window and input indicator allow for quick keyboard adjustments*

Certain languages have complex scripts. Japanese, for example, has two syllabaries and a logographic script that contain well over 50,000 characters between them. These would not all fit on a standard desktop keyboard. Complex languages often use an Input Method Editor to assist a user in entering text.

Input Method Editors are installed along with language support (so make sure you do install the language first), and can be selected as an input source in the Text Entry screen. Japanese support, for example, installs the Mozc Input Method Editor. Entering text is specific to each language Input Method Editor, but for illustrative purposes, we will look at Mozc for entering Japanese (Figure 3-16). Many languages have multiple Input Method Editors, so don't be afraid to try each one and find which works best for you.

Once you've installed Japanese language support, "Japanese (Mozc)" will be added as an input source in the Keyboard settings. Now you can use the Input icon menu to select "Japanese (Mozc)." Click the Input icon again and click "Input Mode (A)" and change the setting from "Direct Input" (which does not interfere with your keyboard) and change it to "Hiragana," which will interpret your typing as Japanese using phonetic romanji transcription rules.

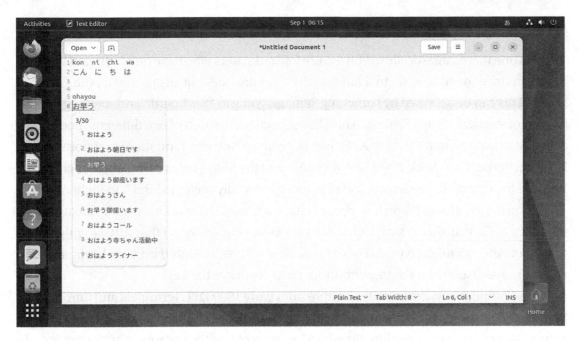

Figure 3-16. *Mozc allows for quickly entering Japanese text phonetically*

In Japanese, you can greet someone by saying "こんにちは," which you would
recognize as "konnichiwa" if you heard it said out loud. Using Mozc, you can write
each syllable phonetically, and as you type "kon," "ni," "chi," and "ha," each syllable is
transformed into the appropriate hiragana character. (Knowing the linguistic reason that
the particle wa is spelled "ha" is unfortunately your responsibility.) You can press Tab
to cycle through various alternatives, or space to cycle through extended transliteration
options. When the correct word is highlighted, you can press Enter and the text entry is
confirmed.

Typing in other scripts can be changed via the input indicator menu or a hovering
preferences toolbar that appears as you type. Typically, kanji can be entered by typing a
word and pressing Space. This will highlight the entire word, and pressing Space again
will bring up a dictionary with various options. Space will continue to cycle through
the listed alternatives. For instance, typing "ohayou" and then pressing Space twice
will result in "お早う" (see Figure 3-16), which is a formal way of writing "ohayō" with
both hiragana and kanji characters. The Input Method Editor includes a dictionary that
contains these mappings.

Adjusting Special Character Entry

There is one more fantastically useful feature for some users who have one keyboard layout but sometimes need to write in a language with characters not supported by the current layout. This can be accessed by launching Settings, going to "Keyboard," and scrolling to the bottom of the right area of Settings. This allows for customization of two different special keys called Alternative Characters (or AltGr) and Compose. You can bind these functions to any key you choose. Caps Lock, Right Ctrl, Right Alt, and the Menu key are very popular choices. Because the Compose key is most useful to me, I personally prefer to bind it to Right Alt.

Some International English keyboards have a physical AltGr key, usually located on the Right Alt key. It allows for quick input of special characters, so that AltGr+s might type ß, or AltGr+$ might type €. These characters will be indicated on your keyboard accordingly—usually on the top or bottom right corner of the key.

The Compose key, however, is a feature from early 1980 DEC terminals and Sun keyboards and allows for simple mnemonic entry of special characters. This ranges from letters to symbols to punctuation. Pressing Compose places the computer in character compose mode, and then the next two letters will create a "composed" character if valid (or produce no input if invalid). For example, Compose, a, e produces the æ in Old English *hwæt*. Compose, n, ~ produces the ñ in Spanish *sueño*. Compose, a, ', produces the á in Spanish *sábado*. Compose, o, ", produces the ö in *Köln*. Compose, -, l produces £ and Compose, =, c produces €. A little bit of practice will save a lot of time for those who are learning a new language or simply occasionally need a character not found on the keyboard in front of them. For instance, Compose, <, " and Compose, >, " produce typographically correct quotes as used around "this" word instead of the straight quotes produced by the " key on its own. Compose followed by three hyphens (-) produces an em dash (—).

You can learn more about the AltGr and Compose key by visiting the Ubuntu documentation at `https://help.ubuntu.com/community/ComposeKey` and view a list of supported Compose key sequences at `https://help.ubuntu.com/community/GtkComposeTable`.

Installing Language Fonts

By default, Ubuntu ships with fonts capable of displaying most modern languages and installing language support will bring in any additional fonts necessary. But there are two packages that can quickly add additional language support so that you never end up seeing a Unicode error box on a web page.

The first font is called "Ancient Scripts," and this provides everything from ancient hieroglyphic and cuneiform script support to musical notation, various symbols, and Emoji support.

The second is called "GNU Unifont" and has a character for every visible Unicode character in the Basic Multilingual Plane. This acts as a fallback font so that it will display any time your computer tries to display characters that are not provided by any other font.

Both can be installed via the command line. Simply launch "Terminal" from the application grid or press Ctrl+Alt+T, and at the command prompt, type:

```
sudo apt install fonts-ancient-scripts unifont
```

Press Enter, and you will be asked for your password. You will not see letters or asterisks (*) while you type. Press Enter again, and you will see a list of additional packages to be installed and a prompt asking whether you want to continue. Press Enter to accept the default of "yes," and the fonts will be downloaded and installed automatically. Once you see the command prompt again, close the Terminal. The next time you launch an application, it should display any Unicode character.

Whether you are monolingual, learning a new language, or comfortable with many languages, the language display and input support in Ubuntu are world class. Your computer experience will be comfortable, familiar, and convenient in the world's most popular languages.

Keeping Track of Your Personal Time Management Using Hamster

Time management is an important skill for everyone to some degree. It can be used to track your daily routine to make yourself more efficient, to pace yourself when working on a project, or to track billable hours when working with a client. All of this can be accomplished by using Hamster Time Tracker (Figure 3-17).

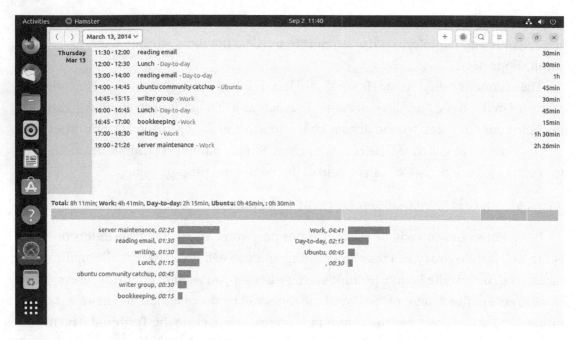

Figure 3-17. *Hamster keeps track of your activities throughout the day*

Hamster can be installed via Ubuntu Software. It may be labeled "hamster-snap" because Ubuntu Software tends to favor snap packages in its listings. Select hamster-snap. If you prefer to use the version that ships with Ubuntu, you can click the "Source" menu in Ubuntu Software's header bar and choose "ubuntu-jammy-universe," or you can install the snap package.

The goal of Hamster is to record your activities and their duration. In Figure 3-17, several activities have been recorded and Hamster is tracking a server maintenance activity.

Activities are started by clicking the + button in the header bar, typing in a description, such as "reading emai.," and pressing Enter or clicking Save. An activity can be associated with a category, and this can be indicated with the at (@) symbol. For instance, "reading email" is unsorted, but "reading email@Work" would be categorized under work. This allows you to record doing the same activity for different purposes. The window lists today's activities and summarizes the amount of time spent on each category under the list. Tags can also be used to further describe an activity.

Once you have an activity, Hamster will record the start time and begin tracking time spent, which is shown in the task list. You can minimize Hamster and perform work. When you are finished, you can open Hamster and click the "Stop tracking" button in the header bar (which looks like a stop sign), and Hamster will record the end time and list the duration of your current activity. This allows you to quickly note your start and stop times throughout the day and leaves the details to Hamster. Double-clicking on any activity will bring up a window where you can edit the activity (see Figure 3-18).

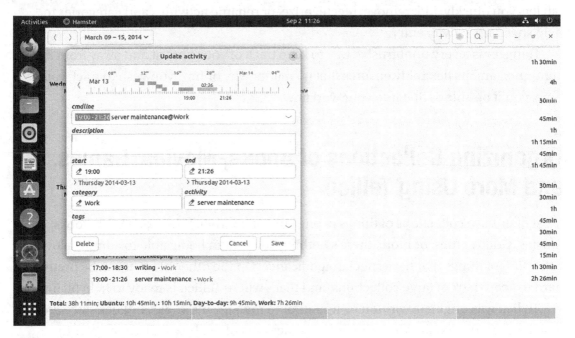

Figure 3-18. *Hamster has a weekly overview where you can quickly edit activity details*

Clicking the date in the header bar displays several view options for today's date, the current week or month, and a calendar picker where you can choose a custom date range. Selecting one of these options will display activities within the date range as well as a bar graph of time tracked at the bottom of the window as well. You can also edit any activity entry here. Clicking the bar graph at the bottom of the window will expand the overview and list various activities along with bar graphs that show the amount of time spent on each in relation to each other.

These overviews are very handy, and you can also use the bar menu ➤ Export… option to save the displayed overview to an HTML file. This pleasant-looking report is perfect for sharing with clients or team members.

Edit ➤ Tracking Settings allows you to customize your overviews and activity entry. By default, Hamster counts a new day as starting at 5:30 a.m., which is perfect for night owls who work into the night, but you can change this time. The "Categories and Tags" tab lets you quickly add, remove, recategorize, or rename activities and categories to help speed up activity entry.

Hamster is a very unobtrusive way to keep track of your time at and away from the computer, and its flexibility ensures that no matter why or how you wish to track your time, you'll be able to fit it into your workflow.

Organizing Collections of Books, Movies, Games, and More Using Tellico

Most of us have collections of things of one kind or another. Whether it's art, books, movies, video games, or more, there's nothing better than being able to admire a lovely collection of things that have special significance. On the other hand, it can be pretty hard to keep track of large collections, and that's where Tellico is ready to help fill in.

Tellico was originally written by its author to manage his books, but has since grown to allow for virtually any kind of collection. Right out of the box, it also comes with profiles for comic books, videos, music, coins, stamps, cards, wine, and board games, and you can create custom collections as well. If you need to keep track of it, you can do it with Tellico.

Once you choose a collection type, adding entries to the collection is simple. The middle of the toolbar will have a "New" button with the icon of the collection type. Clicking it will display a new entry window where you can enter in item details (see Figure 3-19). You can be as brief or as detailed as you would like. Every field is optional. Tellico is smart enough to understand certain formatting as well. For instance, titles are sorted correctly if the first word is an article such as "the" or "a." And the author field is sorted as a name. In the example given, "J.R.R. Tolkien" is displayed and sorted by his last name. Tellico treats it the same if I enter "Tolkien, J.R.R." If a book has multiple authors, just separate their names with semicolons (;), and Tellico will be able to group them correctly.

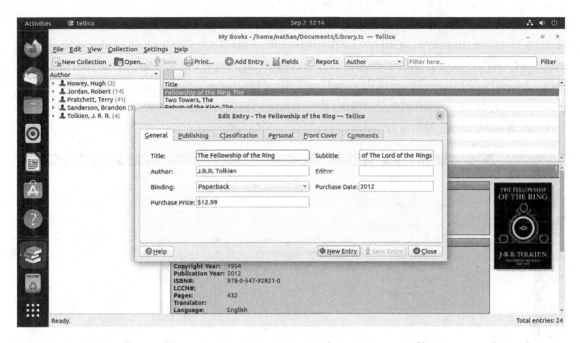

Figure 3-19. *Tellico allows you to manage each item in a collection and track details as well*

You can also use Tellico to keep track of items you lend out. By selecting one or more items and right-clicking on them, you can choose "Check-out...," which will bring up a Loan window. You can enter a name, loan and due dates, and a note. Once it is returned, you can select the items and use the "Collection ➤ Check-in" menu option to mark the items as returned.

It's the unfortunate reality for anyone who tracks collections that adding a new item is exciting, but the data entry required to track an existing collection in a new application is staggering. Tellico makes this easier in several ways. First, it can import data from many different file types. File ➤ Import shows a list, but CSV data can be easily imported and mapped to fields, and Tellico can import entries from GCstar, Alexandria, Goodreads, and many more.

Tellico also has a list of online databases for each default collection type. By right-clicking an entry and choosing "Update Entry," you can choose between various databases to complete the information in the entry. Using the Open Library, for instance, can get author, publisher, genre data, and even cover art. This quickly and easily allows you to fill in the gaps when building a collection.

Every field tracked by Tellico can also be modified and customized. Clicking the "Fields" button displays the list of collection fields and allows them to be edited in innumerable ways. For instance, the Games collection type has a "Platform" field with a drop-down list of various consoles and computer platforms. But this list doesn't include the first couple of console generations or the latest. Figure 3-20 shows how the list is separated with semicolons and how easy it is to add new values.

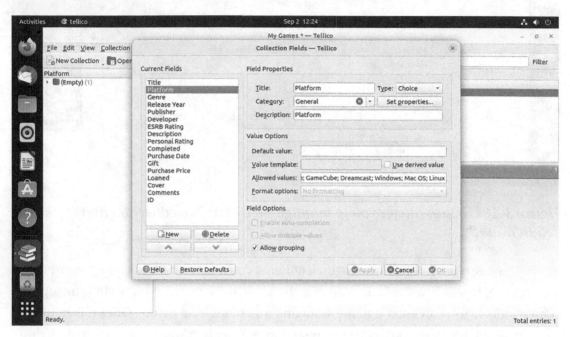

Figure 3-20. *Each collection's fields can be completely customized*

All of this information can be sorted in various ways, and reports can be generated and saved as HTML files or printed. This is useful for making your own checklists or sharing your collection via email or on the Web.

Keeping track of your favorite collections is made easy and simple with Tellico. The combination of common collection profiles, the ability to import details from online sources, and the flexibility of customized fields all combine to make tracking your collections almost as much fun as collecting them.

Managing Your Ebook Library Using Calibre

The digital revolution has transformed many industries, and the book publishing industry is no different. With the advent of electronic publishing, traditional and independent publishers and authors can all publish ebooks. The publishing industry has also standardized around the EPUB format, while Amazon instead opted to extend the old MOBI ebook format. Classic books and new works alike are available in these and other formats, and ebook software is not only available for computers and smartphones, but dedicated reading devices with both e-ink and LCD displays are available. Reading has never been more accessible, but keeping track, managing, and backing up all of your ebooks can be daunting. Calibre can manage your ebook library across your computer and your reading devices.

The first time you run Calibre, it will ask you to choose a name and create a new folder to hold your ebook library. Then, you can choose your ebook device from a list of over 40 supported devices. If your device supports it—such as Amazon Kindle or Apple iOS devices among others—Calibre can be set up to send new books to your device through the Internet. Details vary by device, but the Calibre welcome wizard will assist you with this process. Once you have finished configuring Calibre, press the "Finish" button, and Calibre will initialize and show the library (see Figure 3-21).

Figure 3-21. *Calibre manages both your computer and your device's ebook libraries*

Calibre allows you to work with both your computer and your ebook device. For instance, if you have a Kindle ebook reader that has a significant library on it, you can view your device, select multiple books, and right-click your selection and choose "Add books to library." This will copy the ebooks off of your device and store them in your Calibre library on your computer and will act as a backup. This is valuable even if you use a device like a Kindle or Nook that lets you redownload your purchased books from their respective ebook platform. It also makes the books available to view and read on your computer when they are DRM-free (see Figure 3-22). You can also edit a book's metadata, which can be useful to keep items like author names uniform, or to choose a specific cover image for your library.

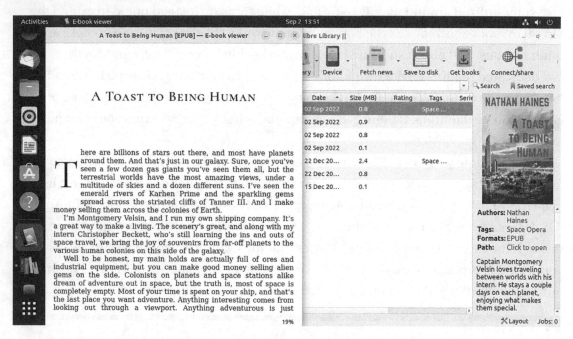

Figure 3-22. *Calibre includes a sophisticated ebook viewer in addition to library management*

If it were only an ebook library management system and ebook viewer, Calibre would be extremely useful. But two other features set it apart. The first is the ability to convert an ebook into various other formats. Whether Kindle, EPUB, MOBI, LIT, PDF, or TXT, Calibre can convert into 17 different formats, and will also "smarten" punctuation to convert straight quotes to curly or "smart" quotes and other such modifications (or unsmarten it, at your preference), set fonts, detect document structure, clean up internal HTML and CSS markup, and otherwise create very nice ebooks even from plain text files. It even knows which formats are supported by which devices, so it can convert on the fly when copying to an ebook reader—but only when necessary.

The second feature that sets Calibre apart is an ebook editor that is simple but very easy to use. You can adjust the text, formatting, headings, tables of contents, chapter divisions, metadata, and all other information in a specific version of an ebook, and you can use this to jazz up public domain books from Project Gutenberg that may be available only in plain text, repair ebooks with formatting errors, or even polish your own ebooks.

Calibre lets you manage your digital library whether you have a vast collection or are just starting out. You can copy and convert books, edit your books, and make the most of your electronic library. This is the ideal solution for enjoying your ebooks on any device.

Printing Labels and Cards Using gLabels

Among the many revolutions that home computers were set to kick off, desktop publishing and printing was one of them. Quite a few programs became quite popular in the 1990s with the advent of high-DPI color dot-matrix printers, and homemade labels and greeting cards were born. While greeting card shops didn't exactly go out of business, being able to pick up a template for business cards, mailing labels, or stickers and print to them is an incredibly simple way to give a project a high-quality, professional touch. gLabels can get you started in a hurry.

Upon opening gLabels, you are presented with an empty window with some tools displayed. When you click the "New" button on the toolbar to start a new project, you are given a list of recent template products you have used, and can use the "Search" tab to choose a predefined template. gLabels comes with a massive database of commercial templates (see Figure 3-23), and will walk you through creating custom templates as well. The first step is to choose a product. As an example we'll look at simple name badges for an Ubuntu get together.

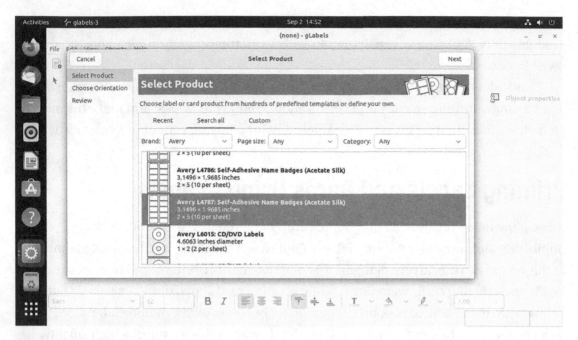

Figure 3-23. *gLabels supports over 10,000 commercial card and label templates out of the box*

The tools are relatively simple, and you can add text, rectangles, lines, circles/ellipses, images, and barcodes to a label. gLabels supports SVG vector graphics, so you are free to design complex graphics in a dedicated program like Inkscape, leaving gLabels for simple positioning and formatting. This lets gLabels remain simple and easy to work with. You can also import photos or other graphics.

When the project has been created, it will show an outline of the label, with a "safe area" outlined in red around the edges. The area outside of the red line is called a "trim area." For consistent results, you'll want to keep all important designs and text inside the red safe area and out of the trim area to compensate for slight alignment changes between your printer as well as the cut of the template.

To add an element, simply click the corresponding button on the toolbar, and then click the label. You can reposition any object just by clicking on it and dragging it to the desired location, and you can use the resize handles to control the size. Holding the Ctrl key as you click a corner handle will preserve the object's aspect ratio so that a circle or image doesn't become distorted.

The object property pane on the right side of the window allows for precise control over the size, position, and properties of an element. For example, Figure 3-24 shows the "Hello, my name is:" text field selected. The object property pane with the "Text" tab selected shows the current text value and can be used to easily read and edit the displayed text independent of the font and colors chosen. The "Style" tab allows for simple selection of a font, font size, color, left/center/right alignment, and line spacing. The "Size" tab sets the dimensions of the text field for long or multiline text, and the "Position" tab allows the position of an object to be defined in points, inches, or millimeters (depending on the settings located in gLabels preferences).

Figure 3-24. *A simple "write your name" badge takes two minutes to design*

Aside from static elements, gLabels also supports data merging, and this allows you to take data from CSV files or your Evolution address book and use them to print custom information on each card. To set this up, use the Objects ➤ Merge properties menu option. Just pick your data format and then choose the data file with the Location option. The Merge Properties window will display a list of records and the field name and data that go along with each record. You can use the "Record/Field" name in text or barcode elements to print that information for each record on the screen. This is perfect for ID badges, mailing labels, moving box labels, and all kinds of other printables that change. You can use LibreOffice Calc to create the list and then export it as a CSV for gLabels.

gLabels may not usher in a new era of desktop printing, but it is an extremely simple and reliable way to handle printing on most of the templates you'll find in stores. It makes short work of any simple design work and uses more powerful programs like Inkscape for more complex designs. No matter your need, gLabels will get the job done.

Backing Up and Restoring Personal Files Using Déjà Dup

If I could offer the most important thing I've learned over nearly three decades of professional computer support experience, it would be to back up your data. The next piece of advice I'd offer is that backing up your files is only the second most important part of a backup. The most important part of a backup is—of course—restoring your files. Ubuntu ships with an integrated reliable and easy solution called Déjà Dup. A graphical front end to the time tested and very robust command-line–based backup project called duplicity, Déjà Dup performs automatic backups, makes recovering missing files painless, and can even encrypt your backup data for peace of mind. Run "Backups" from the application grid. Déjà Dup will display an overview window that prompts you to either create your first backup or restore from a previous backup (see Figure 3-25).

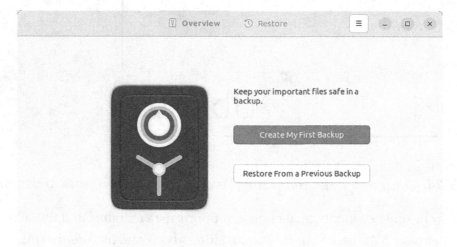

Figure 3-25. *The first time you run Déjà Dup, it guides you to create a new backup or restore from an old one*

Setting up a backup using Déjà Dup is very simple. After you click the green "Create My First Backup" button, a Back Up wizard will appear that will guide you through setting up folders to be backed up (see Figure 3-26). There are only four quick, simple configuration options before you can start backing up your files, and the default settings are all reasonable. The Back Up wizard will guide you through each step.

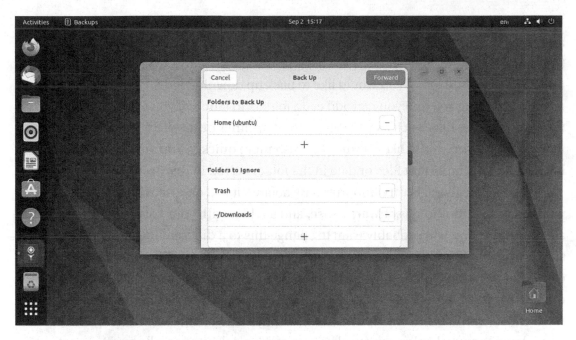

Figure 3-26. *Backup options are simple, and the backup settings window is friendly to use*

The first setting is "Folders to Back Up." By default, Déjà Dup will only save your home folder. This also saves everything inside your home folder, including your documents, pictures, music, videos, and personal application settings. It does not include your Steam library and any installed Steam games and save files, which you can back up and manage with the Steam client, but this is a noteworthy exception because it is preconfigured but not visible. Backing up your home folder is the best option unless you have specific needs, and will generally protect all of your files on your computer. If you want to add more folders such as different internal drives, you can click the "+" button and select more folders to back up. You can remove any folder by clicking the "-" button to the right of it in the list. These settings only affect future backups and do not remove files or folders from an existing backup.

Note   If you install Steam by downloading a .deb file from its website or from the Ubuntu repositories ("Steam installer"), your Steam games will not be backed up. But if you install "Steam (Early Access)" from Canonical, your games will be installed in a different location that is not automatically excluded. If you would like to exclude Steam games from the snap package, add "~/snap/steam/common" to your "Folders to Ignore" list.

The next setting is "Folders to Ignore," and by default it includes your Trash folder and Downloads folder. Note that Folders are separated by a forward slash (/) and tilde (~) stands for your home folder. These are typically good folders to ignore, but you can remove "~/Downloads" if you would like to back up downloaded files you haven't gotten around to sorting yet, and you can add extra folders to ignore if you wanted to exclude folders with large files, such as your Videos folder, either because they are not important to backup or if you would like backups to finish more quickly. You are responsible for backing up any important files or data in the folders listed in this option.

"Storage Location" is very important. By default, it will choose "Google Drive," which requires additional software to use, and a folder with your computer name as a placeholder. You will probably want to change this to a different location before you start backing up files. It is important to keep your backups on a different physical hard drive (not partition) than your primary files. By storing your files on an external hard drive or a remote network location, you can create an off-site backup that allows you to recover data in the case of computer failure or physical damage. The "Storage location" drop-down list will display any attached external hard drives as well as various network options such as Windows Share or SSH for storing a backup on other machines you own. You can also use the command line (see Chapter 6) to install the package `python3-pydrive` to add Google Drive support. In most cases, you can simply choose an external hard drive. Any folder name will do, but I recommend using the name of your computer. This allows you to use the same hard drive to back up multiple computers.

The last option allows you to require a password to restore your files. This allows you to password-protect your backup so that you don't have to worry about anyone accessing your personal files. Déjà Dup will remember your password for future backups, but anyone trying to restore your backup on a different user account or computer will not be able to see the contents of the backup without entering the password first. While this is a smart security precaution, you can also just choose the "Allow restoring without a password" option to simplify the restore process in the future.

Once you have configured your backup settings, Déjà Dup will immediately begin backing up your files (see Figure 3-27). This can take some time, but you can still use your computer in the meantime. Any files you are working on during the backup may or may not have the latest version backed up, so keep that in mind as you multitask.

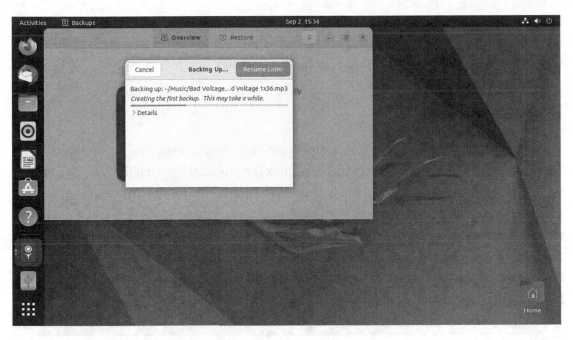

Figure 3-27. *Déjà Dup starts protecting your files the moment you finish setting up your backup policy*

The first time you back up your files, Déjà Dup will perform a full backup. This means that all files in your folder will be backed up. Although your backup is compressed, this process can take quite some time. After this full backup is complete, for future backups, Déjà Dup will scan your existing backup and only backup files that have changed in some manner. This is called an incremental backup and is much faster and smaller. This makes the most of your backup storage space, but requires the original full backup and each subsequent incremental backup in order to recover your data. Once a month, Déjà Dup will perform another full file backup. This minimizes the dependency chain of backups to help protect against file corruption. As the last step in the backup process, Déjà Dup automatically runs a recovery test to ensure that the backup was successful.

Once your backup has finished, Déjà Dup will allow you to back up your files at any time or restore deleted or changed files from your backup. But the overview window shows a "Back up automatically" option. This sets up Déjà Dup to automatically start a backup every 7 days. You can also use the Menu ➤ Preferences option to choose between weekly and daily backups. This allows you to balance the need for fresh backup data with the slight performance hit that running a backup can cause. Preferences also lets you choose whether or not your backups are kept for 6 months, for a year, or forever.

Déjà Dup will not automatically delete old backups unless there is no more space available for newer backups. The "Folders" tab under Preferences allows you to fine-tune the folders included or excluded in your backup settings.

Restoring Files

When you want to restore your files, simply open your backup settings by launching "Backups" from the application grid. Then, click the "Restore" tab. Déjà Dup will display the contents of your most recent file backup (see Figure 3-28). You can select specific files and folders to restore (or press Ctrl+A to select everything shown). If you want to restore an older version of a file, you can use the "Date" list in the bottom-right corner of the window to select from a list of the dates your computer was backed up on. When you have selected the files you wish to restore, you can click the green "Restore" button at the bottom left of the window.

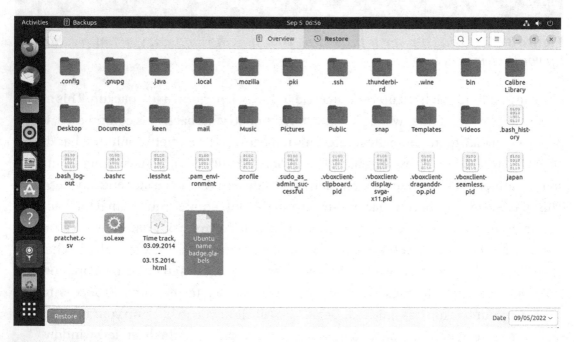

Figure 3-28. *You can recover missing files with a right-click and a menu command*

Once you click "Restore," Déjà Dup will ask whether you want to restore your files to their original locations (this is perfect for restoring files on a new computer or Ubuntu install) or you can restore your backup to a specific folder. This is a good way to recover your files from a different computer without overwriting any files on the new computer. It is also a useful way to fully test an existing backup. Click "Restore" in the header bar to begin restoring your selected files from your backup. Once the restore operation has completed, Déjà Dup will let you know whether the restore succeeded or failed, and you can use the Files application to access your successfully restored files.

To have safe, reliable backups, your backups must be performed regularly and at least one backup should be off-site. Déjà Dup helps make this simple and automatic. While the best backup is the one you never have to use, you can be sure that your files are safe with Ubuntu.

Capturing Screenshots and Recording Your Desktop Using GNOME Screenshot and Kazam

Being able to record your desktop is useful for many things, from saving error messages for technical support personnel to creating a tutorial video to teach others how to perform a task, to taking a screenshot of your desktop background to share with others. No matter the reason, you can take screenshots out of the box with Ubuntu, and Kazam offers desktop recording and advanced screenshot options.

GNOME Screenshot

GNOME Shell includes built-in advanced screenshot and screen capability. It is useful for capturing the entire screen, a single window, or a specific area. It can be launched by pressing the PrtScn (Print Screen) key on your keyboard (see Figure 3-29).

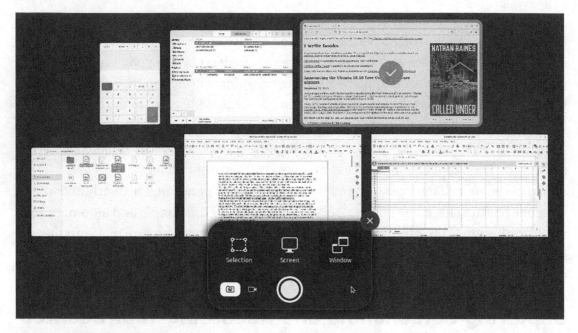

Figure 3-29. *GNOME screenshots are easy to make for windows, full screens, or just portions of a screen*

Pressing PrtScrn will offer a variety of options, including whether or not to grab the entire screen, or just the current window. You can also choose whether or not the mouse pointer should be displayed in the final screenshot with the pointer icon at the bottom right of the screenshot control window. The GNOME Screenshot window will disappear when you click the round "Take Screenshot" that looks like a round shutter button. Once the screenshot has been taken, the captured area will flash white, and the screenshot will be placed in your clipboard as well as saved in your ~/Pictures/Screenshots folder. If you use the video icon in the bottom left of the screenshot control, GNOME will record your screen until you click the red duration timer next to the system menu and will be saved in the ~/Videos/Screencasts folder.

Kazam

Kazam is a very useful tool that performs both screenshots and desktop recording. It is popular with Ubuntu developers for demonstrating new software and features to new users. It also has some convenient shortcut keys for controlling its operation.

When you first launch Kazam, it displays a simple window that contains desktop recording options, which it calls "screencasting." You can access additional configuration options via the File ➤ Preferences... menu option (see Figure 3-30).

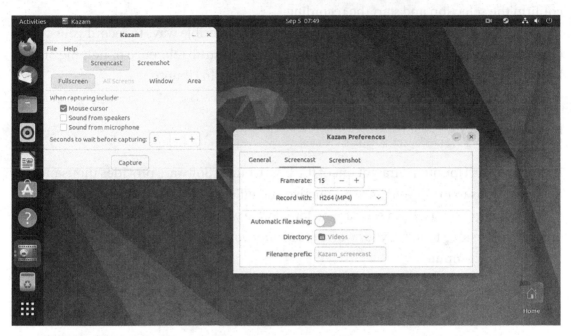

Figure 3-30. *Kazam allows you to record your desktop in various video formats*

Just like GNOME Shell, Kazam can record an entire single screen, multiple monitors, a single window, or a specific area of the screen. You can also choose whether to capture the mouse cursor as well as audio played through the speakers. Kazam can also record the microphone so that you can narrate the screencast as you record it. Each of these options is available from the main Kazam window and can be turned on or off individually. This is especially useful for creating demonstrations for others. Be sure to record a small video to test that the sound is being captured correctly. You can adjust the capture sources via the Preferences window. In the main window, you can also configure a delay between when you click "Capture" and Kazam begins recording your screen. Once you click "Capture," the Kazam window will disappear and a countdown will appear on the screen.

Once your desktop is being recorded, you can simply control your computer as usual until you are ready to finish recording. You can then use the Kazam indicator menu at the top right of your screen to pause or finish recording. Once you finish recording, Kazam will ask if you want to edit your recording or save it for later. If you are not sure whether a specific video editor has been installed, you will want to save the file instead.

Screenshots work similarly with Kazam, and the main advantage of Kazam over GNOME Shell is that it will show you the current dimensions of the selected area and let you resize the selected recording area until it is just right before you press Enter to confirm the selection and start the recording.

Together, GNOME Screenshot and Kazam provide flexible ways to record your computer use. Whether you're saving a screenshot for future reference or helping others by providing assistance, recording your screen is simple in Ubuntu.

Summary

As powerful as Ubuntu is straight out of the box, Ubuntu Software provides thousands of applications to make you more productive and efficient as you work. I hope that these applications give you a head start as you familiarize yourself with Ubuntu. After all, the quicker you're able to finish your work, the sooner you can relax and enjoy spending time on your computer.

CHAPTER 4

Enjoying Media and Other Entertainment

Ubuntu has been shown to have a lot of really useful productivity tools. But it is also home to fantastic entertainment options as well. While the rest of this book focuses on getting things done, this chapter is all about enjoying your computer and getting the most out of your personal media—purchased movies, music, podcasts, and so on. It even covers a few basic suggestions about gaming, whether you are nostalgic for the past or looking forward to the next big retail game.

In addition to sitting back and watching a movie or listening to music, most of us are media creators as well. If we don't have dedicated digital cameras, we all have cell phones that take photos and videos. Our music CDs have to be copied to the computer, or the old digital songs we purchased need to be converted to a compatible format for our new music players. Videos can be transferred to DVD to make them easier for nontechnical friends to watch. And photos can always be made more impressive with a little bit of patience and a bit of color adjustment and cropping. We'll look at a few good ways to get started.

Play DVDs and Media Files

By default, Ubuntu comes with the software needed to play a couple dozen media formats. And the included media player is basic and does an adequate job at letting you watch videos. But there are dozens more compression formats for video and audio, and each of them has various statuses as far as patent and licensing. Unfortunately, this precludes Ubuntu from shipping with full support, because the laws governing such things vary from country to country.

Ubuntu can install support for most formats, and its media player will detect when an unsupported file type is loaded and attempt to search for the software package

143

© Nathan Haines 2023
N. Haines, *Beginning Ubuntu for Windows and Mac Users*,
https://doi.org/10.1007/978-1-4842-8972-3_4

needed to play back the media. However, there's one way to simply install support for most all formats at once. You can simply install the "Ubuntu Restricted Extras" package from the Ubuntu software repositories. This will install support for not only multimedia packages but also additional software such as Adobe Flash Player and Microsoft "core Web" fonts that are allowed to be downloaded from the Internet, but not allowed to be shipped on a disc. Other than a prompt to agree to the Microsoft TrueType Core Web Fonts EULA, installation is automated, but can take some time to download before installation.

To install this additional media support, open a Terminal using the Dash or by pressing Ctrl+Alt+T. You'll see a window with a black screen and a command prompt that shows your username and computer name. It will look similar to the following:

```
nathan@ubuntu-book:~$
```

Next, type the following command to install the Ubuntu Restricted Extras package:

```
sudo apt install ubuntu-restricted-extras libdvd-pkg
```

Make sure that there are no uppercase letters and that all punctuation is correct, and then press the Enter key. Ubuntu will provide a list of additional software that will be installed along with the software. Simply press Enter at the confirmation prompt to accept the default of "Yes," and Ubuntu will download and install the software.

When you get a gray and purple package configuration screen with the TrueType core fonts for the Web EULA, you can continue to the acceptance prompt by pressing Tab, and then Enter. If you accept the EULA from the previous screen, simply press the left arrow key to highlight "<Yes>" and then press Enter. If you highlight "<No>" and press Enter, then the fonts will not be installed but all other software will be. You will also see a similar screen giving you a command to type to configure libdvd-pkg. Just press Enter to dismiss this screen, and pressing Enter on the next screen with "<Yes>" highlighted will ensure that you receive DVD decryption updates in the future. You will see a progress bar at the bottom of the screen while the software is being installed. Once installation is finished, you will see the command prompt again.

At this point, you will be able to play back most media formats, including unprotected DVDs. However, most DVDs are copy-protected, and the decryption software must be installed manually. This only requires one additional step. To install DVD decryption features, type in the following command:

```
sudo dpkg-reconfigure libdvd-pkg
```

Make sure that there are no uppercase letters and that all punctuation is correct, and then press the Enter key. Ubuntu will show an explanation for the installation process and ask if you want to proceed. Press Enter, and Ubuntu will download and compile DVD decryption software. This will take a minute to complete. Once it is finished, you will see the command prompt again (see Figure 4-1). From this point on, you will be able to play any DVD that is compatible with your DVD-ROM drive's region setting.

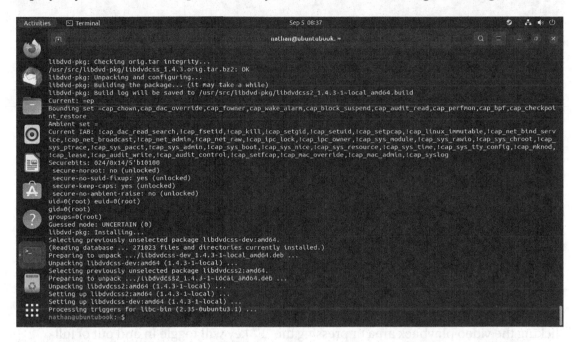

Figure 4-1. *It looks complex, but the hard part of downloading and installing DVD decryption is done for you*

Another helpful tip is to install VLC media player (see Figure 4-2). It supports a dizzying array of file formats—not just video and audio formats but also video discs, streaming media, and subtitle files. It can also dynamically adjust cropping and stretching for aspect ratio and multiple audio tracks. The latest version of this powerful media player is provided directly from the VLC developers, thanks to the snap packaging. (And if for some reason you want it from the Ubuntu repositories, which is tied to VLC 3.0.16, you can choose the source "ubuntu-jammy-universe" when you install it from Ubuntu Software.)

Figure 4-2. *VLC can play almost any media and supports video discs, subtitles, and more*

VLC has many options, but for most videos you won't need to do much more than start playback. The menus are very comprehensive, and you can also right-click the video screen to adjust options specific to the current media being played. Double-clicking the video playback area or pressing the "F" key will toggle in and out of full-screen mode, and this is probably the most useful feature in general. To open a media file, you can drag and drop it onto the VLC window, and Media ➤ Open File... can be used to pick specific files, or Media ➤ Open Disc... can be used to open DVD discs. While Blu-ray is listed as a disc type, commercial Blu-ray playback is difficult to set up and is unreliable due to the content protection system used for most titles.

You may want to set up VLC to be your default media player, and this is easily accomplished, but the setting can be difficult to find. The simplest way is to click the System menu in the top right corner of the screen and choose "Settings." Scroll down on the left panel until you see "Default Applications," and click on that. Then, you can click "VLC media player" from the drop-down menu next to "Video." VLC is so versatile that I always set this up for myself as one of the first things I do on a new Ubuntu computer. I also often select it as the default for "Music" as well, so that I can listen to a single music file I click on, and keep Rhythmbox for a full music album experience.

Regardless of which default media player you choose, you can always open a media file in a specific player by right-clicking on the file and then choosing "Open With." Ubuntu will display installed applications that can open the selected media file.

By installing Ubuntu Restricted Extras, you prepare your computer to work with almost any video or audio file you might encounter. All of the various libraries are installed so that most Ubuntu programs will automatically detect and use them, and you'll never have to worry about finding a "codec pack" that you have to download from an untrusted website. VLC is optional but is the easiest way to play DVDs and other video files. The next time you're ready to relax with some entertainment, you'll be able to sit back and enjoy your content without worrying about which format the files are in.

Organize Your CD and Digital Music Collection Using Rhythmbox

Music is an important part of many of our lives, and over the years there have been many ways to enjoy it, from vinyl records to 8 tracks to audio cassette tapes to CDs. The digital realm has also seen just as many format changes. MP3 is the most ubiquitous format, yet FLAC and Ogg Vorbis are the de facto Free archival and playback formats. Ogg Opus is even higher quality for music, Windows prefers Windows Media Audio format, and Apple and Nintendo media players prefer AAC. Ubuntu happily supports all of these digital formats so that you can enjoy your music no matter where or when you received them.

Ubuntu's music manager is called Rhythmbox, and it provides a unified way to manage your music (see Figure 4-3). By default, it displays all supported music files in your Music folder, and it can also download and play podcasts, interface with Last.fm and Libre.fm, stream online radio streams, and play audio CDs. It can also copy your CDs to your computer in one of several various formats.

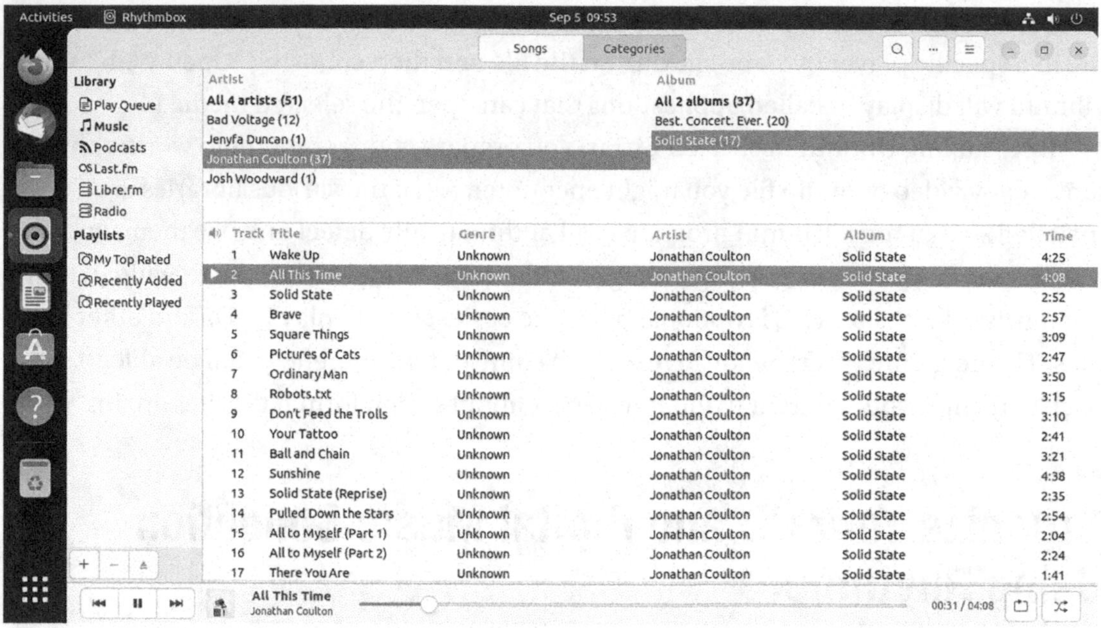

Figure 4-3. *Rhythmbox is a one-stop solution for your music listening needs*

As a music player, Rhythmbox is fairly basic. When launched, it shows your music library stored in your Music folder (see Figure 4-3). The bottom of the window shows previous track, play/pause, and next track buttons as well as repeat and playlist shuffle options, along with the current playing audio file and a progress indicator that you can drag to skip through the song. On the left side of the window under "Library," you can see various music sources as well as saved playlists. To the right of the header bar, the search icon can be used to narrow down the listed audio files. If the Play Queue is empty, the Play button will begin playing the tracks displayed on this screen. The artist and album list can also be used to show specific tracks.

Right-clicking a selected track will bring up a context menu, allowing you to add a song to the play queue or to a new or existing playlist. Once Rhythmbox is playing audio, you can continue working with other programs or even close the Rhythmbox window. Music will keep playing, and you can use the clock menu at the top center of the screen to access play controls without switching back to Rhythmbox (see Figure 4-4). This allows you to quickly pause or skip a track or begin playing a playlist without leaving your current application.

Figure 4-4. *The Sound Indicator gives you fast access to your music while you work*

Copy Audio CDs to Your Computer

Rhythmbox can play audio CDs that are located in your computer's optical drive tray, but it can also copy your music off your CDs and to your computer for more convenient playback. Each of these activities can be activated in the same place.

When you have an audio CD loaded in your computer, the disc will show up under Devices. Rhythmbox will automatically attempt to look up the disc on the Internet to access album cover art and track names. Clicking on the disc will display the track list (see Figure 4-5). You can press the Play button or double-click on a track to begin playing it directly off the CD.

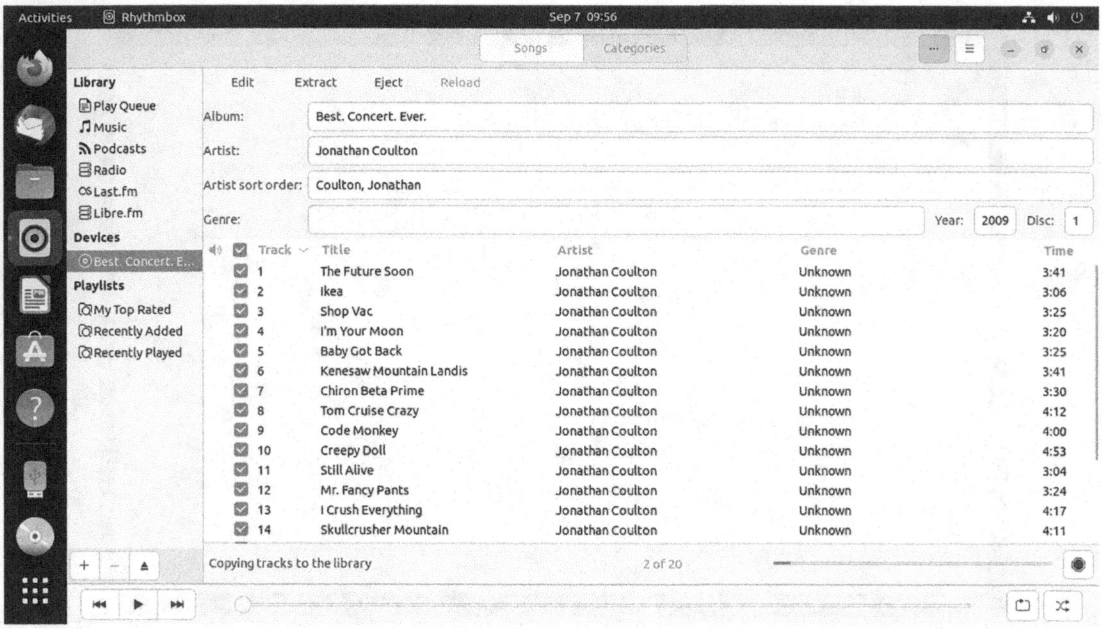

Figure 4-5. *Rhythmbox downloads CD track information from the Internet when available*

If you want to copy CD music to your computer, you can use the "Extract" button. First, make sure any tracks you wish to copy have been selected by checking the check box next to them. You can also edit the album information that will be saved to the digital music files when they are created. Highlighting a track by clicking on it and then clicking the title, artist, or genre a second time will allow you to edit the track details before you begin the copy. Once you are ready to begin copying tracks to your computer, click the overflow menu button ("..") and then click the "Extract" button. Rhythmbox will display the copying progress at the bottom of the window, and you will be able to monitor this even when you switch to other music sources such as the Play Queue, your music library, and so on. You can click the "Stop" button to the right of the progress indicator to discard the current track and stop copying files.

By default, Rhythmbox compresses copied audio using the Ogg Vorbis audio format. This is a high-quality audio codec that is more efficient than MP3, but not as widely supported. By using Edit ➤ Preferences in the Rhythmbox menu, then clicking the "Music" tab, you can change the preferred format by clicking the drop-down menu. You will be able to encode to Ogg Vorbis, Ogg Opus, and FLAC; and if you've installed

Ubuntu Restricted Extras as described earlier in this chapter, you will also be able to choose MPEG Layer 3 Audio (MP3) and MPEG 4 Audio formats as well. Any changes you make to this setting will be used for future copies you make from CDs.

MP3 has the widest range of compatibility with other computers and devices, Ogg Opus has the highest quality of lossy formats, and FLAC is the Free Lossless Audio Codec that saves space without losing any audio information during compression. FLAC is a great way to back up your CDs, and you can also combine the programs Sound Juicer and Sound Converter, available in Ubuntu Software, to create FLAC backups of your music and convert these master files into audio more suitable for your devices. In the future, you can convert from FLAC into new formats without having to use your original media, which can be very useful if you keep your original media in storage.

Listen to Podcasts

Podcasts are on-demand audio programs that can be subscribed to. This lets your music player, phone, or computer check for new episodes on a regular basis and download them automatically so that you can listen to new episodes at your leisure. Podcasts can be found on any topic, and most are free. They make any commute melt away and are an incredible resource for learning, news, and entertainment.

Rhythmbox also allows you to subscribe to and listen to podcasts so you can listen to them at your computer. Clicking the "Podcasts" category under Library will show you a list of all podcasts you have subscribed to. A podcast "subscription" means that your computer will periodically check for new episodes and download them and does not refer to payment. Podcasts are listed at the top of the window, and you can select all available podcast feeds or click on individual titles to filter the episode list at the bottom of the window. Clicking the "Add" button will allow you to search for new podcasts (see Figure 4-6). Clicking the "Update" button will check all podcasts for new episodes immediately.

When looking for new podcasts to add, you can type a podcast title into the search field or the podcast feed URL if you know it. Podcast feeds end in ".xml," and you can copy a link from a podcast's website if it does not show up through a title search. Rhythmbox will display a list of podcasts that match your search term, and you can click each result to see a list of episodes on the bottom half of the screen. Double-clicking an episode will begin streaming the episode for playback, and you can use this to preview a podcast. If you want to add a podcast to your library, click the "Subscribe" button. Clicking "Close" will return to your list of subscribed podcasts.

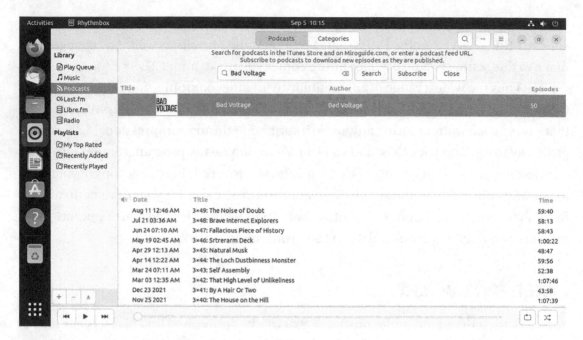

Figure 4-6. You can easily search, preview, and subscribe to new podcasts

Rhythmbox will download the latest episode of a newly subscribed podcast, and you can double-click an episode to begin downloading and playing it. Right-clicking an episode will allow you to download or delete a particular episode, and right-clicking on a podcast feed at the top of the window will allow you to update or delete that feed.

Back Up and Create Music CDs Using Brasero

Optical media such as audio CDs and CD-ROMs were an amazing change in a world where audio cassette tapes needed to be played back in sequence and flipped over halfway through, and hard drives were measured in dozens of megabytes. They delivered high-quality audio and large amounts of data in a small, portable format. However, optical discs are fragile, and recordable discs may only have a lifetime of 2–10 years of reliable storage. Hard drive space is now measured in terabytes, and new recordable discs are cheap. Making backup copies of CDs and creating custom music mixes to keep in the car is just good sense. In Ubuntu, Brasero will help you keep your data safe. It can be installed from Ubuntu Software.

Backing Up a Music CD

There are two ways to back up CDs. The first is to copy the audio off of the disc and store it for later playback. Rhythmbox or Sound Juicer is better suited for this task. The other way is to copy the entire contents of the CD to a hard drive or a blank recordable disc. This is where Brasero excels.

When you first launch Brasero, it gives you five options. We'll look at four of these options in this chapter.

To back up a disc, click the "Disc copy" button. A smaller window will appear and allow you to choose an audio disc to back up from one of your computer's optical drives. Then, you will be able to choose a destination for the information. Brasero will default to a new disc in the same burner, and you will be prompted to replace the original disc with blank media when necessary. If you have two optical drives, you can place a blank disc in the second drive and copy from one drive to another. This does not save time, but it does allow the copy to complete without further intervention.

If you are copying to blank media, you can click the "Properties" button to change the burning settings. You can lower the burning speed if your drive is having trouble burning copies, and if you have an audio CD player that is having trouble with copied discs, lowering the speed can often improve performance in that player. You also have the option of using burnproof, which combines data caching and your optical drive's positioning to prevent slow data transfer from causing a burn failure. "Simulate before burning" goes through the burning process with the laser turned off and is only useful with a slow hard drive or an oversized disc. Because your computer will be used to store the original disc's data before they are written to the blank media, you can choose a storage location for the resulting temporary files. By default, they are stored in the /tmp folder, which is the usual location for temporary data files. Once you are ready to begin the copy, you can click the "Copy" button to create an image and burn it to a new disc. If you click "Make Several Copies," then Brasero will display a prompt after the first copy has been burned, and you can either insert additional blank discs to make more copies or end the copying process.

If you are copying to an image file, the Properties button will allow you to choose a file name and save location as well as a disc format type. You can choose between cdrdao format (which allows for an exact duplicate made including CD-Text and other subchannel information); and bin/cue format, which are the most common formats; and readcd/readom format, which is used by certain Linux tools. Unless you have a specific requirement, the default cdrdao format is a good choice. Brasero requires additional software for the cdrdao and cue formats, and will prompt you to install them if needed. Once the image is complete, Brasero will display a confirmation. You can then back up the image file just like any other file and burn the image to a blank disc in the future.

Burning a Disc Image to Blank Media

If you have a disc image that you would like to burn to a blank disc, then after launching Brasero, you'll click the "Burn image" button. Click the button that says "Click here to select a disc image," and find the image you wish to burn. When you insert blank media, Brasero will display the media type and capacity and allow you to choose a specific disc if you have more than one inserted into more than one optical drive. The Properties button allows you to change your burning settings, and in addition to the preferences described in the previous section, the "Leave the disc open to add other files later" option allows you to create a multisession disc if you want to add more data later. This is compatible with most computer optical drives but usually causes noncomputer audio players to be unable to read the disc until the disc is "closed."

Clicking "Burn" and "Burn Several Copies" functions identically to the "Disc copy" procedure described in the last session.

Creating a Music CD

Creating a new music CD from existing audio files is quick and easy. There are two ways to create music CDs. The first is to create a traditional audio CD that will play in most audio players, and the other is to create a data CD filled with MP3 files that can be played on other computers and in special players. Because MP3 files are heavily compressed, an "MP3 CD" can hold six times more audio than a traditional audio CD. Some players can also read Ogg Vorbis format files as well. Check your playback devices for format compatibility.

After launching Brasero, click either "Audio project" for a traditional audio CD or "Data project" for an MP3 CD. This will show a new window that you can drag audio tracks to (see Figure 4-7).

Figure 4-7. *Creating a music disc is simple: traditional on the left, MP3 data CD on the right*

You can right-click the Files launcher icon and choose "Music" to open your music folder immediately, and copying files to the disc is as easy as dragging them to the Brasero window. For traditional audio CDs, Brasero will copy the album title of the first track you copy as the disc name. For either type of disc, you can change this by editing the title field under the track/file list. As you add files, Brasero will show how many more minutes of audio can be added to the current audio disc, or how much space is remaining on the data disc. The same files are used in Figure 4-6 on an audio CD and a data CD to illustrate the capacity difference.

For audio CDs, the track information will be written to the disc as CD-TEXT information if your optical drives support it. For audio players that support CD-TEXT, it can display the album and current track names during playback. You can select any track, and then click the track or artist name to edit this information without changing the original file. You can also use the toolbar to add a 2-second pause between two tracks, or split a selected audio file into multiple tracks.

Once your disc is prepared, you can either create an image file to be burned later or burn directly to a disc. The drop-down menu under the disc name will allow you to choose between these options. You will be prompted for an image location and file name or for burn preferences before your audio files are converted and the disc is created. These options are as described earlier, except that only the bin/cue image format is available for image file creation.

As storage technology changes, audio continues to be delivered in new and more convenient formats. Whether you now purchase your audio on disc or via digital download or record your own audio to share with others, Brasero allows you to create and back up music discs that protect your original purchases and are compatible with audio players of all descriptions.

Create Video DVDs Using DevedeNG

Video streaming is becoming more and more ubiquitous, and smart TVs and set-top media appliances are increasingly able to play common video formats directly. But video DVD still remains a useful format to share videos in. DevedeNG can create simple DVDs with optional menus in minutes.

Launching DevedeNG displays the Disc type selection window. DevedeNG supports several video disc formats. Most are not very common anymore but are available if you have older video playback devices. "Video DVD" is usually the most useful option.

Clicking "Video DVD" brings up the main window (see Figure 4-8), which allows you to define "titles" that act as stand-alone movies, and for each title you will specify video files that will play in order for each title before returning to the DVD menu. As you make changes, DevedeNG will track the estimated disc usage as you add files. Your video files will also be converted to the proper format once you are finished setting up the disc structure.

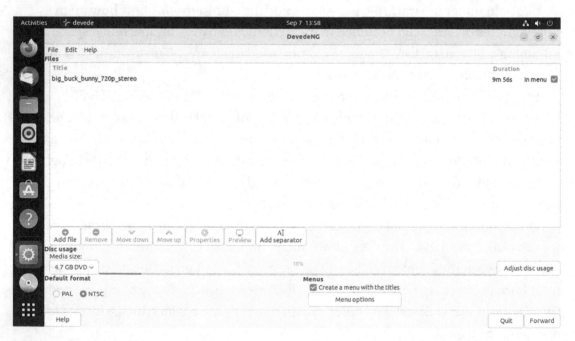

Figure 4-8. *DevedeNG's main menu lets you set up the disc structure and add video files*

The first step is to choose your default format. If you live in an area that uses ATSC such as North America or most of South America, choose NTSC. If you live in an area that uses DVB, choose PAL. Most modern players and televisions support both formats, but playback quality can be slightly degraded if your source files differ significantly in framerate.

Next, you can add a video file. When you click "Add" on the left side of the window, you will be able to select one or more files from the file picker. Each one will be added to the DVD as a "title" when you click OK. You can select a title and click Properties (see Figure 4-9) to give a proper name to the title. This is what will be shown in the generated DVD menu. You have the option of choosing a specific video format if it is different than the disc default and adjusting the file volume, which can be useful if a file has much softer or louder audio than the others on the same disc.

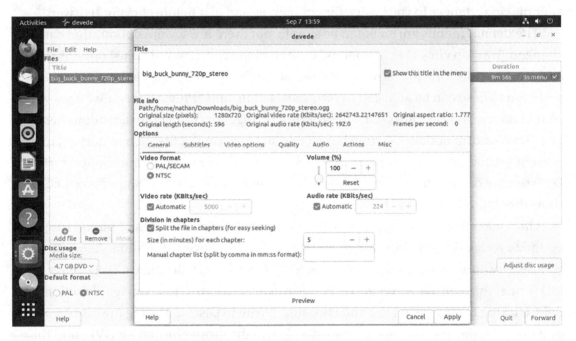

Figure 4-9. *You can control how each file is added to a title*

Each tab has advanced options that are available to explore, but are not usually necessary. You can specify whether to divide the file into 5-minute chapters for easier seeking on the player in the "General" tab and rotate or force letterboxing or stretching for video content that is in a different aspect ratio than the DVD on the "Video options tab." On the "Subtitles" tab, you can add subtitles, and DevedeNG supports several common formats, some of which you can create yourself with software available in

Ubuntu Software. DVD subtitles can be enabled or disabled by the video players, but you can use the "Force Subtitles" to configure subtitles to show by default. This setting is commonly used when a file has partial subtitles for dialog which is in a different language than the rest of the title. The "Actions" tab lets you choose what happens after the current title is finished, so you can go back to the DVD menu, go to the next title, or simply play the video in a continuous loop. The other options are fairly esoteric and shouldn't be necessary unless you are looking for something specific. Clicking "Apply" saves the current title's settings.

The "Disc usage" section allows you to see how much space you have remaining on the disc. You can use the "Media size" drop-down menu to select various disc sizes, and "Adjust disc usage" will increase video quality settings if you have not filled the disc, or decrease them if you are slightly over your disc capacity. You'll want to click this button after making changes to your video files or menus, and just before clicking "Forward."

The default menus are meant to be simple, but there are several options that can be changed. You can click "Menu options" to see a menu preview and adjust options such as the menu title, font, font size, color, shadow, background image, background audio, and more. These can be adjusted to your satisfaction, and "Preview menu" will show you your changes. You can press "OK" to save your changes or "Cancel" to abandon them. The "Disc startup options" section has an option "Jump to the first title at startup" to prevent the menu from being seen unless the viewer presses the "menu" button on the DVD remote or once the first title ends if the ending action is set to "Stop reproduction/show disc menu."

Once you are ready to create your DVD, click the "Adjust disc usage" button to optimize your video quality settings, and then click the "Forward" button. After you choose a location and file name and click "OK," DevedeNG will create a DVD image in ISO format that will allow you to create a disc using Brasero's "Burn image" function or right-clicking the image in Files and choosing "Write to Disc...." During the disc creation process, DevedeNG will convert your video files to the proper format for DVD, and this can take a very long time depending on the source videos and your computer's speed. If you want to run the conversion process overnight, you can check the "Shutdown computer when disc is done" option to save electricity.

Creating DVDs can be a very convenient way to share video files with friends and family, especially with longer video files. DevedeNG makes the process of creating a video disc with menus and multiple titles manageable.

Organize and Edit Your Photos Using Shotwell

One really exciting advance in technology is the spread of digital cameras. From cell phones to iPods to Nintendo handheld videogame systems, cameras are on many of the electronics we buy. The advent of digital photography was exciting for the amateur photographer. No film costs! You could take lots of photos and save the good ones later. This trend continues today with cell phone cameras in every pocket. But this also makes organizing and enhancing photos even more important today. Luckily, Ubuntu comes with Shotwell, a digital photo manager that makes importing and adjusting photos easier than ever.

The first time you run Shotwell, it will offer to import the photos in your Pictures folder. This loads the photos into your library, but Shotwell will not automatically add new photos that are added to your Pictures directory. This keeps your photo library from becoming cluttered, but you can import more photos by dragging them to the Shotwell window or via the File ➤ Import From Folder menu option. You can also use the Edit ➤ Preference menu option to enable the "Watch library directory for new files" setting so that Shotwell automatically adds new photos to your library. Shotwell sorts your photos into events based on their internal timestamps, and this is the primary method for managing your photo library. The events are listed in a sidebar on the left, and clicking an event shows photo thumbnails on the right side of the window (see Figure 4-10).

Importing Photos

When you plug in a camera, Shotwell will automatically detect it and list it under "Cameras" in the sidebar. You can click on a camera to view the photos on the device and import the selected or all photos using the toolbar buttons at the bottom of the window. Shotwell keeps track of photos that have already been imported so you can filter them with the "Hide photos already imported" option, and once an import is complete, it will ask you whether or not you wish to delete the successfully imported photos from your camera or keep them on the camera. If any of the photos were shot in RAW mode, Shotwell will automatically "develop" them in addition to copying the RAW image data. This allows Shotwell to make photo adjustments while retaining your ability to use advanced photo editing software such as GIMP or Darktable to develop and edit the RAW photos if desired.

If you prefer to connect your camera's memory card directly to your computer, simply insert the card into your computer's card reader. Ubuntu will detect and mount the card as a folder, and you can use the Files window to drag and drop photos onto the Shotwell menu or use Shotwell's File ➤ Import From Folder menu option to select a folder and begin importing photos.

Managing Events

Photos are grouped into events, and Shotwell tries to automatically create events based on the date and time each photo was taken (see Figure 4-10). If this information is not available from the photo, Shotwell will show a "No Event" category that you can use to find and sort photos manually.

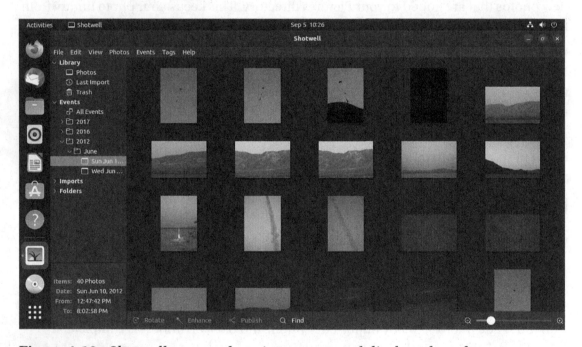

Figure 4-10. Shotwell groups photo into events and displays them for easy browsing

Events are named by date, and you can right-click an event on the left sidebar or double-click the event name to rename any event. You can move a photo from one event to another by dragging its thumbnail onto the new event. Events are sorted based on the earliest photo they contain, but you can use View ➤ Sort Events from the menu to choose whether the list should be Ascending (earliest event first) or the default of Descending (most recent event first).

Clicking the "All Events" item under the Events section of the library will show a list of events with a "key photo" as the thumbnail. This is the first photo in the event, but you can right-click any photo in an event and choose "Make Key Photo for Event" to change this. In the Events menu if you wish to merge two events, simply click one event and then hold Ctrl while clicking the other events to merge. The toolbar at the bottom of the screen contains a "Merge Events" button that will activate, and you can also right-click any of the selected events and choose "Merge Events" from the pop-up menu that appears.

Events in Shotwell cannot be empty, so deleting or moving the last photo in an event will cause the event to disappear. Because you cannot create an empty event, you can simply select one or more photos from your Library or any event and use Ctrl+N, or the Events ➤ New Event menu option to move those photos into a newly created event.

Working with Photos

Individual photos can be viewed in the library or each event, and you can use the zoom slider at the bottom right-hand corner of the screen to adjust the size of the thumbnails, or use the plus (+) and minus (-) keys. Clicking on a photo selects it, and the bottom-left corner of the screen displays basic information about the selected photo. Double-clicking a photo zooms in on it and allows for more editing options. You can also press Enter while a photo is selected to zoom in on it. In this zoomed in view, the left and right arrow keys move to the previous and next photo in the event as do the "Back" and "Forward" buttons at the right of the toolbar, and Esc returns to the thumbnail view.

Shotwell can help you keep track of photos, and you can apply a five-star rating to each one. Selecting a photo and pressing 1–5 will assign the same number of stars to the photo. Pressing 0 will remove the rating. Pressing 9 will mark a photo as "rejected" and hide it from view. You can also right-click a photo and use the "Set Rating" menu to rate any photo. The View ➤ Filter Photos menu option allows you to filter photos by rating, and can be used to show only highly rated photos or to make rejected photos visible again. This can help you choose which photos to keep or edit if you have a large number of photos from an event. In addition to rating photos, you can add tags to help you group photos across events. Simply select a photo and use the Tags ➤ Add Tags menu or press Ctrl+T. A tag window will appear, and you can add one or more tags separated by commas. Once you have defined a tag, you can add the tag to new photos by dragging a photo to the tag in the sidebar.

Editing Photos

Most photos only need minor adjustments, and the toolbar exposes Shotwell's simple editing tools. These tools are mostly automated and allow anyone to make the type of mundane adjustment that any photo might need such as color balancing, cropping, straightening, and so on. While Shotwell doesn't try to replace more advanced photo editing tools, its editing tools cover a lot of needs (see Figure 4-11).

Figure 4-11. *Cropping and enhancing a photo can be done in seconds*

The "Rotate" button allows you to rotate a photo clockwise in 90-degree intervals, and pressing Ctrl while you click the button will rotate the photo in a counterclockwise direction instead. In the thumbnail view, you can select multiple photos by pressing Ctrl while clicking each photo, and the rotate tool will affect all selected photos at once.

The "Crop" button will allow you to adjust the photo's aspect ratio and composition by zooming in on a specific portion of the photo and discarding the rest. An overlay appears when you click the crop tool, and the drop-down menu allows you to choose various aspect ratios, and the "Pivot" button to the right will toggle the cropping reticule between portrait (tall) and landscape (wide) mode. The "Crop" button commits the change.

The "Straighten" tool allows a photo to be rotated 15 degrees in either direction and will crop the photo slightly to maintain its original aspect ratio. After clicking on this tool, you can use the slider along with the grid overlay to rotate the photo by eye, or you can find an edge that represents a horizontal line, click the mouse on one end of the edge, and drag the pointer until the dotted line matches the angle of the edge. Releasing the left mouse button will rotate the photo up to 15 degrees from its original orientation, and you can continue adjusting the rotation using the mouse or the slider if needed. The "Reset" button will remove the current rotation, and pressing the "Straighten" button will apply the new rotation to the photo.

The "Red-eye" button allows you to reduce or remove any "red-eye" effect in a photo caused by light from a camera flash bouncing off the retina of a human's eye. You can adjust each eye individually, and clicking on the tool will show a small circle you drag onto an affected eye. The size slider adjusts the size of the circle, and clicking "Apply" will remove the red-eye effect from the photo. Simply repeat these steps for each affected eye in the photo.

The "Adjust" tool gives you quick control over the color of the photo. The histogram shows you the color range of the photo, and you can slide the sliders to stretch the photo's color range. This produces more contrast in the photo and can often greatly improve a photo's contrast and visibility. The other sliders adjust a color attribute of the photo to help you enhance the photo, and once you are happy with the adjustments you have made, you can click "OK." The "Enhance" tool automatically adjusts the histogram and the shadows sliders, and you can use this tool as a starting point and click "Adjust" to view and change the adjustments.

Shotwell is a nondestructive editor, and this means that your original photos are not modified, but the edits made are stored in Shotwell's database and applied to the photos in real time. This means that your Pictures folder will not contain any of the changes you make in Shotwell, but it also offers several advantages.

Unlike editors that save over the original photo, subsequent edits do not degrade the quality of the photo, so you can continue to refine the look of a photo until you are happy with it. You can view the original photo by holding the Shift key, and you can also revert all changes and restore any photo to its original appearance. Simply right-clicking a photo or clicking the Photo menu and choosing "Revert to original photo" will undo all changes applied to the photo in Shotwell.

You can also apply the color adjustments you've made to one photo to others as well. To do so, select a photo, then use the Photo ➤ Copy Color Adjustments menu option, or press Shift+Ctrl+C to copy the adjustments to the clipboard. Then, you can zoom in on a photo or select one or more photos and use Photo ➤ Paste Color Adjustments or press Shift+Ctrl+V to apply those adjustments to the selected photos. This allows you to keep a consistent look across your photos whether you are adjusting for lighting conditions or artistic style.

Sharing Photos

Because Shotwell does not modify your original files, you will need to export photos before you can share the edited photos with others. You can select photos and use the File ➤ Export menu option to choose whether to export original unmodified or edited photos or choose the photo format such as JPG or PNG, exported resolution, and more. You might lower the resolution before sharing via email or the Web, for example. You can also use the File ➤ Send To... menu option to export a photo and send it to your email client.

Shotwell can also publish your photos directly to a web photo service such as Facebook or Flickr, and even publish videos to YouTube. If you have integrated an online account for one of these services with Ubuntu (see Chapter 3), it will appear as an option when you select photos and use the File ➤ Publish menu option or press Shift+Ctrl+P. The exact process is slightly different for each service, so be sure to follow the onscreen instructions to complete the publishing process.

Advanced Photo Editing Using GIMP and Darktable

As mentioned before, Shotwell can't replace more advanced photo editing tools. And while it does reduce the need for more advanced software, it works alongside them as well. Under Shotwell's Edit ➤ Preferences menu option is an "External Editors" tab. There you can set an external photo editor and an external RAW editor. The drop-down menus will list all photo editors installed on your system. Once you have defined the external editors, you can right-click a photo and choose "Open With External Editor," or where RAW images are available, "Open With RAW Editor" becomes an additional option.

Advanced photo editing is far beyond the scope of this book, but there are two excellent choices that I can recommend to start out with, both available through Ubuntu Software.

The first suggestion for "external editor" is the GNU Image Manipulation Program, or GIMP (see Figure 4-12). This fantastic photo editing tool is comparable in many ways to Adobe Photoshop, and can be used to create edited, color-balanced, and composited photos and artwork. It's useful to know that the palettes can be hidden and restored with the Tab key, which can help you concentrate on your work. If you've used professional photo editing software before, you should quickly feel at home. For a friendly and comprehensive introduction, however, I strongly recommend *Beginning GIMP: From Novice to Professional, Second Edition* by Akkana Peck, also available from Apress.

Figure 4-12. *GIMP allows for advanced photo editing that rivals professional retail software*

When a camera saves a JPG file, the data from the sensor is very heavily processed; however, a RAW image file is aptly named because it contains the raw data captured by the camera's sensor. These data need to be "developed" before they can be used with most other software, and just as a film negative offers so many possibilities to a photographer, a RAW image can be exposed, sharpened, and adjusted in ways a compressed JPG cannot. GIMP can import RAW files for several popular camera models.

The second suggestion, for "external RAW editor," is the program Darktable available in Ubuntu Software, which is comparable to Adobe Lightroom, and allows for complex filters and settings to be applied to RAW image data before it is exported for normal use. This software is complex but powerful, and is the best place to start if you are an experienced photographer familiar with other RAW manipulation software.

With cameras being so common and storage space being so cheap, we all have the ability to create a virtual avalanche of photos, and this can make it hard to find just the right ones to highlight an event or share with others. Shotwell makes it easy to keep your photos organized and make simple adjustments to satisfy most everyday photo needs.

Record and Process Audio Using Audacity

Audio editing can be a bit tricky. It seems like it should be fairly simple, but unlike a photo that we can see, audio can be difficult to visualize. Fortunately, Audacity is a powerful multitrack editor that can be used to record live audio as well as edit, mix, and process existing audio files as well. Audacity can be used for anything from removing pauses from a recording to removing vocals from a song.

When you open a file with Audacity, it is placed in a track and shown in a waveform view. From this you can easily see the volume at various points in the recording. Opening additional files creates new tracks that can be edited together or separately (see Figure 4-13).

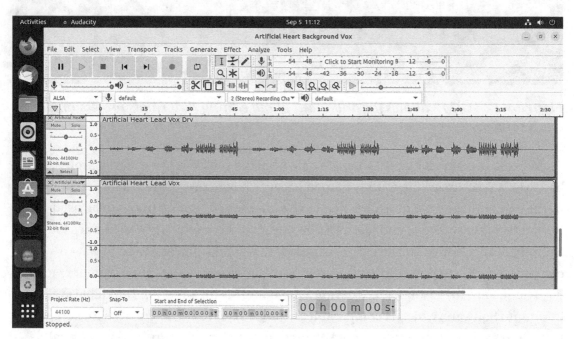

Figure 4-13. *Audacity is a powerful multitrack editor that's good for both quick and advanced projects*

The toolbar is complex, but each button can be hovered over with the mouse pointer until a tool tip appears that shows the button's function and shortcut key. For example, the large round buttons are "pause," "play," "stop," "beginning of track," "end of track," and "record." The tool tips also show keyboard shortcuts; for example, hovering over the "play" button shows you that you can press the spacebar to begin playback.

Clicking on a track places the cursor at that time index. When you click the "play" button or press the spacebar, audio playback starts at the cursor position. When you press the button again, the cursor doesn't move. This lets you use the spacebar to listen to a point in time and determine if it's the right spot without having to place the cursor again. Clicking and dragging the cursor over part of a track will select that audio. You can use the "Zoom In" and "Zoom Out" toolbar buttons to adjust the view to make positioning the cursor easier. Pressing the spacebar with a selection will play only the selected audio to help you select the right audio. You can drag the beginning and end of the selection to adjust the start and stop times. Once you are happy with the amount of audio that you have selected, you can delete, cut, copy, or paste the selection just as you can with text.

Recording audio is as simple as clicking the "record" button or pressing R. Audacity will begin recording audio in a new track at the current cursor position. Audacity shows a live input and output volume level in the toolbar during recording. If you want to add audio to the current track instead of creating a new track, pressing Shift+R will add audio to the end of the existing track. Audacity will play the other tracks in sync with the recording, so it is possible to record a lead track in time with a background track, for example. The View ➤ Show Clipping menu option will highlight any clipped audio in red, so that you can quickly identify poorly recorded audio.

Audacity comes with many filters and audio effects, and the Effect menu lists all of them. The Help menu has a link to Audacity's manual online, and the "Editing" section lists all effects alphabetically and also groups them by function. You can use this to learn how to use effects properly. The manual also includes many practical tutorials that you can use to learn audio editing techniques in general.

While recording audio takes time and practice, Audacity is the best tool for the job. From recording a short voice memo to editing recorded music and building podcasts, Audacity's track editor and effects and plug-in architecture make it easy to work with audio on Ubuntu.

Play MIDI Files

MIDI files are digital instructions that describe music, and while the standard was originally invented so that electric musical instruments could communicate and control one another, the same information is capable of storing musical instructions very efficiently. While the standard is alive and well in the music industry, MIDI files had a brief popular heyday as a way to share music on the computer before actual sound recordings were feasible. Today, MIDI is still useful as a way to generate music from sheet music—as with the Mutopia Project—or to enjoy the soundtracks of classic video games.

MIDI files can be used to control actual hardware. Modern player pianos use MIDI instructions instead of paper rolls to play back a performance by a professional pianist. Sound cards used to have dedicated electronic synthesis hardware, but this is now rare except in professional equipment. Ubuntu has a software MIDI renderer called Timidity that can interpret MIDI instructions and generate high-quality audio.

To install Timidity, open "Terminal" via the Dash, or press Ctrl+Alt+T. Then type:

```
sudo apt install timidity fluid-soundfont-gm
```

Press Enter, then enter your password and type and press Enter again. You'll be prompted to confirm the software installation. Press Enter to accept the default of "Yes." Ubuntu will download and install Timidity and a general MIDI sound font.

Once Timidity is installed, double-clicking a MIDI file will open it in Videos, and the player will use Timidity for its audio playback. Other software that utilizes MIDI playback such as DOSBox or Rosegarden will also automatically detect and utilize Timidity.

MIDI files may not be commonly used for casual playback, but they are still popular among certain music cultures and are easy to find on the Web. By installing Timidity on your computer, you will find that yet another means of entertainment opens up to you.

Explore the Universe Using Stellarium

Stargazing is a pastime that has existed for as long as humans have lived on Earth. The universe has inspired stories and legends from the most ancient records all the way to science fiction novels and movies in the present day, not to mention the intense study through manned and unmanned scientific undertakings. Before the spread of electricity, the night sky was a bright, almost living thing, and on moonless nights the Milky Way galaxy itself was bright enough to see by and cast a shadow on the ground. With the massive amount of light pollution in cities, most of us have to plan a trip to get a dark, starry night sky (and if you haven't had the galaxy cast your shadow, I highly recommend it!). But whether we're planning ahead or just want to virtually study the sky, Stellarium is a virtual 3D planetarium application that re-creates the visible universe around us with stunning graphics.

The first time you launch Stellarium, you'll see a view of the sky in a field as it would appear at your current location if it can be detected via your Internet connection, at your current local time (see Figure 4-14). If your timing is right, you'll enjoy a beautiful, starry view of the night sky. Otherwise you might see a mundane daytime sky or a stunning sunrise or sunset. But personalizing your experience is very simple.

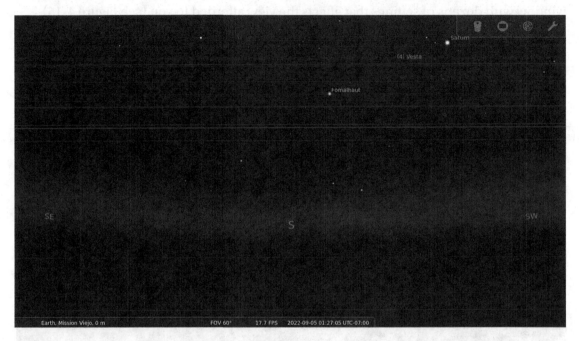

Figure 4-14. *Stellarium simulates a beautiful, realistic view of the sky*

The interface is pretty easy to use. The bottom-left corner of the screen has two bars that appear when you touch the left or bottom edge of the screen with your mouse cursor. On the left is quick access to various configuration and settings, and on the bottom gives you access to various display settings. Placing your mouse over each icon brings up a tool tip that gives the icon name and shortcut key. The left toolbar is the most important if you want to set up Stellarium to match your local conditions. Clicking the "Location window" icon or pressing F6 brings up the location window, where you can set your current location on Earth (or over 120 other planets and stars). This influences the position of the stars above the horizon and can be used to plan optimal viewing positions and times for real stargazing, not to mention virtual field trips across the galaxy.

Once you've set your location, you can click the close icon at the top right of the location window or press Esc. Next, you can then click the "Date/time" icon or press F5 and set an appropriate post-sunset time for your location which matches your seasonal day length in real life. Once you have these options set, the real fun begins, because the next icon is the "Sky and viewing options" icon. Clicking this icon or pressing F4 opens a window with dozens of settings that affects the view afforded to you (see Figure 4-15).

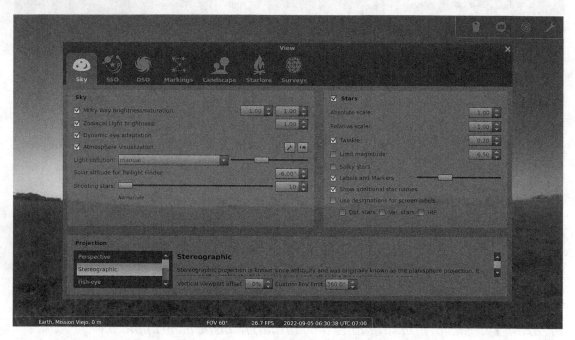

Figure 4-15. *Stellarium's viewing options are worthy of any planetarium*

There are five tabs with various options, many of which have tool tips which appear when you hover the mouse cursor over them. Most notable on this page is the light pollution setting, which allows Stellarium to simulate light pollution. You can enter the Bortle Dark Sky Scale number for your location manually, and Stellarium includes light pollution values in its location database. You can use this light pollution index data for an accurate representation of your star visibility or adjust it to see how the sky would look under different lighting conditions.

The "DSO" tab determines which deep sky objects are shown. The "Markings" tab allows you to toggle various landmarks that can help you visualize the sky, from sky orientation markings to constellation lines, labels, and art. You can also change the projection type used to display the sky. The "Landscape" tab allows you to select various images for the ground. The default landscape is an empty field in Guéreins, France, where the developer of Stellarium lives, but there are other interesting landscapes representing various Earth environments as well as the Moon and other planets. You can also create your own landscape if you have a favorite location. The "Starlore" tab allows you to load different information from different sky cultures, and can be a fascinating way to study ancient legends about the universe. Each culture has its own star names, constellation lines, and constellation art that provide a unique way of looking at the universe around us.

The bottom toolbar is mostly dedicated to toggling specific common settings, and can be used to toggle the display of constellation lines, the atmosphere, ground fog, and so on. Each icon has a tool tip that names the setting and provides a shortcut key where available. For instance, pressing A toggles atmosphere visibility. A blue daytime sky suddenly becomes stark and dazzling without the atmosphere to scatter the sun's light and block out the other stars. Pressing F toggles visible ground fog that simulates poor visibility near the horizon and G toggles the actual landscape, allowing you to view the sky that is still below the horizon. Ocular view simulates the view through telescope or binocular optics—including magnification, field of view, and mirroring—so it is especially useful for planning targets during stargazing trips.

The Configuration window, accessible by pressing F2, allows for various settings to be adjusted, but most notably the "Tools" tab allows you to download more detailed star catalogs with a single click. These catalogs contain an even greater number of stars than ships by default. The scripts tab can play back automated viewing, time, and positional data. The scripts that come with Stellarium are an intriguing mix that demonstrate interesting events such as lunar eclipse (see Figure 4-16), to other astronomical phenomena.

Figure 4-16. *Stellarium simulates real-world events such as planetary positioning and eclipses*

For exploration, the "Search" icon in the left toolbar (also accessible through F3 or Ctrl+F) will quickly find and center the view and track planets, stars, and other objects. Stellarium actually simulates the position of astronomical objects, so you can see the position of the rings of Saturn as visible from Earth, or watch the moons of Jupiter orbit around the gas giant. Stellarium even shows the shadows they cast as they go by. This also means that eclipses are shown in real time. You can use the bottom toolbar to change the passage of time to observe lunar libration, for instance, where the moon's face appears to wobble as it orbits the Earth. Changing the speed of time is also a great way to view sunsets and watch the stars begin to appear in the sky. You can even activate a "Night Mode" that changes the interface to black and red to help preserve night vision.

Stellarium is a wonderful example of professional, high-quality software that satisfies both amateur and professional uses. Observing the sky through software not only helps astronomical study but can also make real trips into nature to study the stars much more rewarding.

Play Legacy PC Games

Linux has a justified reputation for lacking support for games, and this has taken a long time to change. While Ubuntu comes with simple games such as Aisleriot Solitaire and Mines by default, professional and indie game support is increasing all the time. The historic lack of games also leads to the development of emulation software to allow older games designed for other operating systems to run under Linux as well. Even with hundreds of free and open source games available through Ubuntu Software and commercial games beginning to add support for Ubuntu, there are a lot of classic games that are worth revisiting, and "retro gaming" has seen a resurgence in popularity. More importantly, system emulation allows older games from the 1980s and 1990s that you have purchased and still have on CD or floppy disk to still be enjoyed on modern hardware.

A few older games have been rereleased for free, such as the first two games in The Elder Scrolls series by Bethesda Softworks, and other games that were distributed as "shareware"—games that were available to try before purchasing—are still frequently available, such as early Apogee and ID Software games that still feature iconic gameplay. Some game genres, such as adventure games, are now rare or nonexistent when it comes to new releases even though they were once extremely popular.

It is beyond the scope of this book to detail how to transfer data from legacy storage formats and configure emulators, and finding legal sources for legacy software can be difficult, although online auction sites such as eBay can be very effective. But if you are familiar with DOS and adventure games and still have the installation media for your old games, configuring DOSBox will be part of the fun. Others may want to stick with newer software. But even when it comes to purchasing legacy games, there are some nice alternatives to auction sites as well.

Purchase Legacy Games from GOG.com

The resurgence in "retro gaming" and interest in forgotten classics led to the founding of a company named Good Old Games in 2008, which later changed its name to GOG.com. The company wanted to make it easy to experience legacy games on modern computer hardware and operating systems as well as support the rights owners of older games. After initial sales success, they were able to negotiate distribution rights for more and more legacy games. As a bonus for classic game enthusiasts, many games include extras such as scanned manuals, original artwork, desktop wallpapers, and game soundtracks.

Many older games that were updated to run under Windows actually run under DOSBox or ScummVM with carefully optimized configurations. Because GOG.com sells games without digital rights management, many of these games can be installed on Windows or via Wine, and the installed files can be copied to Ubuntu for use directly with DOSBox or ScummVM without Wine. GOG.com also supports Ubuntu, and an ever-expanding collection of software can be purchased and downloaded and installed with a few simple clicks.

When you download a game from GOG.com, be sure to select "Save File" when Firefox prompts you to save the installer. The game will be provided in the form of an install script that will be saved to your Downloads folder. If you open Files and double-click the install script, it will be opened in a text editor. This is a security feature in Ubuntu. To run the installer without the Terminal, you will have to make two simple changes.

The first change will allow Files to run an executable script by double-clicking it. To do this, run Files and then choose Edit ➤ Preferences from the menu, and click the "Behavior" tab. In the "Executable Text Files" section, select "Ask each time." You will only have to make this change once on your computer, and it still offers a measure of security against inadvertently running scripts.

The second change will be done once for each download. In Files, right-click the downloaded install script and choose "Properties." Click the "Permissions" tab, and next to "Execute:," check the "Allow executing file as program" option and click the "Close" button on the title bar. Now you double-click the installer, and Files will prompt you whether you want to run the script or display its contents. Click the "Run" button and follow the onscreen prompts to install your game. Once the installation is finished, you will be able to run the game from the Applications list in the future.

GOG.com offers a small number of games for free, some of which support Ubuntu. This is a good way to see how easy installation is before purchasing other titles and get a feel for how older graphics and sound work on your computer. For more information, visit their website at `www.gog.com/`.

Run DOS Games and Software Using DOSBox

Many classic PC games were released for MS-DOS. With computer hardware being very limited in the 1980s, DOS was a single-user operating system that provided programs with direct access to hardware, and games usually did interact directly with hardware, which is no longer allowed on modern operating systems that strictly control direct hardware access to accommodate many programs running simultaneously. Luckily, modern hardware is powerful enough to emulate legacy hardware and software, and the emulated environment provided by DOSBox is indistinguishable to programs running inside. DOSBox is built to emulate a legacy IBM PC-compatible computer running DOS specifically for the purpose of running games, although this means that many older nongame applications run as well.

From Ubuntu Software, search for and install "DOSBox Emulator." Once DOSBox is launched from the application grid, it displays a window with a startup message and a DOS command prompt. The Z: drive is an emulated drive that contains various DOS utilities such as the MOUNT command which lets you make a folder on your computer accessible via a DOS drive letter. Note that DOSBox uses the older term "directory" to refer to folders. The INTRO command, which can be run by typing "intro" at the prompt and pressing Enter, provides more information about special commands and also offers some examples to show you how to begin.

Typically, you will create a folder inside your home folder to store your installed DOS games, called "dos" or "dosbox," or you can create one folder for each game. This folder can be empty, but it must exist to allow DOSBox a place to store data. Then, you will copy a game's installation files from your installation media into a separate folder in your home folder and mount that folder under drive A. Then, you can switch to the install "disk" by typing "A:" and pressing Enter. The DIR command will list the contents of the current folder, and once you find the setup or installer program, typing the name and pressing Enter will run the program. After the game is installed to your C drive, you can switch to the C drive by typing "C:" and pressing Enter and change to the installation folder by typing "CD" followed by a space and the name of the folder, pressing Enter, and typing the name of the command followed by Enter (see Figure 4-17).

Figure 4-17. *From setting up a game and playing, DOSBox provides an authentic experience*

Because DOS games typically expected unshared access to a CPU that ran anywhere from 8 to 133 MHz and modern computers typically run at 2 or 3 GHz, DOSBox limits the emulated CPU speed. You can press Ctrl+F11 to slow down DOSBox or Ctrl+F12 to speed it up if a DOS game is running at a poor speed. This can affect performance of other applications running under Ubuntu. Clicking the mouse inside the DOSBox window will also "capture" mouse input. If you need to use the mouse in Ubuntu without exiting DOSBox, you can press Ctrl+F10 to release the mouse. You can also toggle full-screen mode by pressing Alt+Enter. Once your game is finished, you can type EXIT at the DOS prompt and press Enter to quit DOSBox.

In addition to the INTRO command, the DOSBox website contains detailed documentation that describes various disk, video, input, networking, and game compatibility notes, so it is the best place to get tips if you cannot get a game running. You can also edit your DOSBox configuration file in ~/.dosbox/dosbox-0.74-3.conf to display graphics with various other options such as different scalers (to increase the graphics size or smooth jagged edges or to emulate old effects such as RGB monitor artifacts or scanlines). For more detailed information, visit www.dosbox.com/wiki/.

Play Adventure Games Using ScummVM

Adventure games started out as interactive books where the play would read a description and then type in a simple one- or two-word command to interact with the story. They typically focus on exploration and puzzle solving while a story unfolds around your character, and the play experience is unique. As computer graphics improved, adventure games began to display graphics and use the mouse. Graphical presentation became more elaborate, and the genre peaked in the 1990s when CD-ROMs became common and digitized voice and video could be included. Unfortunately, this drove production costs up and the genre soon ceased to be profitable. Aside from certain notable exceptions, adventure games are rare today.

ScummVM is a software project that can read the graphic and audio assets of classic adventure games and interpret their scripting languages. This allows many classic games to be enjoyed on Ubuntu, and several games have been released free of charge by their rights holders. Ubuntu Software contains both ScummVM and four popular adventure games that were once available at retail: Beneath a Steel Sky, Flight of the Amazon Queen, Lure of the Temptress, and Dráscula: The Vampire Strikes Back.

In Ubuntu Software, searching for the four games mentioned will return entries for each game. Installing any of the games will also install ScummVM automatically (see Figure 4-18). Once the games are installed, they can be launched by name from the application grid. If you aren't interested in those games but want to play another game that ScummVM supports, you can search for "scummvm" directly.

Figure 4-18. *Ubuntu includes four free, formerly retail adventure games in its repositories*

Each game engine has its own shortcut keys, which are often the only way to access important features such as loading and saving the game. For instance, in Beneath a Steel Sky, F5 accesses the game's menu. Left-clicking a named object will cause your character to examine it, and right-clicking causes your character to use or interact with it. ScummVM also has its own global menu, which can be accessed via Ctrl+F5. The documentation at ScummVM's website details specific commands (called "hotkeys" in the documentation) for many popular games, if you do not still have the game's documentation. In windowed mode, Ctrl+Alt+- and Ctrl+Alt++ will scale the graphics to be larger or smaller, pressing Alt-Enter toggles full-screen mode, and Ctrl+Q quits the current game.

You can copy supported adventure games that you own from their installation media to a folder and add the game to ScummVM. Some games may need additional steps to run properly, which are usually listed in the ScummVM documentation online. You can find more free adventure games and additional notes about specific games and their controls at the ScummVM website at `www.scummvm.org/`.

Play Commercial Games Using Steam

The most convenient way to install commercial games on Ubuntu is often via Valve Software's Steam client. Steam was conceived as a way for Valve Software to sell games directly to players and keep their software up-to-date, and quickly became one of the easiest ways to purchase and manage a computer gaming library. Valve worked on making a dedicated operating system that will power PC-based gaming consoles, called SteamOS. First built on Debian similar to the way Ubuntu is, Valve started encouraging game developers to make games available for Ubuntu so that they would be compatible with SteamOS-based systems in the future. Several years later, Valve also started contributing to Wine via an intermediary step called "Proton," and now approximately 80% of the entire Steam library runs on Ubuntu. Now Valve has released a Linux-based system called the Steam Deck. Any game purchased through Steam can be played on any supported operating system, so if you've purchased games via Steam for Windows or Mac, you will find that many are available on Ubuntu as well. Notable exceptions are certain online multiplayer games that utilize anticheat software to protect the online experience. Still, several anticheat software providers have pledged support for Linux. If a game is advertised as compatible with the Steam Deck, it should run on your desktop with Ubuntu as well.

In Ubuntu Software, install "Steam installer." Once Steam has been installed, launch Steam from the application grid, and the Steam client will be downloaded and installed. Once Steam runs, you can choose to create a new Steam account or log in to an existing account. When you log in, you will see the Steam store or your game library, depending on your preferences. The Steam store will indicate Ubuntu-compatible titles by showing a SteamOS icon by the title listing, and your library will list all of your games, and you can click the "Games" filter at the right of the search field and select "SteamOS + Linux" to view games that are compatible with Ubuntu (see Figure 4-19). Selecting a title and clicking "Install" will automatically download and install the game, and the button will appear as "Play" for installed titles.

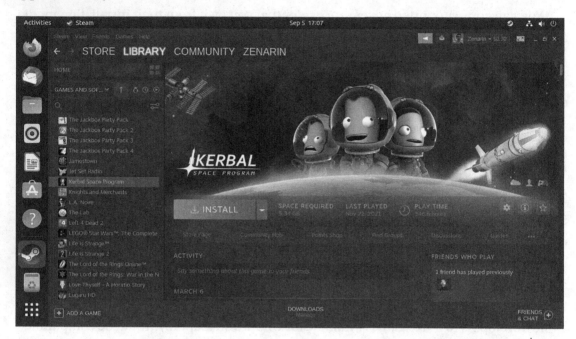

Figure 4-19. *Steam makes buying and playing thousands of games easy*

Summary

Ubuntu turns your computer into a multimedia powerhouse. You can enjoy music and videos and back up your media collection. Ubuntu has the tools you need to create your own music, photos, and video, whether you snap occasional pictures with your phone or are a professional photographer. And Ubuntu Software and Steam allow you to explore new worlds—whether observing the virtual skies in Stellarium or mastering orbital mechanics in Kerbal Space Program through Steam. Ubuntu is powerful and flexible enough to balance work and play.

CHAPTER 5

Command-Line Tricks and Applications

At last we come to the command line! That most powerful and often feared topic of all new Linux users. Fairly or unfairly, the command line has a reputation for being arcane and difficult to use. And it is a half-truth: a lot of arcane utilities have stuck around—and indeed, any Unix or Linux guru can perform magic inside a terminal window. But the other half of this truth is that the most common commands are simple and easy to use, and the command line is therefore both powerful *and* comfortable.

If you've gone through the earlier chapters, you've seen how comprehensive and easy Ubuntu is with pretty much no command-line usage. For daily use, it's pretty simple to get by without ever opening a terminal window or editing a configuration file. Yet if you search the Internet or Ask Ubuntu for solutions to common problems, you'll usually find advice in the form of commands to run on the command line. This seems to conflict with what I just said in the first sentence of this paragraph, but when you understand how the command line works, it makes perfect sense.

When specific actions need to be performed in a precise way, it's very difficult to explain how to perform each step graphically to someone who isn't familiar with a user interface. On the other hand, with specific commands it is possible to make a computer do precisely what is asked. Giving command-line options virtually guarantees that each step is performed in an exact manner. Unfortunately, this also gives rise to the rumor that Ubuntu or Linux can't be used without utilizing the command line, and that scares off a lot of users. Fortunately, the simple fact that we're all the way into Chapter 6 and have already seen tons of practical applications proves that the command line is optional. But for as optional as the command line is for everyday use, it's not unimportant, either. The command line also functions as a way to get work done even when something goes wrong.

© Nathan Haines 2023
N. Haines, *Beginning Ubuntu for Windows and Mac Users*,
https://doi.org/10.1007/978-1-4842-8972-3_5

Computers aren't intelligent or smart. They're fancy calculators that can't do anything without a list of instructions. And when they operate, they only do what you say, not what you mean. A terminal window is your chance to tell Ubuntu exactly what to do, and have Ubuntu do it. In this chapter, we'll look at some very specific tasks that are best done on the command line. They're very simple and extremely useful at the same time. And toward the end of the chapter, we'll take a look at less serious tasks and more fun ones. With luck, you'll find that some of these programs are useful or fun. At the very minimum, you'll understand why many Ubuntu users prefer to use a command-line interface in certain circumstances. Even if you decide not to use the command line in the future, you'll at least see that the command line isn't scary after all.

Introduction to the Command Line

The command line may seem daunting. But the basic commands are very straightforward and easy to remember. This section will teach you a bit about the command line as well as some basic ways to navigate your way around a terminal interface. I'm not going to attempt to teach you all about the command line! That would be a book in and of itself. But I'll teach you what you need to know to understand what's happening in the rest of this chapter. It's my hope that if you are intrigued by what we do cover together, you'll pick up a dedicated book on the subject.

Note   The Ubuntu command line is part of a facet of computer history that stretches back to the 1960s, and more directly from the Multics and Unix operating systems. In the earliest days of command-line interfaces, computer mainframes filled half a room, and user terminals in the same building were hardwired back to the mainframes. The earliest terminals were teletypewriters. You'd type in your command, which was electronically sent to the mainframe, and the resulting output was sent back to your "teletype machine," which typed out the results on printed paper, just like a typewriter. These mechanical terminals were eventually replaced by electronic video terminals (sometimes fondly called "glass teletypes"), which were text-only video displays with built-in keyboards. Today, you run a "terminal emulator" to access the command line. Now you have some context to the brevity of Linux commands and their output. Incidentally, those old teletype machines and video terminals are still compatible with Linux computers.

Accessing the Command Line

There are two different ways to access a command-line interface in Ubuntu, and they function identically. The most common way is simply running "Terminal" from the Activities overview. This will launch GNOME Terminal in a window. For a more immersive view, you can maximize the terminal window. This gives you all the power of the command line with all the power of the modern graphical desktop, such as antialiased fonts and desktop notifications. F11 toggles full-screen mode and is more immersive still.

The other method is to switch to one of your computer's other virtual consoles. Unbeknownst to you, this entire time you've been working on either virtual console 2 or 7, which displays your graphical interface. As the name implies, there are six other virtual consoles at your disposal. To switch out of the graphical interface and into a text interface, press Ctrl+Alt+F3 to switch to an unused virtual console, which is labeled "tty3" (an abbreviation for teletype 3; see the previous note for the historical reference). From here you can use Alt+Left or Alt+Right to switch to the previous or next virtual console, or Alt+Fn, where "Fn" is F1 through F7 to access another virtual console. Note that you need to add Ctrl to the Alt-Fn shortcut when you're already in the graphical interface but don't need it when you're not. This is a fun way to limit yourself to text only if you're learning to use the command line, but also useful if for some reason your graphical interface isn't working or freezes and you still want to use your computer. It also mimics what you'll see if you install Ubuntu server edition on a computer or in a virtual machine. Each console is independent, and any programs you start will keep running no matter which virtual console is active.

Note   Your display server determines if it's using virtual consoles 1 for the welcome screen and 2 for your desktop session, or virtual console 7 for everything. But virtual consoles 3, 4, and 5 should also be free, no matter what graphics system your computer is using.

If you open a terminal window, you will simply see a command prompt, but if you switch to a virtual terminal, you will see a login prompt instead. It will look like the following:

```
Ubuntu 22.04.1 LTS ubuntu-book tty3

ubuntu-book login: _
```

To log in, simply type your username and press Enter. Then, you'll see a password prompt. Enter your password and press Enter. The password prompt won't give any indication that you're typing. This is a security feature that prevents others from seeing the length of your password and makes your password more difficult to guess.

The Ubuntu Command Line

Once you have brought up a terminal window or logged in at a virtual console, you will see a command prompt. On Unix and Linux machines, the command-line interface is provided by a "Unix shell" program. In Ubuntu, the default shell is called "bash." It gives some simple information before prompting you for a command (see Figure 5-1.)

Figure 5-1. *This is your standard Ubuntu terminal window with a bash command prompt*

The command prompt displays the current logged in username, separated from the computer's hostname with an @ sign, all in bright green. Because you can connect to other Unix and Linux machines over the network, this is a useful reminder of which computer you are controlling. A colon (:) separates the hostname from the current working directory, which is in bright blue, and finally a dollar sign ($) announces the end of the prompt. Your cursor shows up on the same line, after the dollar sign, and your Ubuntu system waits patiently for your command.

You work with the command line by typing a command, and if you need to tell the command anything before it gets started—such as the name of a file—that extra information is called an "argument." You separate that from the command with a space before typing it in, followed by another space if you are providing multiple arguments. When you have typed the entire command, you press Enter to tell the computer to run it. You can also specify options in some cases. These are usually preceded by a hyphen (-). Traditionally, an option with a long name is preceded by two hyphens (--). For example, a command might have "-f" or "--find" as synonyms for the same option. Don't worry too much about these details. They'll make sense as you work with specific command line applications.

You can always type the command "clear" and press Enter to erase the terminal window to make the display less cluttered. The shortcut key Ctrl+L also performs the same function. Ubuntu will erase the screen and print your command prompt and any partial command you've typed at the top of the screen. You can type "exit" and press Enter to close your Terminal window or log out of the computer (at a virtual console or remote session) when you are finished. If you close the Terminal window using the red X icon in the title bar, Ubuntu will prompt you if a command is still running, so that you can decide to wait for it to finish or interrupt the command immediately.

Working with Files and Directories (Folders)

Moving around the command line is pretty easy to do, and for most simple uses you'll be looking at files and folders. On the command line, a folder is usually referred to by the older name "directory." When you first open a terminal window or log in to a computer, you'll start at your home directory. This is represented as a tilde (~) in the command prompt as a shortcut because it is so common. Let's take a look together at my system. Follow along, and you'll see different files, but the commands will work the same. My username on the system I used to write this book is "nathan," so my home directory is "/home/nathan," although the prompt just says ~. Note that Ubuntu like all other Unix-like operating systems uses forward slashes (/) to separate each directory, whereas Windows uses backslashes (\) and Mac OS used to use colons (:), although OS X recognizes both colons and slashes (/) now that it is Unix-based, too. If you want to see what is in my home directory, you can run "ls" to print a directory listing for your current directory:

```
nathan@ubuntu-book:~$ ls
Calibre Library   examples.desktop   pratchett.csv
deja-dup          japan              Public
Desktop           keen               Templates
Documents         Music              Time track, 03.09.2014 - 03.15.2014.html
Downloads         Pictures           Videos
nathan@ubuntu-book:~$
```

In the terminal, files are shown in light gray, but directories are bright blue. Executable commands such as programs or scripts would be bright green. I can view the contents of a different directory in two different ways. I can type a space after "ls" and name the directory, or I can change my current working directory and type "ls" again.

When you first log in or open a terminal window, your working directory is set to your home directory, and commands will typically work with the current working directory and its files, which is why it is prominently displayed in the command prompt. To change to a different directory, use the "cd" command. Type "cd" then a space, then the directory you want to change to before pressing Enter. Because my home directory contains a directory called Documents, I can just type "cd Documents" and press Enter to change to that directory:

```
nathan@ubuntu-book:~$ cd Documents
nathan@ubuntu-book:~/Documents$
```

Now the prompt shows my current directory as "~/Documents," and ~ still refers to my own home directory. It helps to keep the command prompt from being too long. Now I can type "ls" again and see a list of files and folders inside my Documents folder:

```
nathan@ubuntu-book:~/Documents$ ls
Artificial Heart          Library.tc      Sales Inquiry.odt    Tea.mm
budget.ods                Library.tc~     sol.exe
demo scale calendar.ics   nanowrimo.odt   Support policy.odt
nathan@ubuntu-book:~/Documents$
```

To change back to my home directory, I can either type "cd .." and press Enter, which will bring me back up one level into the current directory's "parent" directory, or I can type "cd" by itself and press Enter. If you ask your computer to change the working directory with "cd" but don't specify a specific directory, it will change the working directory to your home directory. For a list of some other shortcuts, see Table 5-1.

Table 5-1. Short names for common directories

Directory	Shortcut	Meaning
Home	~	Expands to home directory (e.g., /home/nathan).
Current	.	Refers to the current working directory.
Parent	..	Refers to the directory containing the current directory.
Root	/	The root directory contains all other directories.

Running Commands

You can type the name of any command on your system, and it will run when you press Enter. Even if you type "`firefox`" and press Enter, for example, if you are using a Terminal window on your graphical desktop, Firefox will open a new window to display graphics, and you will see any console messages in the terminal window where it is running. (Some "warning" and "info" messages are normal and no cause for alarm.) You will not be able to type new commands until Firefox exits (or at least until you read the later section on multitasking!).

Once a command has finished, bash will print a new command prompt and again patiently wait for your next command. Computers don't experience boredom, so you should never feel too pressured to take your time or to double-check a command before pressing Enter. Most text commands tend to do exactly what you say without further confirmation and only print feedback if there was some kind of error. This can be confusing if you don't expect it, but the command line assumes that you mean what you say.

In Ubuntu, most of your commands are in the /usr/bin folder or other standardized locations. When you type a command and hit enter, your system will look through a list of folders one by one for that command and run the first match it finds. This list of folders is called the "system path," and it allows you to quickly run commands no matter what directory you're working. As a security measure, Ubuntu only looks in the system path when you type a command. (Otherwise, a software archive might contain a malicious `ls` command. You unpack the archive and then type "`ls`" to see the directory listing, but you've accidentally run the malicious program instead!) To run a specific command that is located outside of the system path, you'll need to give the full path to the command. For instance, I have a nice white noise generator command that I saved

in a file in my Documents directory called "spacedrive." To run it, I can type in "/home/
nathan/Documents/spacedrive" and press Enter, which will let Ubuntu know exactly
where to look. But if I just type "spacedrive" and press Enter, Ubuntu will not find the
command and I'll get an error, even if I'm in my Documents directory, because it isn't in
the system path. Sometimes you'll want to run a script in the same directory. You can use
a period (.) to specify the current directory. So if I'm already in my Documents directory
("cd ~/Documents"), I can run "./spacedrive" and the script starts right up!

Tip   If you create a directory in your home directory called "bin," Ubuntu will
add it to your system path the next time you log in. You can put any scripts you
write there and run them with just their name. You can run "mkdir ~/bin" at
the command line or use Files to create the directory. The next time we see the
spacedrive script in Chapter 6, I'll have moved it to ~/bin.

One last hint is to look at the documentation if you find yourself with questions about
how to use a command. There is a lot of help available, and you can usually type "-h" or
"--help" after a command to see a summary of command usage and options. You can
also read the manual—or "man page"—of a command to get more detailed information.
For example, to find out all about the "ls" command, you can type "ls --help" for a
usage summary or type "man ls" and read the comprehensive manual (press "q" to
quit man and return to the command line). It explains each option in detail, and is the
best way to learn new ways to use commands. The manual is designed to be a reference
guide, so you don't need to memorize every option a command can use. If you want to
do something but aren't sure what the command is called, you can search the manuals of
commands installed on your system with "apropos" and a keyword related to your intent.
For example, "apropos edit" will return a list of man pages with "edit" in the command
name or short description. You can scroll through the list (there will be a lot of false
positives) and when you find a command that looks interesting, read the man page for
that command. It's a great way to explore and learn right from the command line.

Redirecting Output

Most command-line applications print their output to the terminal as text. One of the
most convenient things about using the command line is that you can copy and paste
output to save for later. But sometimes you'll know in advance that you want to save

the output of a program to a file, or you'll want to send the output of one command to another command for processing. This is an iconic feature of Unix that has served Linux very well, and is one of the nicest things about using the command line.

You can redirect the output of a command to a file by using the greater than (>) sign. For example, if you run "`ls ~ > homefiles.txt`", the shell will take the output from ls and place it in the file "homefiles.txt" in the current folder. You can then open up that file in a text editor, or send it to a friend in an email. You should exercise caution, because using > to save output will replace any existing file with the same name. Using two greater than signs (>>) will create the file if it doesn't exist, and append (add on to the end) of the file if it does exist.

One way that redirection comes in handy is using the command "`grep`" to search and display specific information to save you from having to search or scroll through large amounts of data (we'll use grep in an example later). You could save the command's output to a temporary file, but you can use a special character called a pipe (|) to skip that step. When you pipe the output of one command into another program, they both run in parallel, and any output of the first command is treated as input by the second command. You can connect several commands together at one time in this manner, so if you decide to study the command line in the future, you will get a lot of mileage out of this. But for the purposes of this quick introduction, I simply want you to recognize that when you see a pipe, you're asking the second command to process the results from the first command.

See What's Running on Your Computer

Computers are great multitaskers. Almost immediately after the boot process begins, they're doing more than one thing at once. Technically, a single computer processor can only run one instruction at a time (although multicore processors can cheat this a little). But computer time is measured in *billions of operations per second,* and a "multitasking" operating system's job is to schedule tiny little chunks of programs to run, one after the other. Because this all happens faster than human perception, it appears to us as though computers are doing many different things at the same time. Ubuntu gives you access to the same information about which programs are running that Ubuntu itself has. Since Ubuntu has to keep track of all of your programs, there are a few different ways that you can view this information as well.

The easiest way to see what's running on your system is to use the "ps" command. Short for "process status," this command will display a list of currently running processes (programs or parts of a program) on your computer. When run with no additional options, this will show any processes that are running as your user and are attached to the current terminal. It looks like this:

```
nathan@ubuntu-book:~$ ps
  PID TTY          TIME CMD
 2836 pts/12   00:00:00 bash
 3111 pts/12   00:00:00 ps
```

The four columns are simple. PID is the "process ID" for a line. Every time a process starts, it's assigned a number. The first process that Linux starts during bootup is the "init" system, which starts (or initializes) every other process, so it's assigned process id (PID) 1, and the PID goes up by one every time a new process is started. You can use the PID to force a process to shut down with the "kill" command, but it isn't important otherwise. TTY shows the name of the terminal a process is running on. This was more important in the days when many users connected to a single mainframe, but is still useful when monitoring a server that many users connect to over the network. TIME shows the cumulative amount of time that the program has used the computer's processing power instead of waiting on standby. It's measured in hours-minutes-seconds (if there are four numbers listed, the first one specifies days). The last, CMD, shows the name of the running command.

One of the odd things about ps is that it is actually a very old command, and in various versions of Unix over the years, it has displayed different information using different layouts. Because scripts like to run commands like ps and process the output, and many scripts are reused across different operating systems, ps will display Unix-style formatting if it is run with no options or Unix-style options, but will mimic the BSD operating system's ps display if it is run with BSD-style options so that it will be compatible with old scripts. This means that if you want to display all programs that are running as your user by using the "u" option from BSD, the output will look a little different:

```
nathan@ubuntu-book:~$ ps u
USER       PID %CPU %MEM    VSZ   RSS TTY      STAT START   TIME COMMAND
nathan    2836  0.1  0.3  29428  3624 pts/12   Ss   22:59   0:00 bash
nathan    3101  0.0  0.1  25084  1284 pts/12   R+   23:01   0:00 ps u
```

BSD provides a little more information than traditional Unix does. It displays the percentage of computer processing and memory utilization for each process, the virtual and physical memory being used, the current "state" of the process, the time the process was started, and COMMAND displays not just the command name but also the rest of the command line used to start it as well. The details aren't important right now, but you should know that sometimes the display will change and it's nothing to be surprised or worried about. There are a lot of additional options you can use, but "ps aux" displays all processes running by all users on the computer, and this is a good way to see literally everything that's running on your system. You can use it to see what processes are running and which user they are running under.

While ps will give you a snapshot of the processes running on your computer, a more interesting program called "top" will show you the processes that are running in real time, updating the list to show which processes are using the most resources:

```
top - 22:59:43 up 29 min,  3 users,  load average: 1.06, 0.45, 0.29
Tasks: 199 total,   2 running, 197 sleeping,   0 stopped,   0 zombie
%Cpu(s):  9.8 us, 17.3 sy,  0.0 ni, 49.3 id, 18.4 wa,  0.2 hi,  5.0
si,  0.0 st
KiB Mem:   1017500 total,   944564 used,    72936 free,    54172 buffers
KiB Swap:  2095100 total,      412 used,  2094688 free.   422096 cached Mem
```

PID	USER	PR	NI	VIRT	RES	SHR	S	%CPU	%MEM	TIME+	COMMAND
2113	nathan	20	0	1439700	74108	35780	S	33.7	7.3	1:07.87	compiz
1396	root	20	0	344404	54224	14916	S	32.4	5.3	1:01.54	Xorg
2594	root	20	0	44556	2248	1876	S	25.4	0.2	0:35.54	http
2906	root	20	0	4508	1008	640	D	21.8	0.1	0:03.10	updatedb.m+
2008	nathan	20	0	635372	16884	10624	S	9.3	1.7	0:01.95	unity-pane+
2442	nathan	20	0	500820	14720	9004	S	8.6	1.4	0:15.32	update-not+
2536	nathan	20	0	713856	19168	11584	S	5.3	1.9	0:07.33	gnome-term+
7	root	20	0	0	0	0	R	2.0	0.0	0:03.96	rcu_sched
49	root	20	0	0	0	0	S	2.0	0.0	0:00.59	kswapd0
1951	nathan	20	0	290292	4048	2824	S	1.3	0.4	0:02.83	ibus-daemon
3	root	20	0	0	0	0	S	1.0	0.0	0:00.67	ksoftirqd/0
8	root	20	0	0	0	0	S	1.0	0.0	0:02.70	rcuos/0
2011	nathan	20	0	543420	14196	9444	S	1.0	1.4	0:01.11	ibus-ui-gt+
11	root	20	0	0	0	0	S	0.7	0.0	0:01.30	rcuos/3

```
1994 nathan    20   0   816452   17152   10648 S   0.7  1.7    0:01.16 unity-sett+
2051 nathan    20   0   612896   11800    7612 S   0.7  1.2    0:01.66 bamfdaemon
2854 nathan    20   0    31588    1660    1136 R   0.7  0.2    0:00.19 top
```

This is a lot of information packed into a small amount of space, and every last detail is left as an exercise for the reader (running "man top" will display a very detailed manual). But generally, the top section of the screen shows information about the computer itself, and the bottom section shows the running processes under all usernames, sorted from the highest computer utilization to the lowest. This program keeps running until you tell it to stop, and is interactive. You can use the arrow keys to scroll the display up, down, left, and right, and the PageUp and PageDown keys work as well.

The list of processes updates every 3 seconds, and you'll typically use this to find the culprit if a program is causing your computer to run slowly by checking which programs have a high value under the %CPU or %MEM columns. From there you could use the PID of that process to terminate the program, although you should be careful to only terminate programs that you yourself are running or that you know are stuck. Terminating "apt-get" or "dpkg" during a software update could cause major problems. Terminating "firefox" if it's stuck, however, shouldn't cause problems. When you are finished using top, you can press the "q" key to cause it to quit and return to the command prompt.

You can terminate a process using its PID by using the "kill" command, followed by a space and the PID. This sends a signal to the process that means "please stop running," and this is similar to clicking the "Close" button on a title bar. A program might finish its current task or ask you if you would like to save before actually closing. But if a program is really stuck, it may not be able to respond. In that case, "kill -9" followed by a space and the PID will cause Ubuntu to forcibly terminate the program. This guarantees results. Why didn't I give a full command-line example as usual? Because PIDs are different every time, and if you type in an example from a book, there's no telling what (if anything) might be running with the example PID on your system. So be sure to check carefully before using the "kill" command!

Multitask on the Command Line

Unix was a multitasking operating system long before interactive graphical user interfaces were common. In order to run multiple programs at once without actually using different terminals, there are a few different ways to stop the current program, ask a program to continue running in the background, and change which program is running in the foreground. Bash, your command shell, handles these requests.

You run a program by typing its name at the command prompt and pressing Enter. We'll use top as an example because it is easy to see when it is running. If you type "top" and press Enter, it will run in the "foreground," which means that it is actively using the terminal display and listening for keypresses. But you can stop this program by pressing Ctrl+Z. You will then see the following:

```
[1]+  Stopped                 top
nathan@ubuntu-book:~$
```

This means that the program is no longer in the foreground, and the command prompt means that Ubuntu is waiting for your next command. But the old program is no longer running, either. Instead, Ubuntu has stopped scheduling this program to run on the CPU. It still takes up memory, but will not process any information or slow down the computer. You can run other programs, and in fact you can suspend additional programs with Ctrl+Z. They will be stopped as well. For example, if I now run "man top" to read the top manual and want to suspend that temporarily, I can press Ctrl+Z and see the following:

```
[2]+  Stopped                 man top
nathan@ubuntu-book:~$
```

The "2" in brackets means that this is the second job. You can run and suspend as many programs as your computer's memory will allow. As useful as it is to interrupt a program to do something else, sometimes you want the program to keep running in the background while you work. And eventually you'll want to call a program back to the foreground. Bash refers to your running programs as "jobs," and in fact you can use the command "jobs" to print a list of all jobs whether they are running or not. It looks like this:

```
[1]-  Stopped                 top
[2]+  Stopped                 man top
nathan@ubuntu-book:~$
```

There are two jobs listed, and the "current" job is marked with a plus (+) sign. If we don't specify a specific job number, any job control command will take effect on the current job. To indicate a job number, put a percent (%) sign before it. To go back to the man page for top so that it's running in the foreground again, either "fg" or "fg %2" would work. Because job 2 is the current job, specifying its job number to the fg command with "%2" is optional. On the other hand, if I wanted top to continue running in the background, I could run "bg %1", and top would begin processing again, but I would still be at the command prompt. I could continue working with other programs until I was ready to bring top back to the foreground again by running "fg %1".

Sometimes you may want to run a program but have it run in the background right away. To do this, simply add an ampersand (&) to the end of the command line before you press Enter. The command will run in the background until you suspend it or until it finishes on its own. So if I want to run ps in the background, I could simply type "ps u &":

```
nathan@ubuntu-book:~$ ps u &
[3] 10410
```

Bash will print the job number, but instead of printing the command (which you already know because you just typed it!), it prints the PID, so that you can use kill if you need to. Any command you run this way will continue working in the background until you resume control of it with fg or until it stops on its own. When this happens, the next time bash prints a command prompt, it will print a message letting you know what happened:

```
[3]-  Done                    ps u
nathan@ubuntu-book:~$
```

If you run this command, you'll see that ps actually printed to the terminal before it quit. (You may need to press Enter once more to see a command prompt.) Commands running in the background can still print plain text messages. And these job management commands work with all programs, not just text-based command line programs. For instance, you can run the graphical benchmark program "glxgears" in a terminal window. A new window will open, but every 5 seconds the program will print graphics performance statistics to the terminal. By pressing Ctrl+Z in the terminal window, you will suspend the job, and the graphical output will stop. Typing "bg" will cause the program to work in the background, and the processing will start up again. This makes glxgears a perfect program to test out suspending, backgrounding, and foregrounding jobs.

If you've ever wondered how computer users multitasked before graphical interfaces came along, now you have the answer in the Unix and Linux worlds. And being able to suspend and resume programs can be very useful, especially when you're still getting familiar with the command line and want to reference documentation or check files or running programs.

Diagnose a Connection to a Server

Network connectivity can be one of the most difficult problems to troubleshoot, but two command-line tools can quickly give you information about your network pathway to another computer. Simple to use and understand, one is the first thing that network professionals go to when they can't connect to a computer, and the other will give you more information about the route your data takes through the network.

The first tool is called ping. This tool sends ICMP ECHO requests to another computer, which will respond to the "echo" request by sending a reply. The ping command listens for these replies and can measure the round-trip delay. Thus, ping is fancifully named after sonar tracking like you see in movies about submarines. Despite the cute name, this is the simplest way to confirm that you have a working network connection to another computer. You run ping by giving it the hostname or IP address of the system you want to connect to. Then, ping sends one echo request every second and listens for the response. It prints a message for every reply it receives. It continues until you press Ctrl+C (shown in the terminal as "^C"), which sends a "break" signal to the running program. Then, it summarizes the network test results and quits. It looks like this:

```
nathan@ubuntu-book:~$ ping www.ubuntu.com
PING www.ubuntu.com (91.189.89.110) 56(84) bytes of data.
64 bytes from website-content-cache-3.ps5.canonical.com (91.189.89.110):
icmp_seq=1 ttl=49 time=156 ms
64 bytes from website-content-cache-3.ps5.canonical.com (91.189.89.110):
icmp_seq=2 ttl=49 time=155 ms
```

```
64 bytes from website-content-cache-3.ps5.canonical.com (91.189.89.110):
icmp_seq=3 ttl=49 time=155 ms
64 bytes from website-content-cache-3.ps5.canonical.com (91.189.89.110):
icmp_seq=4 ttl=49 time=155 ms
64 bytes from website-content-cache-3.ps5.canonical.com (91.189.89.110):
icmp_seq=5 ttl=49 time=155 ms
^C
--- www.ubuntu.com ping statistics ---
5 packets transmitted, 5 received, 0% packet loss, time 4006ms
rtt min/avg/max/mdev = 155.642/155.924/156.546/0.593 ms
```

For each echo request, it prints the echo size, the reverse domain name and IP address of the target system (e.g., many websites redirect requests to different computers for load balancing), a sequence number, the "time to live" value set on the outgoing request, and the time it took to receive a response. Once it's finished, it shows the number of echo requests (packets) sent, received, and how many packets were lost, as well as statistics for the round-trip time (rtt) measured in milliseconds (ms).

While network troubleshooting is its own book, if you get a response back, you'll know that data can flow back and forth over the network between the target computer and your computer. This means that no matter what else is or isn't working, the network itself isn't to blame. You can use the "icmp_seq" number to see if packets are coming in out of order. If random packets are coming in late, that means the network route between the two computers is unstable. This isn't a problem for web pages or downloads, but it is a problem for games and voice or video chat. If the response time is long or varies wildly between packets, or if there are a lot of "lost" packets, this can indicate network path, router, or server problems as well, and sometimes bad network cables.

If you run ping and nothing is displayed, press Ctrl+C after 5–10 seconds. If ping displays 100% packet loss, then either the remote computer is configured to ignore echo requests, there is no network route between you and the remote computer, or the remote computer is offline. While this is not proof that the remote computer is offline, it's a great way to check for a connection between your computer and your router or your computer and another computer on your same network at home or work.

The other tool that you can use to gather more detailed information about the path between your computer and another is called "mtr" and it works very much like ping, except it traces the route between your computer and the remote system and pings each of those computers as well. You will need to install the "mtr" package via the command line. Type the following command at the command line and then press Enter to install mtr:

```
sudo apt install mtr
```

Type your password when prompted, and press Enter. Ubuntu will provide a list of additional software that will be installed along with the software. Simply press Enter at the confirmation prompt to accept the default of "Yes," and Ubuntu will download and install the software.

Once installed, you can run mtr along with a hostname or IP address the same way you ran ping. For example, if I run "mtr -t www.ubuntu.com", I see the following display update as new packets are continuously sent:

My traceroute [v0.86]

ubuntu-book (0.0.0.0)   Wed May 3 17:38:04 2017

Keys: **H**elp   **D**isplay mode   **R**estart statistics   **O**rder of fields   **q**uit

	Packets		Pings				
Host	Loss%	Snt	Last	Avg	Best	Wrst	StDev
1. 104.236.128.253	0.0%	100	1.6	0.8	0.3	9.5	1.3
2. 198.199.99.253	0.0%	100	0.3	1.2	0.3	29.3	4.2
3. sjo-b21-link.telia.net	0.0%	100	2.0	2.2	2.0	5.6	0.4
4. level3-ic-157355-sjo-b21.c.telia	0.0%	100	1.7	6.4	1.6	52.2	11.3
5. ae-234-3610.edge5.london1.Level3	0.0%	100	159.9	160.8	159.8	197.1	5.1
6. ae-234-3610.edge5.london1.Level3	3.0%	100	159.9	160.5	159.8	184.4	3.5
7. SOURCE-MANA.edge5.London1.Level3	0.0%	100	150.1	151.0	149.9	186.1	4.9
8. eth0.lutin.canonical.com	0.0%	100	148.7	148.9	148.6	154.2	0.6
9. www-ubuntu-com.avocado.canonical	0.0%	100	146.7	149.3	145.5	155.1	3.6

This shows me each network router between me and my destination, and gives me information about the network health of each. The two most important columns are the percentage of lost echo requests (Loss%) and the average response time in milliseconds (Avg). From this I can see if there are any problem points along the way. In this example, I can see that the first four hosts are the path my requests take inside the local network, and the fifth host is where the data hits the Internet and travels to London where the Ubuntu website is hosted. I can tell that the network is very fast on my local network but slows down considerably on the public Internet. I can also see that host 6 is losing packets, but the other hosts do not appear to be. (This isn't immediate cause for alarm—in general this happens all the time and computers resend important data if it is not received.) If I were having trouble loading the Ubuntu website, this would suggest that the web server is fine but data is being lost along the way. But if I was not losing packets and had a low response time (under maybe 400 ms) all the way until the last host which had very high packet loss or response times, that would suggest that the web server itself was the problem. When you are done testing the network pathway, you can press "q" to quit `mtr`.

Both `ping` and `mtr` are extremely useful tools that are the same ones that network technicians use to help diagnose and troubleshoot network performance on the job, and a full analysis and understanding would take a little bit of study. But even a cursory knowledge of what to look for can verify strong or weak network connections and show you where problems lie.

View Information About the Operating System

There are times when you need specific, detailed information about your computer, and this is another example of where command-line use really excels. On the terminal, you can request certain information, or filter out irrelevant information—all more quickly than you could with a graphical tool.

Determine Your Distribution and Version

Sometimes you have access to a computer, but because you didn't install the operating system yourself, you aren't sure exactly what version of Linux is running. You might be able to recognize the distribution by the default wallpaper or the interface, but unfamiliar or heavily modified operating systems will still pose a challenge. One simple command-line tool is common across many different versions of Linux, and can help to answer this question.

The Linux Standard Base (LSB) was a software specification created in 2001 to make software development easier across many different Linux distributions. Not all Ubuntu releases are certified as LSB-compliant, but each version of Ubuntu includes an important tool that can help you identify what version of Ubuntu is running. This command is called "lsb_release." You can use it to request certain information about the operating system, or you can use the option "-a" to display all of the information it will provide. On a standard Ubuntu system, running "lsb_release -a" will display the following output:

```
nathan@ubuntu-book:~$ lsb_release -a
No LSB modules are available
Distributor ID: Ubuntu
Description:    Ubuntu 22.04.1 LTS
Release:        22.04
Codename:       jammy
```

This information is useful in a lot of ways. For instance, the code name is often used when looking for software compatibility. Above, we see that the code name for Ubuntu 22.04 LTS is "jammy." You can also ask lsb_release for specific information. For example, if you were running Ubuntu 22.10 and needed to know the release's code name, you could run "lsb_release -c" and get the following output:

```
nathan@ubuntu-book:~$ lsb_release -c
Codename:          kinetic
```

With an easy way to determine the code name for your release of Ubuntu, you don't have to worry about memorizing it, which can be difficult to keep track of after you've upgraded. An Ubuntu code name is a useful way to narrow down solutions to your specific version of Ubuntu when searching the Web, and is often important to know when working on a server. Because the lsb_release command is available on desktops and servers alike, you might log in to a Linux server and run the command and see the following output:

```
[root@linux-server ~]# lsb_release -a
LSB Version:    :core-4.1-amd64:core-4.1-noarch:cxx-4.1-amd64:cxx-4.1-
noarch:desktop-4.1-amd64:desktop-4.1-noarch:languages-4.1-
amd64:languages-4.1-noarch:printing-4.1-amd64:printing-4.1-noarch
Distributor ID: CentOS
Description:    CentOS Linux release 7.0.1406 (Core)
Release:        7.0.1406
Codename:       Core
```

While CentOS is a very popular Red Hat-based server operating system with some significant differences from Ubuntu (particularly how to install software and where network settings are stored), you'll be able to apply your Ubuntu experience in most cases, and you'll know what to search for on the Web when investigating any puzzling differences.

Determine Your Architecture and Kernel Version

Sometimes you need to know what version of the Linux kernel your computer is running, or whether your installed system is 32-bit or 64-bit. This can be useful when downloading third-party software, for example. You might also want to double-check that you have the proper operating system installed, since it isn't possible to change the operating system without a full reinstallation. Although it's simple enough to click the gear menu and choose "About This Computer" and read the value given after "OS type," this works in all versions of Linux regardless of your choice (or lack of) desktop environment.

Note   Since Ubuntu 18.04 LTS, only a 64-bit desktop image has been available. Ubuntu Server is also 64-bit only on IBM PC-compatible machines but is still available as 32-bit for older Raspberry Pi systems.

The command "uname" stands for "Unix name" and tells you about the operating system kernel that's running. By itself, it simply tells you the name of the current running operating system, but running "uname -r" will display the kernel version number (the "release"), and "uname -m" will display the machine hardware name. "uname -a" will display all available information, but if you are looking for something specific, it's easier to read if you only ask for the information you want.

Running "uname -m" will display "i686" or "armv71" if you're running the 32-bit version of Ubuntu and "x86_64" or "aarch64" if you're running the 64-bit version of Ubuntu. While 64-bit software requires a 64-bit operating system, the 64-bit version of Ubuntu can also run 32-bit applications. So if your computer supports 64-bit software, you should probably have 64-bit Ubuntu installed. If you have a Raspberry Pi Model 3B, then you can use the 32-bit version of Ubuntu if you are constantly running low on memory.

If your operating system is 32-bit but you want to know if your desktop computer supports 64-bit software, you can read the information in the file "/proc/cpuinfo." Typing "cat /proc/cpuinfo" will display the contents of the file and all available information about all processors and cores on your system. However, the information we want is in the "flags" list. Processors that support 64-bit-wide instructions and memory addresses have a flag called "lm," for long mode. But this can be hard to spot in the alphabet soup of features listed by /proc/cpuinfo. To simplify this, we can use the "grep" command to search for "lm." If the processor does not support 64-bit mode, the "lm" flag won't be listed and nothing will be displayed. If it does support 64-bit mode, then grep will only show the "flags" line and will highlight "lm" in bright red. On my 64-bit computer, running "grep -iw lm /proc/cpuinfo" displays the following:

```
nathan@ubuntu-book:~$ grep -iw lm /proc/cpuinfo
flags           : fpu vme de pse tsc msr pae mce cx8 apic sep mtrr pge
mca cmov pat pse36 clflush mmx fxsr sse sse2 ht syscall nx mmxext fxsr_opt
pdpe1gb rdtscp lm 3dnowext 3dnow constant_tsc rep_good nopl nonstop_tsc
extd_apicid aperfmperf pni monitor cx16 popcnt lahf_lm cmp_legacy svm
extapic cr8_legacy abm sse4a misalignsse 3dnowprefetch osvw ibs skinit wdt
arat cpb hw_pstate npt lbrv svm_lock nrip_save pausefilter
```

This repeats four times because I have a quad-core processor, and grep returns each line that contains a match. It would take some time for you to find "lm" there on the second line, but here it's highlighted in bright red. If you're running 32-bit Ubuntu and have a 64-bit processor and at least 4 GB of RAM, you might want to consider installing the 64-bit version of Ubuntu instead. But with these commands you'll understand your computer and software better.

Add New Users via Command Line

Each user on an Ubuntu system has his own username, password, and home folder. This gives each user a little privacy and the ability to customize the system to his own preferences. And while every user can run the software installed by Ubuntu Software, each application stores its settings in the current user's home folder. Creating a new user account to allow someone to log in is simple to do from the command line with the "adduser" command.

Because this modifies the system, you'll need to start the command with "sudo." The sudo command is used to run a command with administrative permissions, and it will prompt you for your password. By using sudo to run adduser along with the login name of the new user, Ubuntu will create the new account and home folder, and then prompt you for some optional information. The full name is used for Ubuntu's login screen, but the rest of the information is a holdover from legacy days and can be left blank. For example, if I wanted to create a user account for my friend Alexander, the setup process would look like this:

```
nathan@ubuntu-book:~$ sudo adduser alexander
Adding user `alexander' ...
Adding new group `alexander' (1001) ...
Adding new user `alexander' (1001) with group `alexander' ...
Creating home directory `/home/alexander' ...
Copying files from `/etc/skel' ...
Enter new UNIX password:
Retype new UNIX password:
passwd: password updated successfully
Changing the user information for alexander
Enter the new value, or press ENTER for the default
        Full Name []: Alexander Brumley
        Room Number []:
        Work Phone []:
        Home Phone []:
        Other []:
Is the information correct? [Y/n]
```

Now Alexander can log into my system with the password I've created for him. If I want to make sure that he has a unique password that he'll remember, I can tell Ubuntu to require him to change his password the next time he logs in. This is done with the "passwd" command's -e option to set the password as expired. The next time Alexander logs in, he'll be forced to change his password before he can complete the login process:

```
nathan@ubuntu-book:~$ sudo passwd -e alexander
passwd: password expiry information changed.
```

On a home computer, I might want to allow Alexander to log in by clicking his name without using a password. I can use the passwd command to do this too, by using the -d option to delete the password for that account. This works the same way as before and prints the same status message. Once the password is deleted, the user can log in without a password in the future:

```
nathan@ubuntu-book:~$ sudo passwd -d alexander
passwd: password expiry information changed.
```

When you first install Ubuntu, you create a user account that is given administrative rights to make system-level changes such as installing new software. Accounts you create with adduser, however, are not able to make these changes by default. To allow users to modify the system, you have to add them to the "sudo" user group. The adduser command can add a user to a user group as well. Simply run the command and specify the user account name first, and the user group name second. This makes the command look a little funny because you have to use "sudo" to run the command, and also specify the group name "sudo" at the end. The entire process is automatic once you press Enter, and looks like this:

```
nathan@ubuntu-book:~$ sudo adduser alexander sudo
Adding user `alexander' to group `sudo' ...
Adding user alexander to group sudo
Done.
```

This change takes effect the next time the account logs in, so if Alexander were already logged in, he would have to log out before he could use sudo on the command line or confirm administrative tasks on the desktop.

With the adduser and passwd commands, it's easy to create new user accounts and set up passwords and administrator rights in seconds. If you spend time working on server tasks, you'll find that these tools make adding users effortless.

Check Your Disk Space

You can use the command line to very quickly find out information about the amount of disk space you have available and how much is being utilized. This is faster than using the Disk Usage Analyzer because the commands are short and you can specify exactly what you want to know.

The best tool for a quick overview of free space on your computer is called "df." Short for "disk free," it displays all of the file systems currently in use on your computer and size information for each of them. By default, the df command displays its sizes in 1,024-byte blocks, but by adding the -H option, the display uses a more human-readable format for the numbers:

```
nathan@ubuntu-book:~$ df -H
Filesystem      Size  Used  Avail  Use%  Mounted on
tmpfs           1.7G  2.2M  1.7G    1%  /run
/dev/sda2       125G   33G   87G   28%  /
tmpfs           8.4G  161M  8.2G    2%  /dev/shm
tmpfs           5.3M  4.1k  5.3M    1%  /run/lock
/dev/sda1       536M   33M  504M    7%  /boot/efi
tmpfs           1.7G  8.9M  1.7G    1%  /run/user/1000/dev/sda1        15G
11G   3.5G   76% /

/dev/sr1         25M   25M     0  100%  /media/nathan/WD Unlocker
/dev/sdb2       606G  524G   83G   87%  /media/nathan/My Passport
```

This is a nice summary of all mounted file systems, including some temporary ones used by the Ubuntu kernel. The system file system is 125 GB, and whether you want to know which device it's running on, whether it contains 33 GB of data or has 87 GB free, or just a quick percentage utilized, everything's right here. The last line contains information on the external drive, which has 83GB available and is mounted at "/media/nathan/My Passport." This is plenty of space for running backups, and I know where to find those files. The file systems that don't start with /dev are used by Ubuntu and can be ignored.

A similar tool is "du," which is short for "disk usage." This tool prints an estimate of disk usage for the current directory and any directories it contains. Like df, the sizes are shown in 1024-byte block sizes, but you can use the "-si" option to make du print sizes in human-readable format. Running the du command shows all folders, even hidden folders and folders inside folders, so the output can be very long. Running the command in the Pictures folder shows the following output:

```
nathan@ubuntu-book:~/Pictures$ du --si
550M  ./Cabrillo Beach
128M  ./2012/06/10
128M  ./2012/06
128M  ./2012
677M  .
```

The period (.) represents the current folder, which is "/home/nathan/Pictures." The summary at the bottom shows that the current folder uses 677 MB, but adding up each of the totals comes to 934 MB. This seems wrong, until you notice that "/home/nathan/Pictures/2012" is empty except for the "06" folder inside it, which is again empty except for the "10" folder inside that contains the actual photos. The size of each folder includes the contents of the folders inside, but the summary at the bottom is correct.

You can also specify a folder path to point du to a different folder than the current location, or specify a file pattern, such as "*.jpg" to get file size information for files that match that pattern. Giving a file pattern shows space information on a per-file basis, and it might be useful to add "-c" to the options to ask du to show the total space used for all files. The display looks like this, with some lines removed for space considerations:

```
nathan@ubuntu-book:~/Pictures/2012/06/10$ du --si -c *.jpg
295k   CRW_5777_CRW_embedded.jpg
279k   CRW_5778_CRW_embedded.jpg
...
377k   CRW_5800_CRW_embedded.jpg
7.7M   total
```

Note   "df -H" and "du --si" display decimal storage units that match Ubuntu's graphical applications that work with storage sizes. But if you prefer binary storage units such as KiB, MiB, and GiB, you can use "df -h" and "du -h" instead.

These two commands give you a quick look at how your computer's storage space is being used, both at the overview level and the specific level as well. These are also tools that are helpful not only on a desktop system, but when working with servers.

Edit Text Files

When spending time in a text-based interface, it makes sense to talk about editing text files. Traditionally, Unix and Linux programs have used text files to store their configuration settings. This allowed the file to be human readable and easy to set up, plus easy to change using text manipulation tools and input redirection using scripts.

Today, many programs still store their settings as text files for the same reasons. Many documents were written in text files as well. With certain well-known exceptions, they are compatible with practically every operating system and easily shared with others. Formatting can be added with special markup such as TeX, HTML, and Markdown. There are many different text editors, and each has its own fans, but the easiest to start out with is definitely nano.

Note   Text editor choice tends to be contentious because people can spend a lot of time working with them. So it's important to pick one that works best for your needs. This is so subjective, however, that countless debates have been fought (and still rage on) over the legendary One True Text Editor. Emacs and vi have steep learning curves but are rewarding. Just know that comparisons online tend to be charged!

To start nano, you can run "nano" along with the name of a file to open. If you do not specify a file, nano will keep your text in memory until you save it to a file. Running nano will display the basic text editing interface (see Figure 5-2). The top line gives you information about the file you are editing (called a "buffer") in the center and whether the file has been modified on the right. The bottom three lines display a status bar that is normally blank, followed by two lines displaying commonly used shortcut keys. On this display, the caret (^) represents the Ctrl key, so ^G for the "Get Help" command represents Ctrl+G. You will also see references to M, which stands for the Meta key. You can use the Alt key as a stand-in for Meta. For example, where the help file specifies M-D as the shortcut to count the number of words, lines, and characters in the current file, you can press Alt+D.

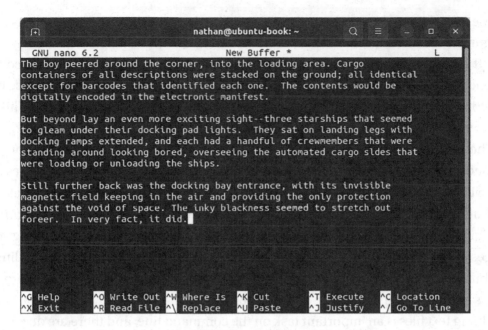

Figure 5-2. *nano is an easy way to edit text files, with onscreen shortcut guides*

Using nano is straightforward. You type and your text appears on the screen. To move the cursor and scroll through help files, the arrow keys and Page Up and Page down keys work in addition to the shortcuts listed on the screen. You can use Ctrl+C to print the current position of your cursor in the file on the status line. This can help you orient yourself in a large file.

If you are using nano to edit a configuration file, you will note that it doesn't wrap lines at the end of the screen but instead uses a dollar sign ($) to show that a line continues to the right of the screen. Placing your cursor on such a line allows you to scroll to the right with the right arrow or End key. The first character on the line will change to $ to indicate that the line extends to the left side of the screen. Configuration file entries must be on one line, so this helps ensure that they are being displayed properly.

If you are writing a document, however, you may want the display to wrap. You can press Alt+$ to turn on "soft" line wrapping. This allows you to see an entire line at once by displaying it on multiple lines without using actual end-of-line characters. This is useful when you are writing in text mode but will import your text to a word processor or other format when you are done.

One other useful feature about nano is that it understands some common text and configuration file formats, such as HTML, Python code, TeX documents, and many more. If you edit a file with an extension of ".html" or ".py," for instance, nano will color-code the text to help you identify keywords, variables, and string literals, and notice other formatting issues that help protect against missing quotation marks or brackets. This can greatly enhance your editing experience without getting in your way.

When you are ready to save a file, press Ctrl+O to write the file out to disk. If you specified a file on the command line, nano will suggest the same file name and pressing Enter will overwrite it. The bottom two lines of the screen display several options as well. Entering a file name and pressing Alt+B will create a backup file, which will copy the original contents of the file to a new file with a tilde (~) at the end before saving your changes to the original file name. By default, Files will not display backup files ending in tilde, but ls on the command line will. Pressing Ctrl+X will exit nano, which will prompt you to save a file if you have made any changes.

Editing text files is an important task on the command line, and there are dozens of different text editors designed to make this easy and efficient. Starting out, nano is a pleasant tool to use and is present by default on Ubuntu. You can use it to write anything, and it is a lightweight editor that loads instantly. Whether it's your first command-line text editor or your favorite, nano will serve you well.

Read Email

Email has changed dramatically over the years. While Internet email as we know it today emerged in the early 1970s, early electronic mail messages were text-only messages that were passed from user mail folder to user mail folder on the same machine. Reading email in a text-only client can be a fun peek back in time that also delivers a unique perspective. Reading email in a text-only mail client is a much more focused experience than you might expect. However, one thing that has not aged very well is the setup process. While the setup on this is not for the faint of heart, the results are pretty fun. There are two popular terminal-based email clients today: Alpine and Mutt. I'm going to focus on Alpine, and you will need to install the "alpine" package via the command line. Type the following command at the command line and then press Enter to install alpine:

```
sudo apt install alpine
```

Type your password when prompted, and press Enter. Ubuntu will provide a list of additional software that will be installed along with the software. Simply press Enter at the confirmation prompt to accept the default of "Yes," and Ubuntu will download and install the software.

One legacy of Alpine is that while it is extremely configurable, it also expects certain information to be entered using specific formatting. The sheer number of configurations can be intimidating as well. The first thing you will need to know is your mail server details. This can be as simple as looking in Thunderbird or Evolution. You'll need your IMAP server and username to receive email, and your SMTP server and username to send email. You can always set up incoming mail and set up outgoing mail later.

To run Alpine, simply type the command "`alpine`" and press Enter. A welcome message will be displayed on the first run only, and you can press E to exit the greeting and show the main menu. At the top of the menu, it will show you the current folder—INBOX by default—and the number of unread messages. Each command can be activated by its shortcut key or by using the arrow keys to highlight a command and pressing Enter. The bottom two lines in the terminal show other commands that can be activated. First, you'll want to press S to enter setup. Then, press C to enter the configuration settings.

The two settings you need to change are "SMTP Server" and "Inbox Path." Both of these need to be formatted in such a way that provides all relevant login information. Let's assume that your IMAP server is "imap.example.com," your SMTP server is "smtp. example.com," and your username is the same for both servers. Each connection setting is built in the same style:

```
imap.example.com/user=username
```

If you are using anything but the standard port, you add a colon (:) after the server name, and you can add /ssl or /tls after your username if you are using encryption. So if you were using SSL to encrypt your mail server connection, the "Inbox Path" setting would be:

```
imap.example.com:465/user=username/ssl
```

Highlight the setting you wish to change, and press Enter to edit the field. Press Enter again to save the value. When you first set the "Inbox Path," you will be prompted for the inbox folder. Press Enter to use the default of "inbox, and you'll see that the path was changed to read:

```
{imap.example.com/user=username}inbox
```

This is the standard format for specifying IMAP folders, and you can use it to point to folders for your sent mail folder (referred to in Alpine as "Fcc" or "file carbon copy").

Once you have set up your mail servers, press E to exit setup. When you exit setup, Alpine will attempt to connect to your mail server and will ask you for your password. Type it and press Enter, and after a few seconds, you should see a status message that your inbox folder is opened along with the total number of messages and the number of new messages. Press I to load the message index. It will display all messages in your current folder (see Figure 5-3).

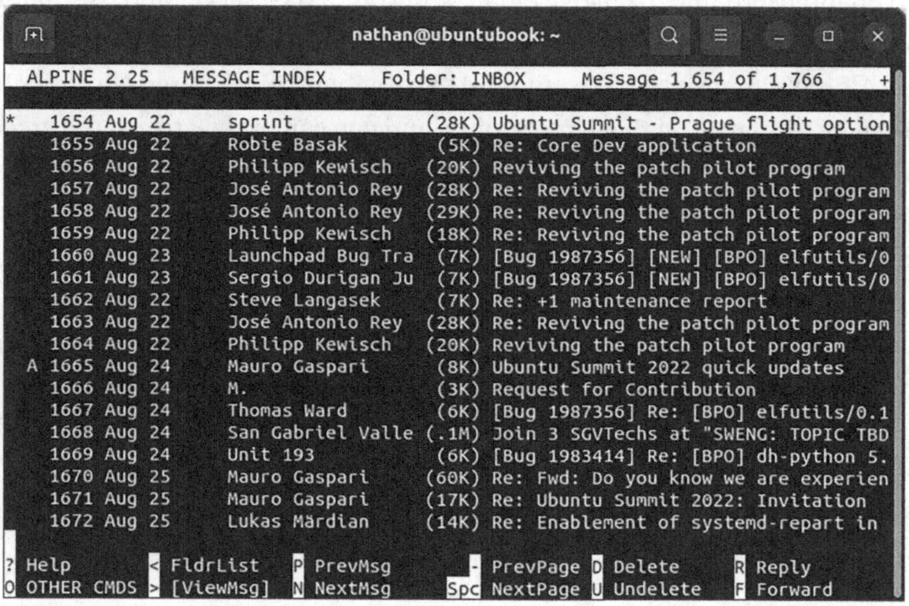

Figure 5-3. *Email without distractions, the way it was in the mid-1990s. Only now with Unicode support*

You can use the arrow keys to move the cursor up and down, and press Enter to read a message. The spacebar scrolls down one page and the minus (-) key scrolls back up one page. Note that messages are listed in order from the oldest at the top to the newest at the bottom. In addition to the Enter key, you can also use the greater than sign (>) to access an email or item and the less than sign (<) to go up one level again. Press C to create a new email or "r" to reply to the highlighted message. The bottom two lines of the screen show you a full list of commands, and you can cycle between the displayed commands by pressing the "o" key. Typing a question mark (?) will bring up the help file and will automatically jump to help on the highlighted object. This is especially useful in the settings screens.

When composing email messages, Alpine uses the pico text editor, and this is the program that inspired the GNU nano editor that you may already be familiar with. Commands are listed at the bottom of the screen, and Ctrl+X will send your email once you are finished writing it. Ctrl+C will cancel the email. The bottom of the screen will prompt you to confirm your actions.

Another interesting way that workflow differed in the past is that actions require extra confirmation. From the message index, you can press D to delete a message, but they are marked as deleted and remain in your inbox. This gives you time to change your mind and press U to undelete them. It is not until you press X to "expunge" your folder that the deleted messages are actually removed. On any of the menus or folder or message lists, you can press Q to be prompted to quite Alpine.

The full-screen text-based email interface in Alpine gives a classic, retro feel that evokes the standard behaviors of mainframes and terminals. What's best of all is that it remains a very classic, efficient way to work with email today. The straightforward presentation and the text-based interface is more than able to stand in for more popular graphical email clients today.

Browse the Web

Some 25 years later, it's hard to remember just how much the World Wide Web changed the Internet and the world at large. Online information retrieval systems used to be built to work with only specific software, and the information retrieved was often only accessible on the same computer architecture with the same authoring software. The Web changed all of that, with a flexible document language that allowed hypertext links to other documents. Because everything was primarily text-based, the documents could be displayed on any computer. These unique properties caused the Web to overtake other potential systems (particularly gopher) and grow into the phenomenon it is today.

A year before Mosaic arrived and 2 years before Netscape Navigator and Microsoft Internet Explorer appeared, a text-based web browser called links was created. It was a very popular alternative to the first graphical web browsers, since not all computer users had access to graphical terminals. Plus, it was fast and efficient and the early Web was mostly text-based as well. Links has been reimplemented several times, and today an enhanced version called ELinks is one of the most powerful and friendly text browsers around. Not only can it be used to experience the Web from the command line, but its menu system and mouse support make it a simple yet refreshing change from slow, graphics-laden websites. You will need to install the "elinks" package via the command line. Type the following command at the command line and then press Enter to install elinks:

```
sudo apt install elinks
```

Type your password when prompted, and press Enter. Ubuntu will provide a list of additional software that will be installed along with the software. Simply press Enter at the confirmation prompt to accept the default of "Yes," and Ubuntu will download and install the software.

With its default settings, ELinks is very plain. The first time you run the command "elinks," it lets you know that you can access the menus with the Escape key, and where to find documentation under the "Help" menu. Once you press Enter to dismiss that dialog, you are prompted for a URL. Just type in a web address and press Enter. Typing in "www.google.com" will take you to the Google home page, for example (see Figure 5-4). This might seem a bit underwhelming at first, but the minimalistic presentation can grow on you, especially if you're looking up information in a hurry. You can also access a web page immediately by supplying it on the command line, for example, typing "elinks https://ubuntu.com/" would open the Ubuntu website by default.

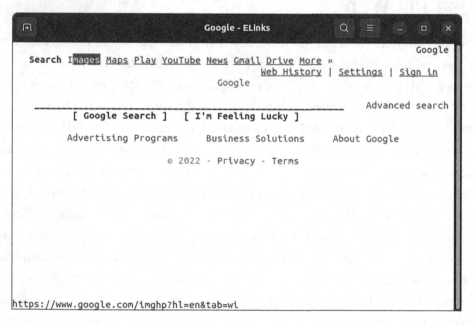

Figure 5-4. *Google wasn't around before 1998, but the Yahoo! and Alta Vista search engines looked much like this*

The top line of the display is the title bar, and displays the title of the web page you are viewing as well as your current position, which is shown in screens full of text. You can press Escape or click on the top line with your mouse to display the menu bar. Clicking on the menu options will open each menu, or you can use the arrow keys to navigate the menus. In all menus and dialog boxes, the highlighted letter of each option can be used to activate that option, and most menu items will display a shortcut key on the right that can be pressed without entering the menus.

The monochrome, plain interface of ELinks cuts out distractions, and most commands are accessible with a single press of the keyboard. But it's possible to make ELinks much more attractive as well. Open the menu by pressing Escape, type "s" to open the "Setup" menu, then type "t" to open the "Terminal Options" window. Then, you can use the mouse or keyboard to enable color mode. If you are using ELinks in Ubuntu while using GNOME Terminal or Console, you should enable "256 colors" mode. If you are using ELinks using a virtual terminal, only 16 colors are supported. You can move the cursor with the arrow keys and activate a selection by pressing Enter, and activate the changes by typing "o" for "OK." Or you can click directly on each option to activate it. Once you test the settings out, you can go back to the Terminal Options menu and click "Save" or type "v" to save your changes. ELinks will load saved settings the next time it is run.

Actually navigating websites is simple. You can use the up and down arrows to move from link to link, and the PageUp and PageDown keys to scroll the web page. The active link will be highlighted, and the Enter key will follow a link. The status bar on the bottom of the terminal will display the link destination or information about the current image or text field. You can select radio buttons or text boxes by highlighting them and pressing the Enter key. Some websites can be awkward to navigate because most navigation menus are implemented as HTML list elements, which show up as bulleted lists in ELinks, but after a little bit of practice, scrolling through to actual content and moving around becomes easy. And even though sites will look different, most well-designed web pages are still readable. The Ubuntu website is a good example of a site that is accessible even in text format (see Figure 5-5).

Figure 5-5. *Carefully designed web pages like the Ubuntu site are usable even in text-only form*

Once you've mastered the basics, ELinks has most of the features you'd expect in a modern web browser. The bookmark manager can be accessed by typing "s" and bookmarks can be visited, added, deleted, and more. Choosing "Add" will bring up a dialog box with the current page's title and address filled in. The main surprise is that the move feature requires individual bookmarks to be selected before they can be moved. Bookmarks can be selected by highlighting them with the arrow keys and pressing the Insert key. Selected bookmarks will be marked with an asterisk (*).

ELinks also has tab support. Typing "t" opens a new tab and asks for a web address. Typing "T" while a link is selected will open that link in a background tab. Once more than one tab is visible, the tab bar appears above the status bar. It lists all open tabs and highlights the current tab. Clicking on a tab name with the mouse switches to that tab, and the less than (<) and greater than (>) keys can be used to display the previous and next tab, respectively. Typing "c" closes the current tab. Documents will load in the background, so tabs are a great way to load a new page while you are still reading the current page.

The download manager appears when you click a downloadable link and choose the "Save" option. After setting a download location and file name and choosing "OK," the download progress is displayed in a window over the page (see Figure 5-6). The file download can be moved to the background, where it can be checked through the download manager later. Choosing "Background with notify" will cause a dialog box to be displayed once the download is finished. The download manager can be accessed via the "Tools" menu or by typing "D" and will manage multiple downloads while ELinks is running. Notably, the "Abort" option will stop the download without deleting the file. The download can be resumed again later.

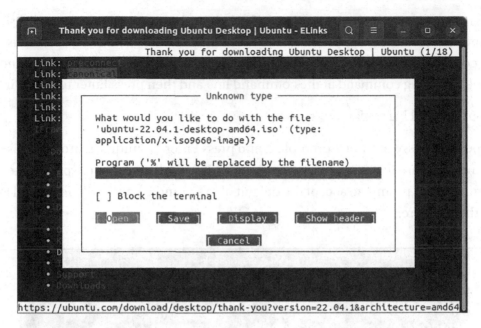

Figure 5-6. *Elinks has a built-in download manager to handle saving large files*

While this covers most of the common features of ELinks, the documentation is easy to read, and Section 3 gives an overview of the user interface along with details on everyday usage, followed by detailed descriptions of the bookmark and tabs features in Sections 4 and 5. You can read the ELinks manual online at http://elinks.or.cz/documentation/html/manual.html-chunked/index.html.

Browsing the Web has come a very long way in the last 25 years, and ELinks is an enhancement of the early text-based browser interfaces. Not only is it useful for testing websites for accessibility and screen reader compatibility, but its speed and bookmark manager make it an interesting way to do research without distracting graphics. Mouse support and a powerful download manager help make it even more approachable for new users.

IRC

Internet Relay Chat is a real-time chat network that brings people together from around the globe. The protocol has been around since 1988 and has been used for socialization as well as coordination. Not only do Canonical employees and Ubuntu members use IRC to coordinate work and communicate during their workdays (see Figure 5-7), but the Ubuntu community also uses IRC to offer technical support, plan events, and simply relax and socialize. IRC support is included with Empathy on the desktop, but to use IRC on the command line, you will need to install the "irssi" package via the command line. Type the following command at the command line and then press Enter to install irssi:

```
sudo apt install irssi
```

Type your password when prompted, and press Enter. Ubuntu will provide a list of additional software that will be installed along with the software. Simply press Enter at the confirmation prompt to accept the default of "Yes," and Ubuntu will download and install the software.

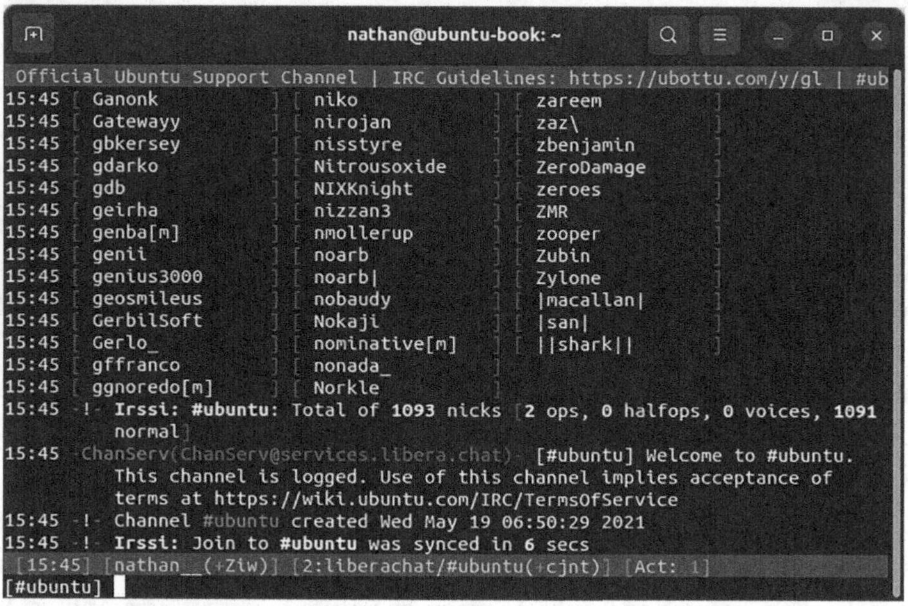

Figure 5-7.   *IRC offers a place for Ubuntu users to discuss Ubuntu and offer each other support*

IRC servers allow users to log in and join other users in "channels" to discuss various topics. Each IRC server has its own administrators and rules of conduct. Servers can be linked together to form an IRC network. Connecting to any server on a network allows you to communicate with other users on the same network. Ubuntu uses the Libera Chat network for official channel hosting, and connecting to irc.ubuntu.com will cause your IRC client to connect to a random Libera Chat server around the world.

IRC clients display server messages in a live window at the top of the screen, and the bottom line is an input area where commands and messages can be edited before being sent with the Enter key. Commands begin with a slash (/) character on the first line, and any command not used by the client is sent to the server for processing. Any line not beginning with a slash is sent to the active IRC channel for others to read.

Connecting to a Server

The "irssi" command starts the irssi IRC client. The first time irssi is run, it will display a message that points you to www.irssi.org/ to find the "startup-HOWTO" under the site's "Documentation" section. This file assumes the user is already familiar with other IRC clients but also gives some useful advice about configuring the software. Irssi also lists the two commands necessary to connect to Libera Chat (/connect liberachat) and join the official support channel (/join #ubuntu).

The first step is to connect to Libera Chat. Once you are connected, you will be able to join channels and talk to other people. By default, irssi will set your nickname (nick) to your username. If someone is already logged in with this name, Libera Chat will rename you by adding underscores (_) to your nick. If this name is already registered on Libera Chat, you will receive a message from the IRC network:

18:29 **Irssi:** Your nick is owned by **nathan** [~nathan@user/nathan]

If this appears, you can change your nick by using the "/nick" command. Simply type "/nick" followed by a space, and then a new nickname containing no spaces. The server will confirm the change:

18:30 -!- You're now known as **nhaines**

Or, it will let you know that the nick is not available:

18:30 -!- Nick **nhaines** is already in use

If your Ubuntu login is in use on Libera Chat or you want to use a different nick, you can change the nick setting in irssi by typing "/set nick" followed by a space and the new nick. Irssi will remember this setting in the future when you connect to a server.

Once you have set up your nick, you can join a channel. If you are new to IRC, you can find a list of Ubuntu-related channels at https://wiki.ubuntu.com/IRC/ChannelList. The Ubuntu support channels are good ways of getting technical support,

215

but are busy and messages scroll by very quickly. The Ubuntu discussion channels are good places to chat with others on various Ubuntu and non-Ubuntu–related topics, and the Ubuntu team channels are places where work is actively done on Ubuntu, usually during Western European business hours. The local Ubuntu channels are run by Local Community teams, and are a good way to meet other Ubuntu users near you.

IRC channel names begin with a hash sign (#), and you can join a channel by typing "/join" followed by a space and then typing the channel name. For example, typing "/join #ubuntu-offtopic" will join the #ubuntu-offtopic channel. A new "window" will open in irssi, and you will see the channel topic and a list of users currently in the channel. Once you have joined the channel, you will see messages from other users. You can type a message and press Enter to send it to the channel. You can leave a channel by typing "/part" and pressing Enter.

Messages are sent to the entire channel at once, but there are several ways of directing messages to a certain user. When you use someone's nick in a message, most IRC clients highlight your message for that user. In a busy room, this can be a good way to clarify that you are asking a question of or responding to a specific person. You can also send messages directly to other IRC users who are logged into the same network with the "query" command. For instance, to send a private message (PM) to me on Libera Chat, you would type:

```
/query nhaines Hello, this is a private message
```

This will appear in a new irssi window. To close a nonchannel window, you can type the "/win close" command.

Irssi uses separate windows to manage each channel. Window 1 is the status window and displays miscellaneous messages from the IRC server. The other windows display messages from channels or other users. You can switch windows by holding the Alt key while typing the number of the window. If this does not work, you can press and release the Escape key and then type the number of the window.

Ending your time on IRC is simple. "/part" can be used to close any channel, but "/disconnect" will close your connection with the IRC server. You can exit irssi with the "/quit" command.

IRC Etiquette

Every IRC network is independent and has its own rules, but IRC has been around for a very long time, and there are certain conventions that are unique to communicating this way. They can catch you by surprise at times, but here are some pointers that will help you while using the Ubuntu channels on Libera Chat.

The most important thing to remember is that most channels are run independently from the IRC network they are on. An IRC network might have certain guidelines—for example, Libera Chat exists to support Free and Open Source software development. Individual channels may have additional guidelines. In particular, IRC is known for being very irreverent, snarky, and sometimes hostile. The official Ubuntu channels all enforce the Ubuntu Code of Conduct and welcome new users.

IRC is an asynchronous communication method. That means that while real-time conversation isn't uncommon, a lot of IRC users will keep their client connected while they are away and check in periodically. This is called "idling" in channel and means that not all of the users shown are actually paying attention to the channel. If you have a support question, but see no other messages, you can leave your IRC client running and check in later to see if there are responses. It may even take hours, but if someone knows an answer, they will see your message when they return to their computer. It may seem counterintuitive, but it's better to ask a question in the public channel instead of sending a private message to an active user. He or she may be busy or may not have an answer, but the public message will be seen by more users.

A side effect of this is that other users generally won't tell you if they don't know an answer to a question. This doesn't mean you are being ignored, but it does mean that they are being "polite" by staying quiet and allowing others to answer. Asking the same question repeatedly is seen as quite rude. On the other hand, many questions are very common. Sometimes asking a question will cause another user to type a "bot command" that causes an automated response, such as a pointer to another channel. This isn't meant to be dismissive, but is a way to quickly provide you with standard information.

Many IRC users consider it rude to send a private message to someone you don't know. While the /query command is useful and is a good way to continue off-topic conversations outside of a channel, it's best to ask permission before using it to contact someone new.

Some channels are workplaces. Ubuntu developers live all over the world, and while the #ubuntu-devel channel is a very friendly place that is exciting to watch, sometimes developers are hard at work discussing the tasks they are working on. Sometimes when an active conversation is in progress, off-topic chatter can be a distraction. #ubuntu-offtopic is a channel that is always safe for random topics.

No matter the IRC channel, it's helpful to read the channel topic and spend time observing the local "culture" and seeing how members treat each other. This will help you fit in and can prevent misunderstandings. For more information about the conduct expected while in official Ubuntu IRC channels and interacting with the community, please see https://wiki.ubuntu.com/IRC/Guidelines. It covers a lot of specific Ubuntu etiquette in detail.

Play Text-Based Games

While the other sections in this chapter show how you can get a lot of work done on the command line, there were also a lot of games written for a text environment, too. Many actually became classics that were expected to be found on any standard Unix system. Ubuntu contains a package called "bsdgames" that you can install via the command line. It contains 40 text games or toys that you can enjoy. Type the following command at the command line and then press Enter to install bsdgames and adventure:

```
sudo apt install bsdgames colossal-cave-adventure
```

Type your password when prompted, and press Enter. Ubuntu will provide a list of additional software that will be installed along with the software. Simply press Enter at the confirmation prompt to accept the default of "Yes," and Ubuntu will download and install the software.

While there are too many games to go over in detail, I would like to highlight a few of them. You can see the list of games installed by running the command "ls /usr/games" in a terminal after you have installed the bsdgames package. You can view the manual pages by typing "man" followed by a space and the name of the game. For example, running "man rain" describes rain as an animated raindrops display. This was used as a screen saver when text terminals were connected to mainframes. Running "rain -d 120" does display an entirely useless yet fairly hypnotic simulation of raindrops landing in a puddle. It's easy to imagine a university student connected to a terminal, writing notes while the display updates (see Figure 5-8). Incidentally, the man page says the optimal speed is a terminal at 9600 baud. I first ran this program dialed into a Linux shell with a 2400-baud modem and couldn't quit it. I had to hang up and dial back in again. You can use Ctrl+C to stop the animation and return to the command prompt, and you won't have to wait 4 minutes while your modem catches up like I once did, either. The command "worms" is similarly a screen saver and is slightly more interesting. It's also best used with "worms -d 120," but the man page, which is read by running "man worms," has other options as well.

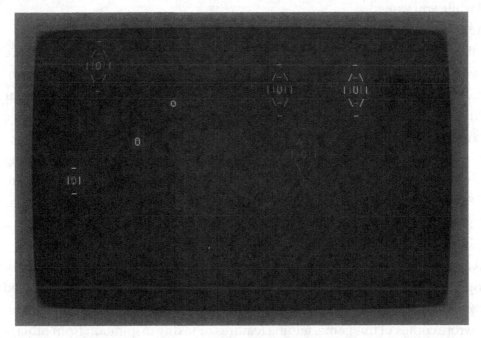

Figure 5-8. *This is pretty close to what "rain" looked like on a real terminal, long ago*

There are many other curious utilities as well. All of them can be ended immediately with Ctrl+C. The "bcd," "ppt," and "morse" commands translates typed input into computer punch cards, older paper tape, or morse code. You can create large banners that could be printed on an old line printer or dot-matrix printer using continuous feed paper with "printerbanner". "arithmetic" and "quiz" are memory tests. The command "pom" prints the current phase of the moon.

Other programs are full-fledged games. The "backgammon" game simulates the famous board game, and even contains rules and a tutorial you can use to learn to play. The game "monop" is very similar to a certain real estate board game, with the same rules, and can be played with multiple players. "canfield", "cribbage", and "go-fish" are the popular card games of the same name, and "hangman" and "worm" are other famous games. Notably, "worm" is the famous growing snake game made popular on early cell phones, but it moves much more slowly and is less stressful.

Other games are more elaborate. "tetris-bsd" is a falling block game, and used to require a fast modem to play. In the mid-1990s, some Linux installers would take an hour or more to install the operating system once it started copying packages. Some of them provided a running copy of this game on a second virtual console which could be played while you waited.

One of the most interesting games is Adventure, which is famous as the first interactive text adventure game to use natural language input. Running "adventure" places you on a path in the woods, between a brick shed and a stream. By typing in movement directions such as "north" or "go building," the computer describes your surroundings. You can pick up and use items, and by following the stream south, you reach a grated entrance to Colossal Cave, filled with treasure, mystery, and danger. By exploring and solving puzzles, you progress through the game. It's worth playing, because it is the direct ancestor of later graphical adventure games such as Beneath A Steel Sky featured in Chapter 4. A later text adventure game is also included, called "battlestar." It has a very distinct feel from Adventure and is interesting in its own right.

Adventure's cave is very closely based on Bedquilt Cave in Kentucky, but another very popular style of game became popular in 1980. A game called "Rogue" allowed you to explore a series of dungeon levels that were randomly generated with each game. Others wrote copies of this game, adding features or taking inspiration from other sources. The most widespread clone or "rogue-like" game was called Hack. Running "hack" drops you into a dungeon with a pet. Together you must explore to the bottom of the dungeon to find a mysterious amulet, and survive the climb back to the top. The game prints a map of your surroundings represented by text characters, and you are only aware of objects in your line of sight, causing the game to expand and unfold as you explore. You'll need to use the "?" key to access the in-game help to teach you the movement keys and other actions available.

Hack was released as an open source game, and another set of developers began to create a version that was named Nethack because the developers mostly communicated over the Internet. This version expanded on Hack to become legendary as a game with hundreds of monsters and items, and even more options. Where Hack is a difficult game to win, Nethack expanded on the formula in untold subtle ways, and is worth installing and playing too. You can install the package "nethack-console" via the command line or Ubuntu Software. The game can then be run with the command "nethack," and the help file and options available are much more detailed (see Figure 5-9). Type the following command at the command line and then press Enter to install Nethack:

```
sudo apt install nethack-console
```

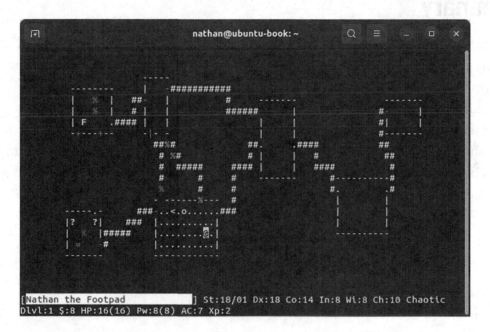

Figure 5-9. *Nethack dungeons are revealed as you explore—as are the true natures of the items you find*

Type your password when prompted, and press Enter. Ubuntu will provide a list of additional software that will be installed along with the software. Simply press Enter at the confirmation prompt to accept the default of "Yes," and Ubuntu will download and install the software.

Hack and Nethack use symbols to stand in for many different objects. You can use the slash (/) key to display a prompt where you can type a symbol and see what it stands for. In Nethack, you can use the cursor to highlight and identify an object on the map instead of typing the symbol. As you explore, you'll find many items that you can use. Armor can be worn; weapons can be wielded. And as you move, you'll need to eat and drink. Food can be eaten and water drank, but your supplies will wear thin. Sometimes you'll find shops where you can buy items. Most of the time your adventurer will die suddenly. But each new game promises a unique experience, and plenty of surprises.

The bsdgames package fits a lot of entertainment into 2.5 MB of disk space. Some games stand the test of time, and others are now more interesting as peeks into an earlier time. But they shaped the free time and culture of the early Unix users that predated Linux and Ubuntu. And they are fun rewards for learning to use the command line.

Summary

The Linux command line isn't as difficult or scary as it's made out to be. While full mastery takes time and patience, there are many tasks that are easier or faster when performed with a text interface. Many commands offer easy-to-read output, and the results can be copied and saved or sent to a file or another program for further processing. And you can use the command line to tell the computer exactly what you want it to do, often saving time and frustration. When you're comfortable on the command line, you have the ability to take advantage of a new way to interact with your computer whenever it is more convenient.

CHAPTER 6

Power User Tools

You'll find that your daily use of Ubuntu is pretty straightforward and simple. You'll run applications; get work done; relax with games, movies, or other entertainment; and generally be productive. And as you become more comfortable with Ubuntu, you'll explore Ubuntu Software and expand what you can do with your computer. The possibilities are truly endless.

As you settle in with Ubuntu, there are a lot of more advanced or technical tasks that will help you experience the full potential of your computing experience. When you search the Internet for answers to questions, these solutions will often direct you to install software from the command line. Occasionally you'll want to use software that is built for Ubuntu but not included in the default repositories. Having become familiar with the Unity interface, you might want to try other desktop environments without actually reinstalling the entire operating system on your computer. This chapter will cover various ways to take control of your computing experience. You won't need to perform these tasks every day, but knowing about them can save you a lot of time when you need them.

Managing Running Processes

As you work with multiple applications, you'll find that Ubuntu handles multitasking very well in general. When your system slows down or a single application begins to freeze, you may need to look at what processes are running and how much of your computer's resources they are taking up. While you saw a useful command-line tool called top in the previous chapter, GNOME System Monitor provides a powerful, easy-to-use graphical version, and it offers additional information about your system resources.

© Nathan Haines 2023
N. Haines, *Beginning Ubuntu for Windows and Mac Users*,
https://doi.org/10.1007/978-1-4842-8972-3_6

A process is an application (program) or part of an application. When you run an application, Ubuntu loads the program data into memory and begins scheduling it to run. Ubuntu will manage how much time and memory each application receives so that many programs running at once are able to share the available resources. GNOME System Monitor summarizes how your computer is being utilized. You can launch it from the Activities overview.

When System Monitor appears, it will show the "Processes" tab, which operates much the same way as top does. This gives you an overview of the currently running processes on the computer. They are identified by command name, icon where available, and the user that started them, the percentage of CPU time they are using, their process ID (shown as "ID"), the amount of memory they are utilizing, their disk usage, and their priority (see Figure 6-1). By default, System Monitor will only display the processes that are being run by the currently logged-in user. The column headers can be used to sort the list; for example, clicking the "% CPU" header will sort the list to show which processes are using the most CPU time. Clicking a header will toggle between sorting by ascending or descending order. You can also use the hamburger menu on the header bar to switch between "Active Processes," which shows only processes which are not sleeping or suspended; "All Processes," which shows all processes running on the system regardless of which user is running them or what they are doing; or the default "My Processes," which shows processes that are being run by the current user. Because an application can be split into several processes or commands, the "Dependencies" option is a toggle that sorts related processes by the master process that owns them and can give further insight into CPU or memory use.

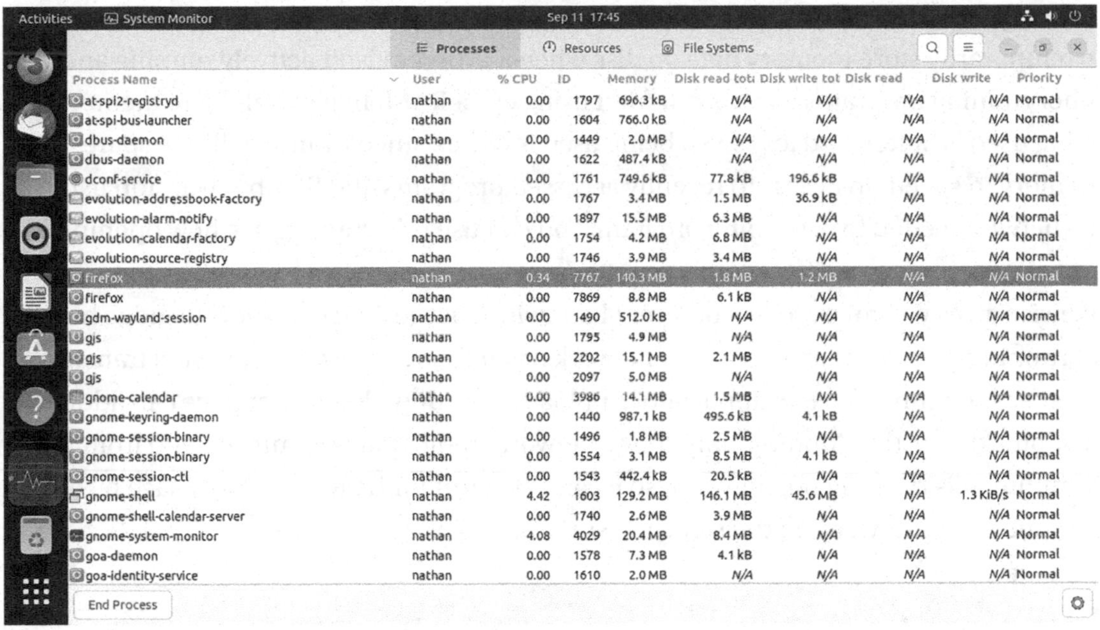
Activities
System Monitor
Sep 11 17:45
Processes
Resources
File Systems
Process Name
User
% CPU
ID
Memory
Disk read tot
Disk write tot
Disk read
Disk write
Priority
at-spi2-registryd nathan 0.00 1797 696.3 kB N/A N/A N/A N/A Normal
at-spi-bus-launcher nathan 0.00 1604 766.0 kB N/A N/A N/A N/A Normal
dbus-daemon nathan 0.00 1449 2.0 MB N/A N/A N/A N/A Normal
dbus-daemon nathan 0.00 1622 487.4 kB N/A N/A N/A N/A Normal
dconf-service nathan 0.00 1761 749.6 kB 77.8 kB 196.6 kB N/A N/A Normal
evolution-addressbook-factory nathan 0.00 1767 3.4 MB 1.5 MB 36.9 kB N/A N/A Normal
evolution-alarm-notify nathan 0.00 1897 15.5 MB 6.3 MB N/A N/A N/A Normal
evolution-calendar-factory nathan 0.00 1754 4.2 MB 6.8 MB N/A N/A N/A Normal
evolution-source-registry nathan 0.00 1746 3.9 MB 3.4 MB N/A N/A N/A Normal
firefox nathan 0.34 7767 140.3 MB 1.8 MB 1.2 MB N/A N/A Normal
firefox nathan 0.00 7869 8.8 MB 6.1 kB N/A N/A N/A Normal
gdm-wayland-session nathan 0.00 1490 512.0 kB N/A N/A N/A N/A Normal
gjs nathan 0.00 1795 4.9 MB N/A N/A N/A N/A Normal
gjs nathan 0.00 2202 15.1 MB 2.1 MB N/A N/A N/A Normal
gjs nathan 0.00 2097 5.0 MB N/A N/A N/A N/A Normal
gnome-calendar nathan 0.00 3986 14.1 MB 1.5 MB N/A N/A N/A Normal
gnome-keyring-daemon nathan 0.00 1440 987.1 kB 495.6 kB 4.1 kB N/A N/A Normal
gnome-session-binary nathan 0.00 1496 1.8 MB 2.5 MB N/A N/A N/A Normal
gnome-session-binary nathan 0.00 1554 3.1 MB 8.5 MB 4.1 kB N/A N/A Normal
gnome-session-ctl nathan 0.00 1543 442.4 kB 20.5 kB N/A N/A N/A Normal
gnome-shell nathan 4.42 1603 129.2 MB 146.1 MB 45.6 MB N/A 1.3 KiB/s Normal
gnome-shell-calendar-server nathan 0.00 1740 2.6 MB 3.9 MB N/A N/A N/A Normal
gnome-system-monitor nathan 4.08 4029 20.4 MB 8.4 MB N/A N/A N/A Normal
goa-daemon nathan 0.00 1578 7.3 MB 4.1 kB N/A N/A N/A Normal
goa-identity-service nathan 0.00 1610 2.0 MB N/A N/A N/A N/A Normal
End Process

***Figure 6-1.** System Monitor shows you what's running and how it affects your computer*

Right-clicking a process brings up a context menu with several different options related to process management. The bottom section of the menu mirrors the operations we discussed in Chapter 5. Stopping a process suspends it so that it stops running until it receives a signal to continue. Ending a process sends a request to the process to finish up and cleanly exit, whereas killing a process causes Ubuntu to stop executing the process and clear its memory for other use. As before, it's better to end a process unless it's completely unresponsive and doesn't react to end requests, because killing a running process can lead to lost or corrupted data. Changing a process's priority will instruct Ubuntu to schedule more or less CPU time for it when system resources are limited. You can use this to make a process run faster or more smoothly, or to ensure a long-running process such as a video conversion doesn't slow down the rest of the system if you don't mind the time it takes to finish a task.

The "Resources" tab gives you a graphical overview of how your system has been performing over the past 60 seconds (see Figure 6-2). The CPU History graph is nice because it shows you how each CPU is being utilized. Ubuntu will try to schedule different applications to run on separate CPUs to maximize your system's resources. It also shows how much memory has been used over time. Memory is physical RAM used to keep programs running smoothly, and swap memory shows disk space that is used to temporarily store memory data on disk when a program isn't actively running and other running programs can benefit from using extra RAM. In general, more memory being used is better, and less swap being used is better, since Ubuntu will use spare memory to speed up access to recently accessed programs and files but will stop using it when it's needed by a running program. You can use this graph to see how opening and closing programs affect your computer's memory resources. Network history likewise gives you an overview of recent bandwidth usage. You can use it to judge how all running programs are using your network if you suspect slower than usual transfer speeds. Sometimes several applications uploading or downloading at once can add up very quickly. System Monitor only shows network traffic that is coming to and from the computer it is running on, however, so it can't account for heavy network usage by other computers and devices on the same network.

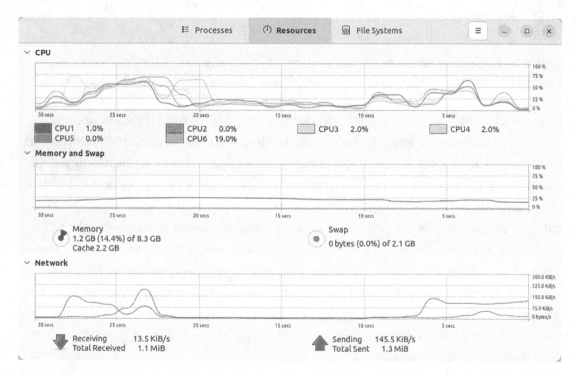

Figure 6-2. *The Resources tab shows your computer usage over the last 60 seconds*

The "File Systems" tab shows you a quick overview of the file systems that are mounted and in use. From their device name and mount point to their size and a breakdown of available and used capacity, this can be a quick look at what disks and partitions are being used and how much space you have available.

GNOME System Monitor gives you an up-to-the-second look at how your computer is being used and how your resources are being utilized. You can use this information to close programs you aren't using to speed up your system, change the priority of running programs, or decide whether you need to buy extra memory or storage space for your computer. This system utility will keep you in the know for when you want a comprehensive overview of your computer's performance.

Managing Disks and Thumb Drives

You will be able to use Ubuntu to read and write to most disks you use with your computer, but sometimes you will need to set up a blank disk or repartition or reformat a disk. Ubuntu makes this easy with Disks utility. This utility provides a way to view the layout of each drive in your computer, manage file systems and formats, and view the status and health information of each drive.

You can launch "Disks" from the application grid. When it appears, the left side of the windows will list all drives connected to your computer, and the right side will show specific information about the selected drive (see Figure 6-3). The three-vertical dot button in the top right of the header bar opens a menu with various features that can be performed on the entire selected disk. You can use this to perform a full disk format that replaces the drive's partition table, to create or restore full disk images, or to run a benchmark test that determines the speed of the drive. If an optical drive or external drive is selected, an "Eject" and "Power off" button will appear in the header bar next to the vertical dots button.

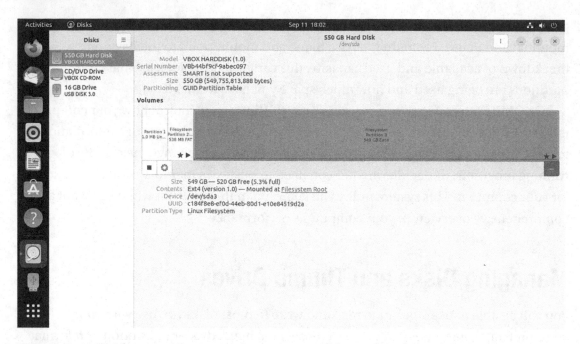

Figure 6-3. *Disks provides a quick overview of drive details and data allocation*

This menu also lets you open the SMART Data & Self-Tests window, which shows the current health of the drive and lets you start the drive's internal self-tests. The Drive Settings option lets you change power-saving preferences that can affect the energy usage of your drive as well as performance. You should not change these settings from the defaults unless you understand each option and its effects clearly. The "Power Off…" option saves any data waiting to be written the selected disk and disconnects the drive, telling it to power itself off. You can safely remove an external drive once it disappears from the Devices list on the left.

Partitions are displayed as rectangles proportionate to their size, but very small partitions are not shown to scale. Any partition that is mounted (in use) will have a small media control-like "play" icon that looks like a triangle in the bottom right-hand corner. System boot partitions will also have a small star icon in the corner. You should not unmount or edit system partitions while the system is running. If you do need to change or resize these partitions, you can boot from your Ubuntu install media and use Disks to make any necessary changes.

Underneath the partition map, you may see a "Mount selected partition" (triangle) or "Unmount selected partition" (square) icon, a "Create partition in unallocated space" (plus) icon, an "Additional partition options" (gear) icon, and, far to the right, a red "Delete selected partition" (minus) icon. Select a partition by clicking on it. If the partition contains a file system, you can use the mount and unmount icons to change whether the file system is available to use. If the file system is not in use, you can delete the partition or use the "Additional partitions" button to edit the file system or format the partition.

Formatting a partition allows you to choose between three file system formats. FAT is compatible with practically all devices and operating systems, but no single file can be over 4.3 GB in size. NTFS is used by Windows and lacks the file size limitation of FAT but cannot be written to by OS X without additional software. Ext4 is compatible with most Linux systems, and despite the label, it is perfectly fine to use Ext4 on removable drives, although they will only be readable on another Linux system. The "Encrypted" option creates an Ext4 filesystem inside an encrypted LUKS container. Ubuntu will prompt you for the decryption password each time you mount the encrypted filesystem. You can use the "Other" option to specify a specific filesystem type if you need something different for a special purpose. Ubuntu should be able to read every format listed, but won't have the software necessary to create every new file system by default. For instance, exFAT is very popular for large USB disks used on Windows and for some game consoles. Ubuntu can use disks already formatted with exFAT, but can't create new exFAT file systems without additional software.

Tip   If you want to format disks with the exFAT file system, you'll need to install the utilities to do that by running "sudo apt install exfatprogs" in a Terminal. See "Installing Software from the Command Line" below for more detailed instructions.

Disks displays your computer's attached disks and enables the most common disk operations as well as a large number of very technical options, such as complex formatting, changing file system mount parameters, and adjusting performance characteristics. While caution should be used when working with drives containing important data, Disks is a powerful tool that can be used for anything from simple formatting to working to rescue or repair a computer's drives while booted from the Ubuntu install media.

Using Multiple Workspaces

Monitors feature much higher resolutions than in days gone by. The advent of high-definition television has made a resolution of 1,920 by 1,080 pixels standard, and now 3840x2160 "4K" monitors are popular. Just 25 years ago, 640 x 480 and 800 x 600 were far more common. Special features, such as "virtual desktops," were developed to help deal with limited screen space. In Ubuntu, this feature is called "workspaces" and is a standard part of your desktop.

When you run graphical applications, they display in one or more windows. As you arrange windows on the screen, they fill up your computer's desktop. You can set up a desktop to work for a specific task, but when you switch to a different task, you need to rearrange your windows again. This can be inefficient if you are constantly rotating between tasks. Ubuntu automatically provides you a new workspace whenever you need one. These additional workspaces extend to the right in a horizontal row.

To see the applications running on your current workspace, as well as previews of the other workspaces available to you, move your mouse to the very top left of your monitor, and click the Activities button to open the Activities overview. You will see your current workspace, and all open windows on that workspace will be spread out so you can select one and bring in into focus (see Figure 6-4).

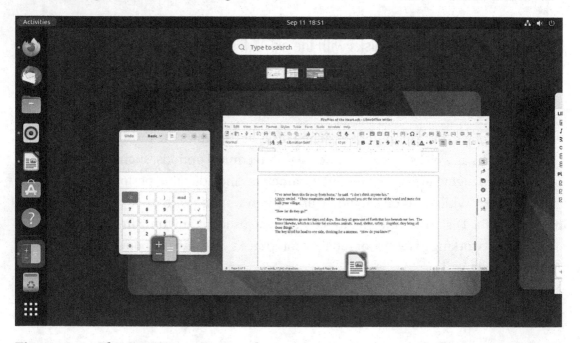

Figure 6-4. *The Activities overview shows you your current and all active workspaces*

If you only have one active workspace, you will see the edge of an additional workspace on the right side of your screen. You can drag any open window to the edge of the screen to move it to the new workspace. If you have more than one active workspace, you will see a small thumbnail view of all workspaces under the search field. You can click these thumbnails to change your active workspace. You can also drag windows from your current workspace onto any of the other workspace thumbnails.

Ubuntu manages your workspaces automatically. You will always have an empty workspace to the right of all your workspaces that you can begin using at any time, and any empty workspace will be removed automatically. Workspaces are organizational in nature and do not take up significant memory or other resources, so you can use as few or as many as you find convenient.

Everyone has a favorite way to use multiple workspaces, but one popular use is to use each workspace to perform different categories of tasks. For example, if you're planning a day of working at the computer, you might set up one workspace with your word processor and web browser, a second workspace with your email client, a third workspace with Rhythmbox for background music, and the last workspace with Solitaire or Mines for your periodic breaks. With each workspace focused on a different activity, you can take a break by switching to a workspace. When you're ready to resume work, you can switch back to your first workspace, and all your applications are running and arranged just the way you had them. This can greatly increase your productivity—as long as you're honest about the time you spend on your "work break" workspace! Don't forget that there's no need to use every workspace just because they're there. You can use only two or three if you like.

Using workspaces is fairly simple. When you launch an application, it appears on your current workspace, and you can switch to a different workspace whenever you like. The easiest way to switch is to click the Activities button at the top left of your screen or press the Super key. Click on your desired workspace and then press the Super key again. Clicking the application grid also gives you larger workspace previews (see Figure 6-5). You can click on a workspace to switch to it immediately, or drag windows between workspaces, although this is less easy than in the Activities overview. Once you select a new workspace, your view will zoom back into your new workspace, and you'll be able to work with those windows.

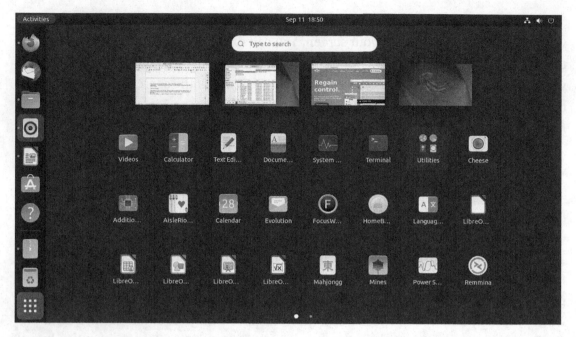

Figure 6-5. *The application grid lets you instantly switch between workspaces by clicking on them*

The Unity Dock will show all running applications, but the Alt+Tab window switcher will only show applications on your current workspace. Clicking the Launcher icon for an application on another workspace will automatically switch you to its active workspace, with a sliding animation that helps you keep track of which workspace is active. This gives you a nice balance: workspaces simplify Alt+Tab switching as you focus on a task, while the Dock gives you instant access to everything running on your computer. If you want quick keyboard access to all applications on all workspaces, the Super+Tab application will show everything running on your computer.

There are additional ways to move an application to other workspaces as well as dragging and dropping them in the Activities overview. You can also right-click the title bar of any window and choose from several options. "Always on Visible Workspace" will place the window in the same location on all workspaces. "Move to Workspace Left/Right" lets you move a window to an adjacent workspace. This is a good way of setting up workspaces when you've already been working in a single workspace for a while but want to change your workflow to start using the others.

Once you get accustomed to working with multiple workspaces, you can switch between them even faster by pressing and holding Ctrl and Alt and pressing the left or right arrow key. Ubuntu will show a small indicator of your workspaces as your view slides to the new one. Holding Shift while you press Ctrl and Alt will bring the active window with you to the new workspace. This keyboard shortcut is a little more obscure but can be useful when moving a window around after your workspaces are set up.

Ubuntu lets you slightly customize the way multitasking with workspaces work. One interesting setting is how to use workspaces when you have multiple monitors attached to your computer (see Figure 6-6).

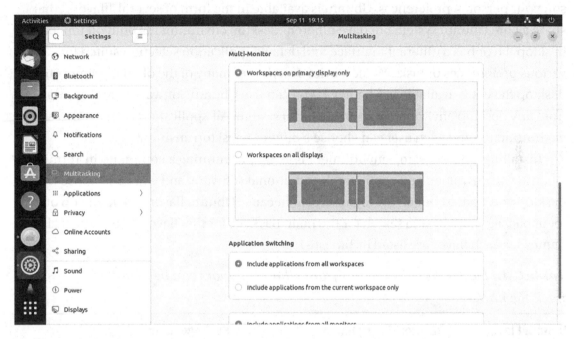

Figure 6-6. *You can adjust workspace multitasking to better suit your preferences*

By default, only your primary display is affected by workspaces. This leaves your secondary displays alone as you switch between workspaces. This is incredibly useful if, for instance, you are using a secondary display for reference during research, or possibly for watching video while you work on your primary display. But you may find it more valuable to treat all of your monitors as a single workspace. For that, open Settings, click Multitasking on the left, and then scroll down to the Multi-Monitor section. You can choose between "Workspace on primary display only" and "Workspaces on all displays." Try out each setting for yourself.

Workspaces are an advanced feature that you can use for even greater productivity on Ubuntu. Not only do they simplify application switching and multitasking, but they can help you optimize your workflow as you move from task to task—making you more efficient as you focus on work and reducing your downtime between tasks.

Installing Alternate Desktop Environments

One of the most compelling things about Ubuntu and Linux in general is the amount of customization that is available. By installing different software on top of the kernel, you can create an operating system that suits your needs perfectly. Even the default Ubuntu graphical interface is just one option out of dozens that you can change to suit your personal preferences. Ubuntu is available in the form of several "flavors" that share a core Ubuntu system but have different desktop environments built on top. Each desktop flavor has a different interface and default application selection suited for various preferences or tasks. While a brief overview of many of the officially supported desktop flavors is available in Chapter 1, you can use Ubuntu Software to add software from any desktop environment to any Ubuntu system. All applications run in all desktop environments, and each user can choose a different desktop environment.

Installing a new desktop environment is as easy as running a command in Terminal. Ubuntu will download and configure the additional software, and you can choose which desktop you wish to run on the login screen. Because Ubuntu flavors are made up of a lot of packages, it's best to search for the main package for that flavor. The main package names for each flavor are listed in Table 6-1.

Table 6-1. *Desktop environments from Ubuntu flavors can be installed by package name*

Ubuntu Flavor	Desktop Environment	Package name
Ubuntu	GNOME with a custom Ubuntu session	ubuntu-desktop
Kubuntu	KDE Plasma Workspace	kde-standard
Xubuntu	XFCE Desktop Environment	xubuntu-desktop
Lubuntu	LXDE	lubuntu-desktop
GNOME	Ubuntu with the GNOME session	gnome-session
Ubuntu MATE	MATE Desktop Environment	ubuntu-mate-desktop
Ubuntu Unity	GNOME with the Unity interface	ubuntu-unity-desktop
Ubuntu Studio	KDE with media creation tools	ubuntu-studio-installer(run separately)

For example, to add the KDE desktop environment to any Ubuntu system, you would open Terminal, then type "`sudo apt install kde-standard`", enter your password and press Enter, and then press Enter again at the confirmation prompt. Ubuntu will download and install all additional programs that were included on the Kubuntu install media (see Figure 6-7). Approximately 1.4 GB of additional software is needed on top of an Ubuntu system. If you are asked to select a display manager, press Enter to keep your default display manager. (This software manages your graphical login screen and user sessions.)

Figure 6-7. *Kubuntu and KDE can be installed like any other application with just one terminal command*

Once additional desktop environments have been installed, they can be selected on a per-user basis at Ubuntu's login screen. When you select a user and are prompted for your password, the bottom right of the screen has a button with a gear icon on it. Clicking on this brings up a menu that displays all installed desktop environments (see Figure 6-8). Clicking "Plasma" will choose the KDE Plasma desktop environment and return you to the password prompt. Once you enter your password and log in, the KDE Plasma Workspace will be your active desktop environment. Ubuntu will remember your choice until you change it again at the login screen, and every user can choose their preferred desktop environment.

Figure 6-8. *You can choose between installed desktop environments before you log in*

All software on your computer is available regardless of which desktop environment you run, so you can experiment to see which interfaces you prefer. You may even want to install several desktop environments, evaluate them, and then perform a clean install of that Ubuntu flavor on your system. Regardless, changing your desktop interface and the entire look and feel of your Ubuntu system is as simple and straightforward as installing any other software.

Installing Software from the Command Line

One of the best things about Ubuntu is that it includes thousands and thousands of software packages. Even software that isn't included in a default install can be quickly and easily added to an existing system and receive updates through Ubuntu's Software Updater utility. This is one of Ubuntu's greatest strengths, because a default installation can be customized, but still kept easily up to date. I've mentioned that many programs leverage the strengths and capabilities of other programs, and Ubuntu Software is no different. Ubuntu is built using a software packaging system that was created for Debian long ago. And while all of the software in the Ubuntu archives has been compiled specifically for Ubuntu, the tools used to install and manage the installed software on an Ubuntu system are the same: dpkg and apt.

An even newer technology used in Ubuntu is snap packages. Snap packages allow you to install software in a safe, confined manner that is separate from your main Ubuntu system without any additional effort on your part. Snaps are an especially safe and convenient way to try new software because they have security confinement and automatic updates but do not carry the risk of conflicting with preinstalled software. This means that third-party developers can package software for Ubuntu and deliver updates right to your computer without the risk of requiring the third-party developer to have administrative access to your computer while their application is being installed.

The following sections will talk about software that is included with Ubuntu as Debian packages. Instructions for working with snap packages will follow afterward.

Understanding Ubuntu's Software Collection

The Debian package tool (dpkg) is used to install and uninstall Debian packages on a Debian-based operating system like Ubuntu. However, the Advanced Package Tool (apt) also manages keeping track of what packages are installed on the system, checking for updated packages, downloading newer packages and any additional packages they need to run, and downloading them from the Internet and making sure they haven't been tampered with. Then, it runs dpkg to do the actual installation. The end result is that we can learn how to use apt instead of working with dpkg directly.

We would normally use Ubuntu Software to install software from the Ubuntu archives. But installing software on the command line is especially efficient. While the end result is identical, it is much easier to explain how to install software on the command line. For that reason, it is extremely common to see command-line instructions given in online tutorials. That makes it important to understand what is happening when an article or online solution asks you to open a terminal window and run commands to install software.

Ubuntu software is contained in a variety of software repositories. A repository is a list of available software packages and their relationship to other packages, along with the packages themselves. Ubuntu can use this list to download and install new software packages as well as determine when installed packages have been updated. The software in Ubuntu's repository is separated into various groups: main, restricted, universe, and multiverse. The "main" group contains the core Ubuntu software that is directly supported by Canonical. This includes the default desktop as well as the most important server software. The "restricted" group has firmware and other software that isn't Free Software or Open Source and is distributed by Ubuntu and Canonical to help ensure that Ubuntu can run on a variety of hardware. The "universe" group is filled with community-supported software, and "multiverse" is software that may not be fully redistributable because of software license or patent issues.

Each Ubuntu release has three repositories. One uses the release's short codename (e.g., "jammy" for 22.04 LTS), which is an archive of Ubuntu as it existed at the moment of that release. The matching repository, "jammy-updates," contains any packages that have been updated since 22.04 LTS was released. The last repository, "jammy-security," contains updated packages that have been updated because of security issues. Each repository contains software from all four groups. Because apt combines these lists of software packages into one database, you can use apt to install and upgrade any software that is included in Ubuntu regardless of where it comes from.

Tip   While most online instructions still use `apt-get`, `apt-cache`, and other tools, this book prefers the `apt` command—introduced in Ubuntu 14.04 LTS—because it has color-coded output and a progress bar that is easier to read for command-line newcomers. The two commands produce the same end result, although `apt-get` has more advanced options. The use of `apt-get` in online instructions *may* be a sign it is out of date!

Keeping Software Up to Date

Before you search for or install a software package, you should ensure Ubuntu's software index is up to date. By default, Ubuntu updates its software list once per day, but you can manually update the index by running "`apt update`." This will download the current list of packages from the Ubuntu repositories. Because this modifies system files, you must run it with sudo and type your password, followed by pressing Enter:

```
sudo apt update
```

Ubuntu will check each of its repositories and only download package lists that have changed since the last time the command was run. Once this is finished, you can upgrade or install new software. The Ubuntu updates repository only keeps the latest couple of updates to any single package, so if an upgrade or install fails with a "Package not found" error on a computer that hasn't been turned on in a while, running apt update before repeating the upgrade or install command will often succeed.

With an updated package list, Ubuntu knows which packages are available and can replace older software on your system. The command to do this is "apt upgrade." If you run this with sudo, apt will list all updated and new packages and ask whether you wish to proceed with the upgrade. Here is an example of an upgrade where Ubuntu's Linux kernel will be updated:

```
nathan@ubuntubook:~$ sudo apt upgrade
Reading package lists... Done
Building dependency tree... Done
Reading state information... Done
Calculating upgrade... Done
The following NEW packages will be installed:
   linux-headers-5.15.0-47 linux-headers-5.15.0-47-generic
   linux-image-5.15.0-47-generic linux-modules-5.15.0-47-generic
   linux-modules-extra-5.15.0-47-generic
The following packages will be upgraded:
   linux-generic-hwe-22.04 linux-headers-generic-hwe-22.04
   linux-image-generic-hwe-22.04 linux-libc-dev
4 upgraded, 5 newly installed, 0 to remove and 0 not upgraded.
4 standard security updates
Need to get 115 MB of archives.
After this operation, 584 MB of additional disk space will be used.
Do you want to continue? [Y/n]
```

"Y" is the default option, so pressing Enter will begin the upgrade. Ubuntu will download all of the listed packages from its software repositories, and install them, with a progress bar printed at the bottom of the screen. Once it is complete, your system will be up to date.

Occasionally, apt will say that certain packages are being held back. This happens when certain packages must be removed and replaced with newer versions with new names. This isn't common but occasionally happens with certain system libraries. You can run "sudo apt full-upgrade" or "sudo apt-get dist-upgrade" to install the held-back packages. If apt reports that a lot of packages are going to be removed, and it doesn't look like most of them are being replaced with similarly named versions, it's worth stopping and checking online for any issues, or simply waiting another day to check for updates and try again.

Searching for Software

There are nearly 70,000 software packages in Ubuntu 22.04.1 LTS, and finding new software to install can be difficult. Sometimes a package name is the same as the application title, such as "thunderbird" or "inkscape." But sometimes a package name is different, such as "nethack-console." Using the command line to install an application is the quickest method when you know the exact package name, but apt can also be used to find software as well.

Every package has a name and a short and long description, which is part of the information stored in the Ubuntu repositories. Using the commands "apt search" will search the names and descriptions in the package database on your computer and will print a list of package names and their short descriptions. For more information on any package, you can run "apt show" followed by a package name. This displays a lot of information, including the installed size and the package's long description. This allows you to narrow down a package name for software you wish to install. Using the command line to search for applications is more bare-bones, but is much faster than using Ubuntu Software.

You can also use "apt policy" to find out more information about the installation status and availability of a package. If I run "apt policy libreoffice-writer", for instance, I see the following:

```
nathan@ubuntubook:~$ apt policy libreoffice-writer
libreoffice-writer:
  Installed: 1:7.3.5-0ubuntu0.22.04.1
  Candidate: 1:7.3.5-0ubuntu0.22.04.1
  Version table:
 *** 1:7.3.5-0ubuntu0.22.04.1 500
        500 http://us.archive.ubuntu.com/ubuntu jammy-updates/main amd64
        Packages
        100 /var/lib/dpkg/status
    1:7.3.2-0ubuntu2 500
        500 http://us.archive.ubuntu.com/ubuntu jammy/main amd64 Packages
```

I can clearly see from the "Installed" field that LibreOffice Writer 7.3.5 is installed. The "Candidate" field tells me the latest version that Ubuntu wants to install. Because it's the same as the installed version, I know that my browser is the latest available in the Ubuntu repository. The version table shows me that LibreOffice Writer 7.3.5 was included in jammy-updates. Because it isn't in jammy-security, I know it there haven't been any serious security issues since the release of Ubuntu 22.04 LTS and the fixes are bug-related. I should install it unless I have a good reason not to. And I can also see from the last two lines that Ubuntu 22.04 LTS originally shipped with LibreOffice Writer 7.3.2.

Even when a package is not installed, `apt-cache policy` provides the same information. Using FocusWriter as an example shows the following:

```
nathan@ubuntubook:~$ apt policy focuswriter
focuswriter:
  Installed: (none)
  Candidate: 1.7.6-2
  Version table:
     1.7.6-2 500
        500 http://us.archive.ubuntu.com/ubuntu jammy/universe amd64
        Packages
```

The "Installed" field clearly indicates with "(none)" that FocusWriter is not installed on the computer and that using `apt` or Ubuntu Software to install it will result in FocusWriter 1.7.6-2 being installed.

Installing New Software

Installing software from the Ubuntu repository is simple on the command line. If you know exactly what you want to install, you can start the process in mere seconds. The command "`apt install`" will automatically download the latest version of a package along with any additional packages it requires, and install them in the most efficient order.

Because it modifies system files, "`apt install`" must be run with "`sudo`", along with the name of the package you wish to install. Then, `apt` will determine what needs to be installed, and if the package can be installed by itself, it will begin the download and installation immediately. If the package requires additional packages that you did not specify, it will pause after printing a summary and wait for your response. Pressing Enter will begin the install. Installing FocusWriter looks like this:

```
nathan@ubuntubook:~$ sudo apt install focuswriter
Reading package lists... Done
Building dependency tree... Done
Reading state information... Done
The following additional packages will be installed:
  libdouble-conversion3 libmd4c0 libpcre2-16-0 libqt5core5a libqt5dbus5
  libqt5gui5 libqt5multimedia5 libqt5network5 libqt5printsupport5
  libqt5svg5
  libqt5widgets5 libxcb-xinerama0 libxcb-xinput0 qt5-gtk-platformtheme
  qttranslations5-l10n
Suggested packages:
  myspell-dictionary qt5-image-formats-plugins qtwayland5
The following NEW packages will be installed:
  focuswriter libdouble-conversion3 libmd4c0 libpcre2-16-0 libqt5core5a
  libqt5dbus5 libqt5gui5 libqt5multimedia5 libqt5network5
  libqt5printsupport5
  libqt5svg5 libqt5widgets5 libxcb-xinerama0 libxcb-xinput0
  qt5-gtk-platformtheme qttranslations5-l10n
0 upgraded, 16 newly installed, 0 to remove and 4 not upgraded.
Need to get 0 B/18.4 MB of archives.
After this operation, 58.6 MB of additional disk space will be used.
Do you want to continue? [Y/n]
```

This tells us that 15 extra packages will be installed. Pressing Enter will begin the download and installation. If you wanted to know more about the additional packages, you could type "n" and press Enter, and then run "apt show libqt5printsupport5" for example. Using "apt show" reveals that it helps applications provide printing support. apt also listed three other suggested packages that work with FocusWriter or offer additional functionality. Suggested packages are not installed by default, but they can offer additional functionality, and you can install them manually. If installing a package would require the removal of software, those package names would also be listed. Altogether, apt will download 19 MB of packages, and once they are uncompressed, installed, and configured, they will use 59 MB of disk space. This also takes into account any software that may be upgraded, replaced, or removed by apt.

Installing more than one package at a time is as easy as listing more than one package on the command line. When I install Ubuntu on a new computer, one of the first things I do is run "sudo apt install gimp inkscape vlc ubuntu-restricted-extras". By directly asking Ubuntu to install these packages, I save a lot of time over opening Ubuntu Software, searching for each one by name, and clicking "Install."

Occasionally, you may want to download packages now but not install them until later. You can do this by running "sudo apt -d install [packagename]" or "sudo apt -d upgrade". The "-d" option tells apt to download the packages but skip installing them. The next time you run a command to upgrade or install those packages, they will not be downloaded again unless a newer version has been released.

Removing Software

Removing software is just as simple as installing it. The command "apt remove" uninstalls software packages and frees up disk space. When you run this command, it deletes the application and associated system files. It doesn't typically delete any configuration data in your home folder. This means that you can still back up this information, and should you reinstall the software again in the future, your old settings will still be used. If you want to completely remove a package and its configuration files, you can use the command "apt purge [packagename]". This will leave no trace of the specified software on your computer.

Ubuntu's basic software management tool apt is an easy-to-use and powerful way of managing your computer's software at all steps: searching, downloading, installing, upgrading, and removing. This technology lays a foundation for Ubuntu's ease of use and reliable security and bug fixes. By working with these tools directly, you can save yourself time and quickly install and remove software so that you can get to work.

Working with Snap Packages

In addition to Ubuntu's software repositories, Ubuntu Software also grants access to a large collection of software from the Snap Store. This is an online service provided by Canonical that lets third-party developers and software enthusiasts package their software so that it can be used in every Ubuntu still supported by Ubuntu and Canonical—instead of requiring a separate package for each version of Ubuntu the developer wants to support. When a snap package is installed from the Snap Store either in Ubuntu Software or on the command line, Ubuntu will automatically check for and install updates several times a day.

Working with snap packages on the command line is easy, because unlike Debian packages which have a list of other software and libraries they need to run, snap packages include everything they need to function. This means that searching, installing, and removing snaps is much simpler than working with Debian packages.

First, to find a snap, you can run "snap find [search term]" to search the Snap Store's catalog. This searches snap package names, software titles, and descriptions to return a list of snap packages. For example, if I run "snap find skype", I might get the following result:

```
nathan@ubuntubook:~$ snap find skype
Name            Version               Publisher     Notes
    Summary
skype           8.88.0.401            skype✓        -
    One Skype for all your devices. New features. New look. All Skype.
skyperious      5.3                   suurjaak      -
    Skype chat history tool
spreedme        0.29.5snap1           nextcloud✓    -
    Spreed.ME audio/video calls and conferences feature for the Nextcloud Snap
fakecam         2.2.0                 diddledani✪   -
    Fakecam
ferdi           5.8.1                 getferdi      -
    Ferdi
```

To find out more about a snap package, you can run "snap info [snap package]":

```
nathan@ubuntubook:~$ snap info firefox
name:      firefox
summary:   Mozilla Firefox web browser
publisher: Mozilla✓
store-url: https://snapcraft.io/firefox
contact:   https://support.mozilla.org/kb/file-bug-report-or-feature-
request-mozilla
license:   unset
description: |
  Firefox is a powerful, extensible web browser with support for modern web
  application
  technologies.
commands:
```

```
  - firefox
  - firefox.geckodriver
snap-id:       3wdHCAVyZEmYsCMFDE9qt92UV8rC8Wdk
tracking:      latest/stable/ubuntu-22.04
refresh-date: 8 days ago, at 17:24 PDT
channels:
  latest/stable:     104.0.2-1    2022-09-06 (1810) 185MB -
  latest/candidate: 105.0-2       2022-09-15 (1849) 187MB -
  latest/beta:       105.0b9-1    2022-09-12 (1836) 187MB -
  latest/edge:       106.0a1      2022-09-16 (1852) 193MB -
  esr/stable:        91.13.0esr-1 2022-09-02 (1791) 161MB -
  esr/candidate:     102.3.0esr-1 2022-09-12 (1839) 183MB -
  esr/beta:          ↑
  esr/edge:          102.2.0esr-2 2022-09-02 (1793) 182MB -
installed:           104.0.2-1               (1810) 185MB -
```

This tells me several things. For instance, now I know that Firefox is a web browser. Second, I know that the publisher is Mozilla. The green check mark next to the publisher name means that Canonical has verified that the publisher's identity. Some snap packages are created by community members, not the original software developer.

If you already have a snap installed, you will see "refresh-date" above "channels," and this will tell you the last time the snap was installed or updated on your computer. The last line, "installed," will tell you what version of the snap you have on your computer, and you can compare that with the latest versions listed in each channel.

The "channels" information is more interesting. The Snap Store has the ability to track several different versions of a program. This means that if a developer sets it up, you can install specific versions of the software. Firefox has a "latest" track and an "esr" (extended support release) track. Each track has four channels: stable, candidate, beta, and edge. Most software only publishes to the stable channel, but some use the other channels as well. Typically, "edge" is the latest version of their software built with the latest development work, "beta" is software that's been tested and is shaping up, "candidate" is software that is expected to be stable but needs final testing, and "stable" is the actual, tested release.

Firefox has two tracks. The "esr" track is an older version of Firefox that is very stable and is only receiving security updates. The "latest" track is for the latest release, and Mozilla uses the "stable" channel for final releases, the "beta" channel for the next version of Firefox being developed and finalized, and the "edge" channel for the next

245

version after that. You can install the version of Firefox that works best for your computer usage, and you can also easily install an upcoming version of Firefox, try it out, and keep it or move back to the stable version without risking any instability to the rest of your Ubuntu system.

To install a snap from the Snap Store, you simply type "`snap install [packagename]`", and Ubuntu will download the snap package, install it, set up any access it needs to your computer via "snap interfaces," and then check for new updates periodically. If you installed a desktop application, the application will be available from the application grid as well as the command line.

If you want a specific version of a snap, you can specify that before you install. "`snap install --beta [packagename]`" will install from the beta channel of a snap. If you want to install a specific track, you can specify it directly. For example, to run the latest Firefox ESR release, you would run "`snap install --channel=esr/stable firefox`".

Sometimes a snap will use many tracks. For example, the Nextcloud snap is a rather sophisticated server all bundled up in a single snap. It has tracks for each of its major versions, and the "latest" track is slow to update, sometimes taking weeks, in the name of stability. But if you want to receive maintenance updates but stay on a specific version until you decide to change versions with the "`snap refresh`" command, you can install a specific track.

If a snap is already installed, you can check for updates at any time. Sometimes you will be notified that an update is available for a snap, but it is running. But Ubuntu doesn't automatically monitor your running applications so that it can install the update once you close it. Instead, if you want to update your snaps on demand, you can close the application and run "`snap refresh`". This will search for updates to all of your installed snaps (unless they are currently running) and download and update them. If you only want to update a single snap, you can do that as well by running "`snap install [packagename]`" when it is not running.

If you want to change tracks or channels for an installed snap, the "refresh" command can do that, too. "`snap --channel=esr/stable firefox`" will switch your computer's version of Firefox to the ESR release, for example, and then begin using that track and channel for updates.

Ubuntu keeps the last version of a snap around in case an update causes trouble. If a snap update doesn't work on your computer, you can run "`snap revert [packagename]`" and the snap and its program data will immediately revert to the previously installed version. Ubuntu will continue monitoring the snap for updates and will update once the latest version is replaced.

Removing snapped software is simple as well. "`snap remove [packagename]`" will make a compressed snapshot of the snap and your snap data. Ubuntu will keep this snapshot for 31 days. If you later find that you want to restore a snap and all of its data, you can run "`snap restore [packagename]`", and everything will be restored. If you do not want a snapshot to be created for purposes of disk space or otherwise, you can run "`snap remove --purge [packagename]`", and Ubuntu will not create a snapshot.

Lastly, snaps are isolated from your Ubuntu system for your security. This means that aside from being able to request basic features via "slots" (such as desktop integration or access to your home folder), snaps cannot automatically request access to more advanced slots (such as the ability to monitor what is running on your computer or to access removable drives on your computer). However, you can grant access to these either in Ubuntu Software (which is the most convenient method) or on the command line.

Most snaps that require extensive additional permissions will explain this in their description. For example, the OBS Studio snap requires several connections to interfaces for the best experience. It lists these in its description. For example, to grant OBS Studio's snap access to your cameras, you would run:

```
sudo snap connect obs-studio:camera
```

You can also revoke access to a snap package with the "disconnect" command. For instance:

```
sudo snap disconnect obs-studio:camera
```

In the end, snaps provide a secure way to install third-party applications that will run on Ubuntu in a manner that allows you to manage what resources it can access, much like you would with a mobile app on your cell phone. This provides the latest software, directly from the developers, no matter what version of Ubuntu you are running, without the risk of conflicts with other software on your Ubuntu system, which means that you can continue getting the latest software even if you are using an older version of Ubuntu. This helps you get the most out of your Ubuntu system, on your own schedule and terms.

Expand Your Software Options

Ubuntu comes with a wide array of software—nearly 80,000 packages at your disposal, thanks to large software repositories. Sometimes, it's not enough. Ubuntu's update policy means that major versions of software are locked in a couple of months before release and the Ubuntu repositories only see minor maintenance or security updates to ensure stability. LibreOffice 7.3.2 was included in Ubuntu 22.04 LTS and received updates up to 7.3.5. Ubuntu won't receive further updates of LibreOffice even though the current version at the time of publication is 7.4.0. Other software was not able to be packaged for Ubuntu for various reasons. Some weren't available or stable enough to include during Ubuntu 22.04 LTS's development cycle. Others are released directly by third-party software manufacturers. When an application makes an Ubuntu package repository available, you can add the repository to your system and gain access to the included software.

A third-party Ubuntu repository will have two components. The first is a link to the repository, and the other is a GPG encryption key to sign the packages and ensure a package hasn't been corrupted or tampered with. With this information you can add the repository to your software sources and interact with it using Ubuntu Software and apt. Ubuntu's Launchpad project also offers a feature called "Personal Package Archives." This service allows developers to create Ubuntu packages for testing or updates outside of the Ubuntu release process and is slightly easier to add because Ubuntu can import the signing key automatically.

Some third-party software, such as Google's Chrome installer and Valve Software's Steam installer, add themselves to the software list during the install, allowing Ubuntu to automatically detect and download updates. To manually add a repository, launch "Software & Updates" from the Dash and click the "Other Software" tab. You will see any optional repositories that have been added to your system, as well as a checkbox indicating whether each source is enabled or disabled (see Figure 6-9).

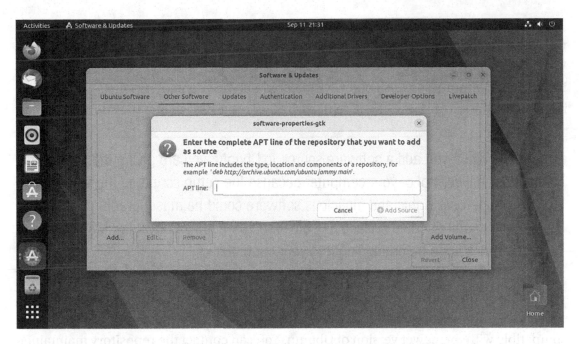

Figure 6-9. *Software sources can be added automatically or by hand*

To add a repository, click the "Add..." button. Ubuntu will ask you for the "APT" line that describes the repository. This usually begins with the word "deb." To use Oracle's VirtualBox repository as an example, Oracle provides repository information on its website in the VirtualBox downloads page at `www.virtualbox.org/wiki/Linux_Downloads`. Following the instructions on that page, in the "APT line:" field, you would enter:

```
deb http://download.virtualbox.org/virtualbox/debian jammy contrib
```

Once you've entered that into the field, click "Add Source." Ubuntu will ask you to enter your password to confirm your request. Once you click the "Authenticate" button, Ubuntu will add the repository to your system. Next, you will need to add the repository's signing key. If the repository maintainer uses one, it should be available in the same place as the repository information. For example, Oracle provides a link to the signing key on the Linux download page as part of repository setup instructions. Download this key with your web browser and go back to the Software & Updates window and click the "Authentication" tab. Click the "Import Key File...," select the .asc file you downloaded and click "OK." Ubuntu will add the key, and when you click "Close," you will receive a prompt that says "The information about available software is out-of-date." Click the "Reload" button, and Ubuntu will update its software list, including the new source you just added.

Once the Software & Updates window closes, you can install packages in the new repository using Ubuntu Software, Software Updater, or apt just like any other package. VirtualBox is now available in an additional "virtualbox-5.1" package that can be installed. If Ubuntu 16.04 LTS's older "virtualbox" package containing version 5.0 was installed before, virtualbox-5.1 will replace the older software so that they do not conflict.

Caution   When you add a software source to Ubuntu, you are giving the source maintainer full control of your computer because the setup scripts in the packaging run with superuser rights and malicious software could be masquerading as something useful or could replace any other software on your system. Make sure you trust the source before adding it to your computer.

When you upgrade to a new major release of Ubuntu, these additional software sources are automatically disabled because there is no guarantee that they are compatible with the newer version of Ubuntu. You can contact the repository maintainer or carefully test the software on the newer version of Ubuntu and reenable each source on an individual basis. Sometimes you can use the "Edit" button to update the release name, from "jammy" to "kinetic," for instance, if you were upgrading to Ubuntu 22.10. If the new source is not available for the newer version of Ubuntu, the currently installed packages will remain but will not update until their availability changes.

Ubuntu is able to receive updates to the software it provides, but is also flexible enough to receive updates from other sources as well. Used with caution, this is the perfect way to keep up with updates to Chrome, Steam, VirtualBox, and many other software projects.

Creating Application Launchers for Programs

Sometimes you might have written a script or found an interactive command-line application that you want to be able to launch using the Activities overview or pin to the Ubuntu Dock. While some command-line applications (such as Elinks) are available in the Activities list after installation, the vast majority of command-line applications do not show up in Activities. Other software that isn't available through Ubuntu's package management runs in place but without a desktop launcher. Most software without a launcher will never be missed, but if you want to set up a custom icon, you can do so by creating a ".desktop" file.

A .desktop file is a text configuration file that describes a program to a desktop environment. Most modern desktop environments automatically detect .desktop files in either a system folder or a per-user folder. To demonstrate, let's create a script named "spacedrive" that generates a pulsing white noise similar to a starship engine. Then, we'll create an application launcher file so we can run it using GNOME Shell instead of the command line.

First, install the package "sox." This small sound file utility can convert sound files but can also be used to generate sound effects. To install SoX, open "Terminal" via the Dash, or press Ctrl+Alt+T. Then type:

```
sudo apt install sox
```

Press Enter, then enter your password and type press Enter again. You'll be prompted to confirm the software installation. Press Enter to accept the default of "Yes." Ubuntu will download and install SoX and the libraries its needs to playback sound.

Next, click Files in the Launcher and create a new folder named "bin" in your home folder if it does not already exist by typing "mkdir ~/bin". If you just created "bin," you should log out and log back in. Ubuntu will automatically add "~/bin" to your system path if it exists, but only when you log in. Then, launch Text Editor from the application and enter the following into a new file:

```
#!/bin/sh
echo -n "\033]0;spacedrive\007"
/usr/bin/play -n -c1 synth whitenoise lowpass -1 120 lowpass -1 120 lowpass -1 120 gain +14
```

Save that in your ~/bin folder with the name "spacedrive". In Files, open the "bin" folder and right-click "spacedrive", and then choose Properties from the pop-up menu. Click the "Permissions" tab, and click the "Allow executing file as program" check box until it has a check mark in it, then close the "spacedrive Properties" window. If you have created this script correctly, you can launch Terminal from the Dash and type "spacedrive" and press Enter. You should hear gently pulsing white noise with a status and volume indicator. This will continue to play until you press Ctrl+C in the Terminal window.

Once this works, go back to Text Editor, and click the "Create a new document" icon in the toolbar. In the new text file, enter the following with no blank lines at the top:

```
[Desktop Entry]
Version=1.0
Name=spacedrive
Comment=Engages your starship's engines for relaxing background noise.
Exec=spacedrive
Icon=/usr/share/pixmaps/faces/launch.jpg
Terminal=true
Type=Application
Categories=AudioVideo;Audio;Music;
```

Save this to your Desktop folder with the name "spacedrive.desktop". On your desktop, you will see the file appear with a faded icon of a NASA space shuttle and a red X in the corner. If you try to run it, you will receive an error that says the application launcher does not have the right permissions to be launched. Right-click the file and choose "Properties," and go to the "Permissions" tab and allow the file to be executed as a program as you did with the "spacedrive" script. Then, right-click the file again and select "Allow Launching." The file icon will become clear, and the label will change from "spacedrive.desktop" to "spacedrive." The file name has not actually changed, but its appearance on the desktop has. You have now created an application launcher.

To make the file available in the application grid, you can move it to the ~/.local/share/applications folder. It will immediately be available in the Dash, and you can even drag it to your Launcher at the left side of the screen. Once the script is running, pressing Ctrl+C or closing the terminal window will end the sound effect.

The .desktop file follows a specific format, but you should be able to modify the spacedrive.desktop file to suit your own needs. The "Name" line will be the way your application appears in the Dash and Launcher, and the "Comment" line is used for extra search keywords by Unity and often shows up as a tool tip when hovering your mouse over a menu item in other desktop environments. The "Exec" line should be the exact path and filename you use to run the script or command from a command prompt. If the application is in your path (such as applications installed by the package manager or items in your "bin" folder), you can specify just the name, but if they are outside your path, you must give the full path, for example, "/home/nathan/bin/spacedrive".

The "Icon" line is optional and can point to any file. If no path or file extension is given, Ubuntu looks in /usr/share/pixmaps for a matching file and adds the right extension. The "Terminal" line indicates whether or not to display a terminal window, and can be either "true" or "false." If the application is graphical or runs without interaction, you will probably make this "false." If you need to interact with the script or command, you will want to make this "true."

The line "Type" needs to be "Application" in order to function as a launcher, and "Categories" should be one of the main categories in the specification. You can use semicolons (;) to separate additional categories on the same line as in the example. A list of valid categories to use on this line are available at:

```
https://specifications.freedesktop.org/menu-spec/latest/
```

Having a shortcut for a favorite command or script can be a huge convenience. Using simple .desktop files can allow for custom launchers that range from the simple to the complex, and come in handy—especially when you are working between with software that doesn't use Ubuntu's software management.

Working with Virtual Machines

Finding the best software to suit your workflow can be fun but challenging. And in the end, you might find that you need to use software that is only available on other operating systems. You may also want to experiment with different operating systems or software changes while keeping your primary computer usable. Dedicating a computer to one operating system or dual booting a single system is one option, but moving between computers or stopping work to reboot into another operating system is inconvenient. Other times you may just want to test something temporarily. The best way to do this is to create a virtual machine where your changes don't affect your primary computer. There are many virtualization technologies, and Ubuntu supports many of them. VirtualBox is very popular, as is the VMware family of commercial products. KVM support is used in a lot of cloud computing solutions, and in fact there are many commercial virtual server providers such as DigitalOcean and Linode. All of these solutions have their uses, but VirtualBox is one of the most user-friendly ways for a beginner to work with virtual machines (see Figure 6-10).

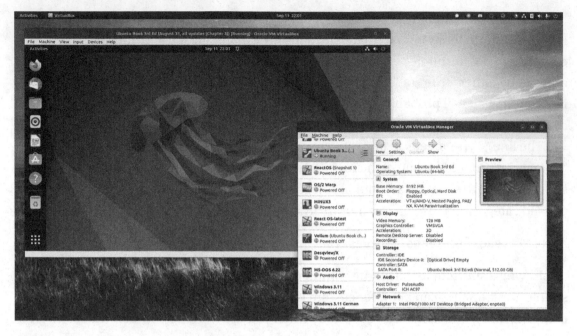

Figure 6-10. *This Ubuntu 22.04.1 LTS virtual machine was the model for this book*

A virtual machine is a simulated computer that runs like a program. Once created, it behaves just like a real computer. You can define how much memory it has, create virtual disks and define their sizes, and connect virtual and real hardware to the virtual machine. While a virtual machine uses your computer's CPU, memory, and disk space, it is isolated from the rest of your computer. In fact, the first thing you do after you turn on a new virtual machine for the first time is install an operating system—just like a new physical machine. Because of the way they share resources, the computer running VirtualBox is called the "host" computer, and the virtual machine inside VirtualBox is called the "guest" machine.

To work with VirtualBox, you can install it from Ubuntu Software, or use apt to install the package "`virtualbox`." If you want to use the latest version available from Oracle, you can use the earlier section "Expand your software options" as a guide to adding Oracle's VirtualBox repository to your system. When this book was written, "`virtualbox-6.1`" was the latest version of VirtualBox, but check the official website at `www.virtualbox.org/` for updated instructions. Only members of the "vboxusers" group on your system will be able to run VirtualBox. The install process should automatically add your user account to the group, but you will need to manually add other users to this group before they can run VirtualBox, too. The first time you install VirtualBox on an Ubuntu computer, you will need to log out of Ubuntu and log back in so that the "vboxusers" group permissions take effect. Then, you will be able to launch VirtualBox through the application grid.

Creating a Virtual Machine

The first time you run VirtualBox, you'll see a welcome screen (see Figure 6-11). This screen gives instructions for creating your first virtual machine. Click the "New" button on the toolbar and the "Create Virtual Machine" wizard will appear. The wizard explains each step in detail. On the first page, you can give your machine a friendly name that will appear in the machine list, and select your target operating system from the drop-down menus. When you hit "Next," you'll be prompted for the amount of memory installed in the virtual machine. The important thing to remember is that when the virtual machine is running, it takes all of the allocated memory from the host operating system. The recommended memory size is based on the minimum requirements for the operating machine you specified, but you can choose any size you like. Smaller sizes can cause poor guest performance, and larger sizes can cause poor host performance that affects the entire computer and running virtual machines. When the virtual machine is powered down, it doesn't use any memory.

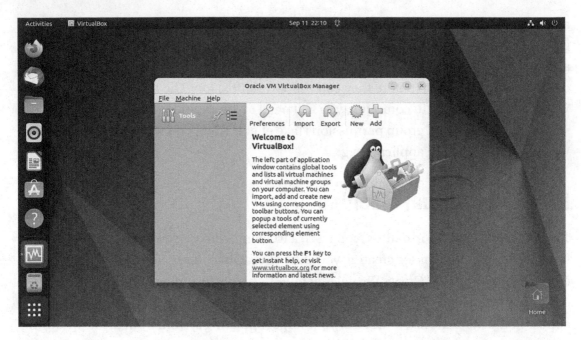

Figure 6-11. *VirtualBox guides you through each step of the creation process*

Next, you can create a virtual hard drive for the machine. The recommended size is once again based on the minimum requirements of the virtual machine. Once you choose whether to create a new virtual hard drive, a "Create Virtual Hard Drive" wizard appears and guides you through the process. Unless you have a specific need for a different format, you can safely create a VDI (VirtualBox Disk Image) format disk. If you create a "dynamically allocated" drive, then the drive file size will start at 2.1 MB regardless of the virtual capacity and will only grow when written to. A "fixed size" virtual drive file will be as large as the capacity you choose on the next screen. It can be useful if you are working with a virtual machine that will save a lot of data, because it can be faster to write to, and you won't cause the host operating system to run out of disk space unexpectedly. Once you create the disk drive, the wizard will close, and you will be back at the main VirtualBox window with the details of your new virtual machine displayed on the right of the window.

Some operating systems rely on 3D acceleration to display their user interface. Both Windows Vista and later along with Ubuntu 12.10 and later will be much faster with 3D acceleration enabled. You can select a virtual machine and click the "Display" settings header, and then enable the "Enable 3D Acceleration" feature. If you will install Windows on the virtual machine, you can also select "Enable 2D Acceleration." Once you install the VirtualBox Guest Additions, your virtual machine will function much more smoothly. See the dedicated section for more details.

Running Your Virtual Machine

Selecting a virtual machine and clicking the "Start" button on the toolbar will virtually power on the machine. A display window will appear to server as the virtual machine's monitor. You can type and use the mouse inside the window. Both the Ubuntu and Windows installers recognize the virtual mouse, so you'll be able to click inside the display window at any time. If you are not running an operating system that supports the virtual mouse, the virtual machine will "capture" the mouse when you click inside the window. This can also happen with the keyboard. To free both the mouse and the keyboard, press the Right Ctrl key.

A new virtual machine will have a blank hard drive. The first time you start a virtual machine, VirtualBox will ask you to select the location of your operating system install media (see Figure 6-12). You can choose an optical drive on the host machine or an ISO disc image if you have it in your files. Clicking "Start" will insert the disk into the guest's virtual optical drive and power on the virtual machine. At that point, you will proceed to install your guest operating system as you would on a physical computer.

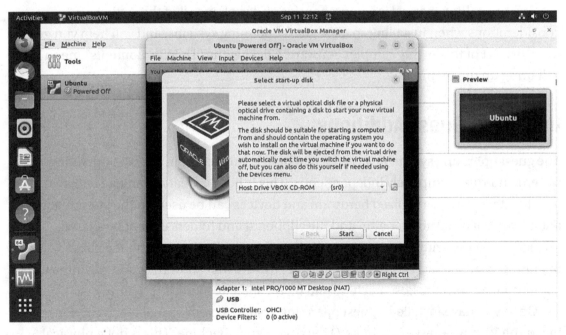

Figure 6-12. *Just like a real computer, you have to install an operating system on a virtual machine*

Once you have installed an operating system, a virtual machine is almost identical to using a physical machine. You can close the virtual machine window to power off the virtual machine, although if the guest operating system allows for an automatic shutdown, you should always use it instead of forcing a power off. Your virtual machine has audio, video, and network, and storage hardware, and if the guest operating system supports USB, you can connect USB devices plugged into your host machine directly to the guest machine's USB ports by using the Devices > USB Devices menu and clicking on the desired device. Once your guest machine is finished with the device, you can detach the device from your virtual machine the same way. It automatically reattaches to your host machine.

VirtualBox has a dizzying array of options and features, and if you are used to building computers, you can customize much of the virtual hardware. In the main VirtualBox window, you can right-click on a virtual machine and choose "Settings" from the pop-up menu. Most settings have a tool tip that appears when you hover your mouse over them. These tips not only explain the option but often offer advice on avoiding configuration problems.

The VirtualBox manual is comprehensive and explains all of the settings, considerations when installing specific guest operating systems, and will help you get the most out of this highly complex software. Clicking the "Help ➤ Contents" menu item will bring up the manual.

Installing Guest Additions

The guest operating system in a virtual machine is isolated from the host operating system and runs completely independently. This is both a great advantage and a disadvantage. Only virtualized hardware and devices can be used on the guest machine, and features like 3D acceleration and the clipboard and folders cannot be shared. VirtualBox comes with a set of guest additions that can be installed on the guest operating system to add virtualized hardware drivers that allow the guest machine to communicate with the host machine and better share resources.

Once you have installed a guest operating system in your virtual machine, you can insert the Virtual Guest Additions CD into the virtual machine. This is not a physical CD but can be inserted with the "Devices ➤ Insert Guest Additions CD image..." menu item when the operating system is running. The guest operating system should ask if you want to run the software on the CD. Choose yes, authorize the system changes, and the installer will appear. On Windows guests, this will look like a typical program installer, and you will be able to choose whether to install 3D acceleration. Follow the onscreen prompts to install the guest additions. On Ubuntu and other Linux operating systems, a terminal window will appear and show the installation progress. If it doesn't, open the CD in Files, right-click the file window and click "Open in Terminal," and run "sudo VBoxLinuxAddtions.run". If the installer complains about needing additional software to build the kernel modules, run "sudo apt install build-essential" and then rerun VBoxLinuxAdditions.run. Once installation has completed, you can close the windows, eject the CD, and restart the guest machine to fully enable the guest additions. More detailed and up-to-date instructions for installation and guest operating system compatibility are available in the VirtualBox manual. When VirtualBox is upgraded on the host OS, the guest additions should be updated on your guest OSes as well. Your guest operating system will notify you if a newer update is available, and you can simply repeat the installation process. The installer will remove the old additions and replace them with the new ones.

Guest additions offer many benefits. The keyboard and mouse will no longer be "captured" by the virtual machine, and your virtual machine will have access to more graphics modes, including the ability to automatically adjust to the virtual machine window being resized. On Windows and Linux, you can also enable "Seamless Mode," which removes the guest operating system's desktop background. This allows you to work with the guest application windows as though they were running on your host system. While this has some restrictions, it can greatly simplify switching between applications on the host and guest machines. Guest additions even allow for the sharing of clipboard data and folders between the host and guest, and VirtualBox 5.0 added direct drag-and-drop support for small- to medium-sized files. Once again, the VirtualBox manual will have more details as well as the latest updates on functionality.

For operating systems that rely on 3D acceleration to display their user interface, you should ensure that 3D acceleration enabled in the virtual machine settings. While the virtual machine is powered off, select the virtual machine and click the "Display" settings header, and then enable the "Enable 3D Acceleration" feature. For Windows guest machines, you can also select "Enable 2D Acceleration." Graphics acceleration will speed up the interface and also allow you to play many 3D accelerated games inside the virtual machine.

VirtualBox allows you to work in multiple operating systems at the same time. With the installation of guest additions, you can expand those operating systems to provide better access to your physical hardware and offer extra convenience features that make working with wildly different software much more pleasant.

Recommended Uses

VirtualBox gives you a computer in a window. In fact, you can run as many virtual machines as your physical computer's hardware resources can accommodate. The possibilities are truly endless:

- You can try different operating systems. If you wanted to work with Windows, or a different flavor of Ubuntu, you can safely test the install process and user experience by trying it in a virtual machine first. If you love Ubuntu but have one or two Windows applications that won't run under Wine, you can run them in Windows with a virtual machine without having to dual boot.

- You can run older or newer operating systems. Do you have old DOS games or are just feeling nostalgic? You can create a virtual machine and install MS-DOS or FreeDOS. Do you want to see what Ubuntu looked like a decade ago? You can install Ubuntu 6.06 LTS as a guest operating system. The computer this book was written on always ran the latest versions of Ubuntu during writing, but three virtual machines running Ubuntu 22.04.1 LTS, Windows 11, and macOS helped ensure that all screenshots and instructions were taken from a clean, freshly installed operating system that will match your experiences (see Figure 6-10).

- You can experiment. Snapshots save your machine's state so you can revert if things go wrong. Test upgrades or recovery processes. You can build a virtual machine with extra storage, or floppy drives, or two network cards.

- You can learn. Ever wanted to run an Ubuntu server? You can use a virtual machine to install Ubuntu Server and use your host operating system's web browser to look up learning and reference material. You can run two virtual machines side by side to communicate. You can write programs and run commands and upgrade operating systems without risking your data or your computer's stability.

- Being able to create and destroy virtual computers in seconds is the ultimate power user tool. Whether you set up different virtual machines to handle various tasks or you occasionally create machines to test something before deleting them, the only limit is your imagination.

Summary

There are always tips, tricks, and shortcuts that perform tasks faster or in more specific manners. Being a power user isn't about knowing every secret, but learning these features and using them when they help (and ignoring them when they don't!) is part of the process of becoming a power user. Not everyone will use every single feature or program in this chapter, but choosing the ones that work for you will help you accomplish more with Ubuntu, be more efficient, and achieve more with your computer.

APPENDIX A

Ubuntu Releases

Ubuntu is the result of tens of thousands of software projects coming together and receiving polish and integration. From the incredible work done by the Debian project to the focused effort by the Ubuntu community, this takes time and care. Canonical drives much of the design for the Ubuntu desktop and the foundational work done to support cloud, server, and embedded platforms. But the bulk of the actual development and coding is done by the Ubuntu community as well as the greater Free Software community.

Release Schedule

Every 6 months, Ubuntu syncs its software repositories with Debian and works to polish and improve the software, sending general fixes back "upstream" to Debian whenever possible. After another couple of months, the software has improved and a new Ubuntu release is made.

When the Ubuntu project officially launched in 2004, it promised a new release every 6 months, with security and maintenance support for 18 months. Each release was given a version number matching the year and month of its release, so the first version of Ubuntu which was released in October 2004 was called Ubuntu 4.10.

After only 6 months of development, the release was very promising but still had some rough edges. The developers jokingly gave it the code name "warty warthog." The software repository was named "warty." Ubuntu 5.04 followed 6 months later in April and was a marked improvement. To celebrate the extra maturity of the software, it was codenamed "hoary hedgehog."

Ubuntu releases are typically referred to by their release number or the adjective part of the code name. Thus, Ubuntu 22.04 LTS, the "Jammy Jellyfish" release, is referred to as both "22.04" and "jammy." Each release code name is alliterative and often chosen

© Nathan Haines 2023
N. Haines, *Beginning Ubuntu for Windows and Mac Users*,
https://doi.org/10.1007/978-1-4842-8972-3

to reflect the goals for the release. For example, LTS names are chosen to evoke their extended lifetime support. "Dapper" received extra polish, "hardy" saw greater adoption on servers, and "lucid," "precise," "trusty," and "xenial" all speak to the Ubuntu's clear focus and direction as it continues to evolve.

Long-Term Support

As Ubuntu began to grow in popularity as a desktop system, there was a desire to start running it on servers as well. Servers require a more reliable platform because performing a major software upgrade on a server every 6 months takes a lot of planning and downtime, and third-party hardware and software developers found it hard to target Ubuntu because of the rapid release schedule. It was decided that a long-term support release was required, and that Ubuntu 6.04 would be supported for 3 years instead of 18 months, and that the server components would be supported for a total of 5 years. Weeks before the release, the developers decided to delay the release for a few more weeks to allow for final polishing. The planned Ubuntu 6.04 was released in June 2006 as Ubuntu 6.06 LTS. Additional releases came every 6 months as planned; and 2 years later, Ubuntu 8.04 LTS was released, which allowed Ubuntu 6.06 LTS users to upgrade directly, skipping the intermediate releases.

In April 2014, Ubuntu 12.04 LTS was released with the promise of 5 years of support for the desktop as well as the server, and the non-LTS releases saw their support lifetime drop from 18 months to 9 instead. It also received an additional 2 years of extended support, which was raised to 5 years for Ubuntu 14.04 LTS and every LTS release since. Ubuntu 22.04 LTS continues with 5 years of support for both the desktop and the server, followed by an additional 5 years of select security updates during an Extended Security Maintenance lifetime, and a reliable foundation for computing everywhere.

List of Ubuntu Releases

Here is a list of Ubuntu releases from Ubuntu 4.10 to Ubuntu 22.10, along with their code names, release cycles, and release and end-of-support dates (see Table A-1). It is very important to use a supported version of Ubuntu on any computer with a network or Internet connection.

Table A-1. *Each Ubuntu release has a version number, a code name, and lifetime support*

Release	Code name	Released on	Supported until
4.10	Warty Warthog	October 26, 2004	April 30, 2006
5.04	Hoary Hedgehog	April 8, 2005	October 31, 2006
5.10	Breezy Badger	October 12, 2005	April 13, 2007
6.06 LTS	Dapper Drake	June 1, 2006	(Desktop) July 14, 2009 (Server) June 1, 2011
6.10	Edgy Eft	October 26, 2008	April 26, 2008
7.04	Feisty Fawn	April 19, 2007	October 19, 2008
7.10	Gutsy Gibbon	October 18, 2007	April 18, 2009
8.04 LTS	Hardy Heron	April 24, 2009	(Desktop) May 12, 2011 (Server) May 9, 2013
8.10	Intrepid Ibex	October 30, 2008	April 30, 2010
9.04	Jaunty Jackalope	April 23, 2009	October 23, 2010
9.10	Karmic Koala	October 29, 2009	April 30, 2011
10.04 LTS	Lucid Lynx	April 29, 2010	(Desktop) May 9, 2013 (Server) April 30, 2015
10.10	Maverick Meerkat	October 10, 2010	April 10, 2012
11.04	Natty Narwhal	April 28, 2011	October 28, 1012
11.10	Oneiric Ocelot	October 13, 2011	May 9, 2013
12.04 LTS	Precise Pangolin	April 26, 2012	April 2017/April 2019
12.10	Quantal Quetzal	October 18, 2012	May 9, 2013
13.04	Raring Ringtail	April 25, 2013	January 27, 2014
13.10	Saucy Salamander	October 17, 2013	July 17, 2014
14.04 LTS	**Trusty Tahr**	**April 17, 2014**	**April 2019/April 2024**
14.10	Utopic Unicorn	October 23, 2014	July 23, 1015

(*continued*)

Table A-1. (*continued*)

Release	Code name	Released on	Supported until
15.04	Vivid Vervet	April 23, 2015	February 4, 2016
15.10	Wily Werewolf	October 22, 2015	July 28, 2016
16.04 LTS	Xenial Xerus	April 21, 2016	April 2021/April 2026
16.10	Yakety Yak	October 13, 2016	July 2017
17.04	Zesty Zapus	April 13, 2017	January 2018
17.10	Artful Aardvark	October 19, 2017	July 2018
18.04 LTS	Bionic Beaver	April 26, 2018	April 2023/April 2028
18.10	Cosmic Cuttlefish	October 18, 2018	July 2019
19.04	Disco Dingo	April 18, 2019	January 2020
19.10	Eoan Ermine	October 17, 2019	July 2020
20.04 LTS	Focal Fossa	April 23, 2020	April 2023/April 2030
20.10	Groovy Gorilla	October 22, 2020	July 2021
21.04	Hirsute Hippo	April 22, 2021	January 2022
21.10	Impish Indri	October 14, 2021	July 2022
22.04 LTS	**Jammy Jellyfish**	**April 21, 2022**	**April 2027/April 2032**
22.10	Kinetic Kudu	October 20, 2022	July 2023

Index

A

Additional Drivers, 18
Advanced photo editing, 159, 162, 164, 165
Adventure games, 172, 173, 176, 177
Alpine, 206–209
Alternative characters (AltGr), 122
Ancient scripts, 123
Apple Silicon-based Macs, 57
Argument, 183
Audacity (multitrack editor), 166, 167
Audio editing, 166
   using audacity, 166, 167
Automatic repair, 54

B

Backup partition, 54
balenaEtcher, 4, 5
Bash, 182, 185, 191, 192
Beginning Ubuntu installation
   advanced features, 12
   default selection, 9
   detect keyboard layout, 9
   disk partitions, 12
   download updates while installing, 10
   "Erase disk and use ZFS", 13
   Ethernet connection, 10
   full-disk LUKS-based drive
      encryption, 13
   install third-party software, 10
   MP3 playback, 11
   repartition, 13

   Ubuntu installer, 8
   video and audio codecs, 11
Bethesda Softworks, 172
Binary-only network card firmware, 11
BIOS, 6, 40, 41, 49, 57, 58
Bootloader, 7, 13, 49, 50, 52, 54
Brasero
   backing up music CD, 153, 154
   burn to a blank disc, 154
   music CD, creating, 154, 155
bsdgames, 218, 222

C

Calendar view, 104, 105, 107
Calibre, 129–131
Canonical Ubuntu Desktop, 8
CD-Text, 153, 155
Celluoid, 33
CentOS, 198
Command line, 179
   access, 181, 182
   "adduser" command, 199–201
   commands, 185, 186
   df command, 201, 202
   du command, 202, 203
   editing text files, 204–207
   files and directories (folders), 183, 184
   IRC, 213
   Linux, 196
   LSB, 196
   "mtr" package, 195

© Nathan Haines 2023
N. Haines, *Beginning Ubuntu for Windows and Mac Users*,
https://doi.org/10.1007/978-1-4842-8972-3

Printed in the United States
by Baker & Taylor Publisher Services